D0712856

Literature, Religion, and Postsecular Studies
Lori Branch, Series Editor

Hard Sayings

The Rhetoric of Christian Orthodoxy in
Late Modern Fiction

Thomas F. Haddox

 THE OHIO STATE UNIVERSITY PRESS • COLUMBUS

Library of Congress Cataloging-in-Publication Data

Haddox, Thomas F. (Thomas Fredrick)
Hard sayings : the rhetoric of Christian orthodoxy in late modern fiction / Thomas F. Haddox.
p. cm. — (Literature, religion, and postsecular studies)
Includes bibliographical references and index.
ISBN 978-0-8142-1208-0 (cloth : alk. paper) — ISBN 978-0-8142-9310-2 (cd)
1. Christianity in literature. 2. O'Connor, Flannery—Criticism and interpretation. 3. Spark, Muriel—Criticism and interpretation. 4. Updike, John—Criticism and interpretation. 5. Percy, Walker, 1916–1990—Criticism and interpretation. 6. Gordon, Mary, 1949-—Criticism and interpretation. 7. Robinson, Marilynne—Criticism and interpretation. I. Title. II. Series: Literature, religion, and postsecular studies.
PN49.H23 2013
813'.54093823—dc23
2012047044

Cover design by Jerry Dorris, AuthorSupport.com
Text design by Juliet Williams
Type set in Palatino and ITC Leawood
Printed by Thomson-Shore, Inc.

9 8 7 6 5 4 3 2 1

CONTENTS

ACKNOWLEDGMENTS

No book is produced alone, and whatever merits this one may possess derive in large part from the contributions of friends, colleagues, and family members who discussed it with me, offered constructive criticism, and encouraged me to persevere. Among my colleagues at the University of Tennessee, I particularly want to thank Misty Anderson, Dawn Coleman, Allen Dunn, Amy Elias, Heather Hirschfeld, Russel Hirst, Mark Hulsether, Keith Lyons, Chuck Maland, Jeff Moody, and Steve Pearson for reading sections of the manuscript and taking the project seriously; and Stan Garner, who as head of the English Department did much to create a congenial environment for its completion.

Looking farther afield, I am grateful to Robert Donahoo and Avis Hewitt, who invited me to present some of the material in this book at conferences; to Anthony DiRenzo and David Malone, whose conversations with me at conferences proved to be especially helpful; and to Marshall Bruce Gentry, who was very hospitable when I came to Milledgeville back in the summer of 2004 to examine Flannery O'Connor's manuscripts. Ralph Wood, whose work I have followed for several years, has provided, from afar, the scholarly standard to which I aspire.

Two portions of this book have been previously published. A section of chapter 1 first appeared, in a different form, under the title "On Belief, Conflict, and Universality: Flannery O'Connor, Walter Benn Michaels, Slavoj

Žižek," in *Flannery O'Connor in the Age of Terrorism,* ed. Avis Hewitt and Robert Donahoo (Knoxville: University of Tennessee Press, 2010): 231–39. Sections of chapter 2 first appeared, in a different form, under the title "Religion for 'Really Intelligent People': The Rhetoric of Muriel Spark's *Reality and Dreams,*" in *Religion and Literature* 41 (Autumn 2009): 43–66. I am grateful to both publishers for permission to reprint this material here.

I am grateful to Sandy Crooms at The Ohio State University Press for her enthusiasm and professionalism, to the two anonymous readers who evaluated my manuscript and whose suggestions improved it considerably, and to Maggie Diehl and Maggie Smith-Beehler for their meticulous copyediting. And above all, I am grateful to my wife, Honor McKitrick Wallace, and to my children, James, Elizabeth, and Anthony, for their incomparable love and support. I present this work to them with love, zeal, and apologies for the time it has consumed.

The cover of this book is a photograph of the Kaiser-Wilhelm-Gedächtniskirche in Berlin, an image reflective of the multiple ironies surrounding the situation of Christianity in the late modern world. The old church, permanently damaged in an air raid in 1943, dates only from 1891 and was named not for Jesus Christ or for a Christian saint, but for Kaiser Wilhelm I of Germany. As such, it is a symbol of the often dubious relationship between the church and the modern state that used to characterize much of Christendom. The modern concrete, steel, and glass tower to the right is not a secular office building but the "new" Gedächtniskirche, consecrated in 1961. The small cross on its summit is not visible from the angle of this photograph and seems, even when visible, like an architectural afterthought—perhaps appropriately enough for a building that Berliners like to call "der Lippenstift" (the lipstick). Yet even granting these mordant ironies, the building remains a Christian house of worship and, through its very imperfections, a testament to the difficulties of speaking the hard sayings of Christianity in a late modern context.

INTRODUCTION

Christian Orthodoxy and the Rhetoric of Fiction

This is a book about the work of six writers of fiction—Flannery O'Connor, Muriel Spark, John Updike, Walker Percy, Mary Gordon, and Marilynne Robinson—and its relationship to what I call "Christian orthodoxy." I define Christian orthodoxy as the conviction that the central dogmas and moral imperatives of historic Christianity are true and binding and that we ignore their truth and their claims upon us at our peril. Orthodox Christian believers affirm, at a minimum, that there is one God, who has revealed himself in the Old and New Testaments; that there are three persons, Father, Son, and Holy Spirit, in the one God; that Jesus Christ is both God and man; that his salvific death and resurrection were real historical events, not mythic narratives or metaphors; that those who believe in him and repent will have eternal life; and finally, that such believers, commanded to live in accord with Jesus' moral teachings, constitute the Church, the Body of Christ, wherein salvation is found.[1] Moreover, orthodox Christians do not regard these as merely intellectual propositions but strive continuously to make of their belief and their actions an integrated whole. Christian orthodoxy, in short, is both a narrative that claims to tell the truth about the human predicament *and* a mode of life lived in obedience to God.

---

1. Beyond these minimum propositions, of course, orthodox Christians—whether Catholic, Protestant, or Eastern Orthodox—disagree considerably about particulars of doctrine and practice.

I consider the novels and short stories discussed in this book as case studies in what Wayne Booth long ago called "the rhetoric of fiction," investigating how their authors position themselves in relation to Christian orthodoxy and attempt to persuade their intended audiences of the truth and the desirability of its doctrinal claims. The first four writers—O'Connor, Spark, Updike, and Percy—began their careers in the 1940s and 1950s and have to varying degrees identified themselves as advocates for Christian orthodoxy. Gordon and Robinson, who began writing in the 1970s, have a more complicated stance toward Christian orthodoxy—indeed, Gordon often writes in explicit opposition to it—but they too see it as essential to their projects, whether as a force to be challenged in some of its particulars or as something to be appropriated for other purposes. All six writers, I maintain, have much to teach us about the relationship between Christian belief and literary rhetoric in what I call the late modern period—a time that begins roughly with the Second World War.

It would be easy enough—and partially accurate—to explain the broad differences between O'Connor, Percy, Spark, and Updike on the one hand and Gordon and Robinson on the other by referring to the cultural upheaval in the West known as "the Sixties," which temporally divides the first group of writers from the second. Such an explanation would, however, align too neatly with a classification of the first four writers as "modern" in orientation and the last two as "postmodern." I maintain that as Westerners of the late twentieth and twenty-first centuries, all six writers inhabit a late modern world still with us—a condition defined by liberal and democratic forms of government, religious toleration, and an expansive cultural pluralism underwritten by an increasingly global capitalism.[2] This world has much in common with the one predicted by sociology's "secularization thesis," which held that as modernization proceeds, a "disenchantment of the world" (Max Weber's phrase) comes to sever religion from the public sphere and to weaken its cultural influence. Marx, Weber, Freud, and Durkheim all advanced versions of the secularization thesis,

---

2. Part of what makes this period "late modern" is the perception that some political-economic regimes—mercantilism, fascism, or Soviet Communism, for instance—have been decisively discredited, leaving no viable alternatives to finance capitalism. "Late modern" thus suggests a certain shrinking of horizons, and in this sense it echoes the term "late modernism," which Fredric Jameson regards as a disappointing interval between the utopian high modernisms of the early twentieth century and the postmodernism that soon supplanted them (*Singular Modernity* 165–66). I too perceive shrunken horizons and disappointment, but I define "postmodernism" very differently from Jameson, as one strong current within the late modern rather than a phenomenon in its own right. I also mean to evoke the urgency intrinsic to Christianity—the sense that ever since Christ's resurrection, the hour has been "late."

which, despite their considerable differences, all foresaw religion's ongoing attenuation. It is now a commonplace that in the mid- to late twentieth century, the secularization thesis was widely accepted by intellectuals in the West, including many who were avowedly Christian.[3]

From a contemporary perspective, the secularization thesis has become less persuasive. It seems most persuasive when applied to contemporary Europe and Japan, far less so when one considers the United States and Latin America, and least convincing when one views the Middle East, Africa, and Asia, where an intensification of religious belief and feeling in all of the world's major religions proceeds in apparent defiance of modernization. Important correctives have recently come from Peter Berger, who insists that "Modernity is not necessarily secularizing; it is necessarily *pluralizing*" (23), and especially from Charles Taylor, who in *A Secular Age* rejects "subtraction stories" in which modern human beings have "lost, or sloughed off, or liberated themselves from certain earlier, confining horizons, or illusions, or limitations of knowledge" (22) and predicts that "the dominant secularization narrative, which tends to blame our religious past for many of the woes of our world, will become less plausible over time" (770). Yet if the portrait I have sketched of the West since the mid-twentieth century *sounds* like a wholly secular world, this is because I wish to emphasize the difference between Christian orthodoxy and the proliferation of any religious belief or intimation. I would argue that in the contemporary United States, for instance, profession of and emotional investment in Christianity remain strong, but that many avowed Christians have in fact adopted a kind of narcissistic spirituality that does not challenge a fundamentally secular order. The contemporary world may not be thoroughly secular in Weber's sense, but it is primarily therapeutic—and therein lies its attraction for many.[4]

---

3. See, for instance, Harvey Cox's *The Secular City* for an exemplary Christian endorsement of secularization—indeed, an argument that secularization continues the demystification set in motion when Jewish monotheism divided God from nature and the cosmos (15–32).

4. I use the term "therapeutic" in the sense developed by Philip Rieff. The term implies narcissism and a disconnection from social endeavors, but I do not mean to equate it with "pietism" or "contemplation," nor do I mean to suggest that all strategies of coping with the pains of life are ignoble. Rieff locates the origins of "the triumph of the therapeutic" in Freud's work and distinguishes sharply between "our present inwardness" (that is, therapeutic culture) and "ancient faith." For Rieff, "the therapy of all therapies is not to attach oneself exclusively to any particular therapy, so that no illusion may survive of some end beyond an intensely private sense of well-being to be generated in the living of life itself" (*Triumph* 261). In therapeutic culture, religion contributes toward this "private sense of well-being" and may even be perceived as necessary to social order. But the question for Rieff, as Christopher Lasch puts it, is "not whether religion was necessary but whether it was true" (228).

Such conditions tend to produce neither militant atheism nor even a general indifference to religion, but rather what Amy Hungerford calls "postmodern belief." Hungerford describes postmodern belief as a "belief in meaninglessness," a valorization of the form over the content of religion. She argues that American literary culture since 1960 is strongly marked by this "belief without meaning [which] becomes both a way to maintain religious belief rather than critique its institutions and a way to buttress the authority of the literature that seeks to imagine such belief" (xiii). Whether embraced consciously or not, postmodern belief works to reconcile individual religious feelings with the pluralism of American life. It does so largely by stressing the nonsemantic, aesthetic aspects of religious practice and even of religious language—striving, like the New Critical poem that Hungerford considers its analogue, to "be" more than to "mean" (xviii).

As a description of a broad swath of recent American literature and its relationship to belief, Hungerford's account is convincing, and her readings of texts by writers such as J. D. Salinger, Allen Ginsberg, Don DeLillo, and Toni Morrison are often illuminating. My quarrel is not with her literary history but with her evaluation of "postmodern belief" and its textual exempla. While Hungerford perceives in her chosen literary texts and in the culture that nourishes them "the very richness and success" of postmodern belief (xv)—even arguing that it is "in good measure responsible for the continuing relevance of American literary culture since the 1960s" (xxi)—I perceive instead the proliferation of an eclectic but vapid "spirituality" that may pay lip service to some features of Christian orthodoxy but empties out the radical specificity of its truth claims. Against Hungerford, I maintain that to take Christian orthodoxy seriously means to entertain (if not necessarily to accept) the primacy of truth over desire, utility, and custom, and to remain open to the content as well as the forms of Christian belief.

In a pluralistic society, writers with orthodox Christian commitments will try to anticipate the commitments and desires of their intended audiences, to speak to their own historical and cultural situatedness. They will neither neglect nor minimize the narrative dimension of Christianity, its unfolding in time as a story of redemption. Yet they will not proffer their arguments only as a set of aesthetic or therapeutic satisfactions—in attempting to persuade, they will insist, in Ralph Wood's words, on "the premise that the Christian Story is absolutely and definitively true, not only for me and my kind, but potentially for every human being" (*Literature* vii). Because the six writers I examine take Christian orthodoxy seriously, even when they do not endorse all of its propositions, their arguments are, even to many sympathetic readers, "hard sayings."[5] My task will be to evaluate their claims to persuasive authority in a climate in which the value of persuasion itself has been called into question.

I write as a Roman Catholic Christian, and the disproportionate weight given to Catholic writers reflects my own commitments and scholarly interests, though it also reflects the fact that, for whatever reason, more avowedly Catholic than avowedly Protestant fiction writers of literary merit have addressed such questions since 1945.[6] Because I maintain that Christian orthodoxy and reason are compatible, I am opposed to the widespread notion that theology is an idiosyncratic and personal endeavor that should be excluded in principle from public deliberation and from other forms of inquiry.[7] Accordingly, I reject both the positivism of much contemporary scientific thought, which sees religious and metaphysical discourse as irrelevant at best and pernicious at worst (as in the "New Atheism" of Richard Dawkins or Daniel Dennett); and the romantic irrationalism of much that goes by the name "postmodernism" (for instance, the work of Jean-François Lyotard or Gilles Deleuze).[8] These two currents of thought, however ostensibly opposed, in fact complement each other well—as seen in those strands of libertarian thought that yoke together a positivist understanding of economic behavior with a commitment to the primacy

---

5. My title, of course, alludes to the Gospel passage in which some of Jesus' disciples, hearing him teach that those who eat his flesh and drink his blood will have eternal life, respond, "This saying is hard; who can accept it?" and then abandon him (John 6:60). This remains a "hard saying" even within Christianity, as the history of theological dispute about transubstantiation reveals.

6. This fact is, in some respects, surprising. Walker Percy has, in an amusing section of *Lost in the Cosmos* called "Why Writers Drink," proposed that painters and sculptors are the "Catholics" among artists, while writers are the "Protestants." Language, less material than painting or sculpture, focuses solely on the word (or Word) but lends itself more readily to gnostic temptations and distortions (147–48). The images produced by painters and sculptors, moreover, can be viewed as possessing an implicit sacramental force (a Catholic view) or as temptations to idolatry (a Protestant one). When I consider my own relationship to the works that I examine here, I have to conclude that my theology is Catholic, but my aesthetic sensibility is Protestant.

7. See, for instance, John Rawls's *Political Liberalism*. Even when not explicitly acknowledged as a principle, this exclusion informs a good deal of contemporary opinion in Western societies about the relationship (or lack thereof) between religion and public life.

8. I will have more to say about postmodernism, but for now I would insist that the most common slogan associated with it—Lyotard's "incredulity toward metanarratives" (xxiv)—makes no sense. To be conscious of the contingency of one's beliefs, of the possibility that they could be different or could change, does not imply that one holds the beliefs less firmly, that one is less convinced of their truth. One can only become incredulous toward one metanarrative by replacing it with another; a *general* incredulity toward metanarratives is impossible.

and unanswerability of desire, often rendered polemically as "freedom" or "choice." Moreover, both of these currents work to discredit acts of persuasion. The first suspects that facts speak for themselves and that persuasion always amounts to coercion, demagoguery, or seduction; the second resents what it considers persuasion's pretense of objectivity, as if human beings could ever have sufficient distance from their desires to consider them in the cold light of someone else's argument, or would consent to do so if they could. Both, in short, are suspicious of ordinary human beings' capacity to listen and to make competent judgments, and both—whether cynically, joyously, or unwittingly—endorse a way of life centered upon bread and circuses: experts should run the world, and one should trust them implicitly in order to pursue one's desires without worry and with maximum liberty.[9] In a world so ordered, religion can be only a private matter of therapy and self-fashioning.

If, however, Christianity proclaims the truth—as O'Connor, Percy, Spark, and Updike affirm, and as Gordon and Robinson are prepared to consider—then these writers' fiction confronts a central problem of rhetoric, which Richard Weaver sums up in a question: "[I]f truth alone is not enough to persuade men, what else remains that can be legitimately added?" (15). One might reply that Weaver's question is misguided, that to pursue the truth as one does in philosophy and theology should suffice. Perhaps even to pose such a question with respect to fiction shows, as Simone Weil once suggested, that humans have returned "to the age of Protagoras and the Sophists, the age when the art of persuasion—whose modern equivalent is advertising slogans, publicity, propaganda meetings, the press, the cinema, and radio—took the place of thought and controlled the fate of cities and accomplished coups d'état" (64). Plato's desire to banish the poets in *The Republic* is only the earliest extant attempt to draw a line between imaginative writing and philosophy, and even he has Socrates call the opposition between the two "ancient" (396). Moreover, it cannot be denied that many Christians have shared his desire, while others have

---

9. My understanding of the terms "persuasion" and "judgment" is influenced by Bryan Garsten, and I will cite here his definitions: "*Persuasion* in the strict sense identifies a way of influencing that is neither manipulation nor pandering. . . . By *judgment* I mean the mental activity of responding to particular situations in a way that draws upon our sensations, beliefs, and emotions without being dictated by them in any way reducible to a simple rule" (7). Garsten is interested primarily in the role of persuasion in democratic politics; he wishes to preserve a space for it, against those theorists of deliberative democracy who, following Rawls, believe that political arguments in a democracy must be rooted in a shared conception of public reason. It should be clear that from the standpoint of political philosophy, I agree with those who hold that religious discourse and argument have a legitimate place in the public sphere—but the primary thrust of my argument is about religious persuasion in and of itself, rather than its possible political applications.

endorsed imaginative writing only when it functions as transparent allegory or dogmatic exposition—in short, when it is aesthetically bad according to contemporary literary standards. On the other hand, readers who value aesthetic complexity often consider it incompatible with didacticism: as Marian E. Crowe puts it, "Even people who don't mind being preached to in church, object to it strongly when they sit down to read a novel" (2). Given these pitfalls, why turn to fiction at all—particularly when philosophers and theologians who argue for an authentically Christian and historically grounded understanding of both reason and faith have done important work? Alasdair MacIntyre, for instance, has argued (above all, in *Whose Justice? Which Rationality?*) that the tradition initiated by Aristotle and subsequently enlarged and revised by Augustine and Aquinas has continued to maintain its explanatory power and capacity for self-correction in the face of less coherent, less persuasive challenges from the younger tradition of liberalism. Doesn't the consideration of fiction in this context merely muddy the waters?

Although I find MacIntyre's argument compelling, I am aware that relatively few people will ever engage it, that in our contemporary moment most who struggle with questions of belief and rationality do not turn to philosophy or academic theology for aid. Moreover, I fear that too many are not particularly interested in truth—that even if they have never read William James or Richard Rorty, they, like Rorty, would endorse the Jamesian view that truth is "a compliment paid to sentences that seem to be paying their way" (Rorty, *Consequences* xxv), rather than something that exists irrespective of our emotional investment in it.[10] To this extent, philosophy and theology are already at a disadvantage because of their traditional insistence that truth—which necessarily excludes and divides—is an object of primary importance. Postmodern belief would regard such claims as unwarranted arrogance, affirming instead only those philosophers or theologians who abjure or relativize any notion of truth.

Fiction, on the other hand, reaches a wide audience and can have great persuasive power. Indeed, fiction in the broadest sense seems inescapable in argument, for philosophers, theologians, and Jesus himself have had frequent recourse to it, whether in the form of allegory, counterfactuals, or

---

10. Rorty of course recognizes the ironic nature of such a claim—is it "true," after all, that truth is only a compliment?—but refuses to argue with those who challenge it. Instead, he wants to seduce his critics to this point of view. Perhaps, then, it is more accurate to say not that many are uninterested in truth but that, like Rorty, they inoculate themselves from challenges to their own "truths" by labeling them preferences—and then maintaining that preferences cannot be questioned, because tolerance demands it. Here again persuasion as such is precluded, and the effort to influence people is redescribed as either coercion or seduction.

other protofictional narratives. Jesus' parables are the obvious example, but even Plato, often understandably viewed as the enemy of rhetoric, finds the fictive and rhetorical mode of allegory useful for his arguments in the *Phaedrus* and *The Republic*. The popularity of such novels as *The Da Vinci Code* and the *Left Behind* series is only the most recent evidence of fiction's ability to provoke religious argument and even to serve as surrogate theology—sometimes despite factual errors, commitment to false premises, flawed reasoning, or bad faith on the part of the author. And even if a reader begins from something like a Rortyan standpoint, distinguished fiction might nevertheless lead readers to love truth for its own sake. (That the work of the six writers examined in this book is more aesthetically distinguished than the productions of Jenkins and LaHaye or Dan Brown I take to be an uncontroversial claim.)

Some of the most interesting recent arguments in narrative theory, to be sure, have bracketed any connection between fiction and truth, even when they have not invoked aesthetic worth as the alternative to truth. Richard Walsh, for instance, describes "fictionality" as a distinct use of rhetoric (rather than a set of generic or formal features), and the "age-old problem of fiction's claim upon our attention" as "the problem of reconciling fictionality with relevance" (16). Readers find fiction compelling neither because they mistake it for a set of propositional truths—after all, most sentences in novels, referring to nonexistent people and events, are "false"—nor because they view it as an unproblematic imitation of the real world, but rather because they perceive its relevance to their interests. I find Walsh's argument suggestive but potentially misleading in its implication that relevance and truth are so neatly separable. (I am tempted to reply: Truth is always relevant.)[11] He is correct to maintain that "[f]iction does not achieve relevance globally, at one remove, through some form of analogical thinking, but incrementally, through the implication of various cognitive interests or values that are not contingent upon accepting the propositional

---

11. For the same reason, I am hesitant to endorse fully Nicholas Boyle's very different argument that a "Catholic approach to literature" would affirm that "[l]iterature is language free of instrumental purpose, and it seeks to tell the truth" (125). Much turns, no doubt, on the precise resonance of the phrase "instrumental purpose." For Boyle, "[B]oth sacred and secular literature . . . do not talk about the things of this world as, directly or indirectly, capable of fulfilling the desires of the speaker of the writer but talk about them in a way that Kant, who had something like this insight . . . called 'disinterested'" (125). Seeking to tell the truth may not be "instrumental" in that it will often not fulfill one's own all-too distorted and self-destructive appetites. But if Boyle means merely that in reading literary texts, readers may come to love the truth, without respect to how well it approves their cravings for power, then I am happy to concur. I would only add that having the right relation to the truth must be a matter of urgency, and that one should not simply reject exhortations to the truth on the grounds that they might be described as "instrumental."

truth of the utterance itself and upon the deployment, investment, and working through of those interests in narrative form" (30). The writers I examine certainly affirm particular truths that do not depend upon accepting the reality of the characters and the events they depict—which is what I understand Walsh to mean by "the propositional truth of the utterance itself." Moreover, these writes' efforts will succeed only to the degree that they establish these truths, through context-specific appeals, as relevant to readers. While the time that elapses in reading does preclude an "analogical thinking" that establishes relevance immediately, readers can and do make general statements about the truth claims of fiction as they read, statements which can later be corrected or refined. Taking Walsh at his word, then, when he holds that "a pragmatic approach to fictionality . . . does not, and should not, conflict with what we currently do as readers and critics" (37), I see no reason not to investigate both the persuasive strategies that these writers employ and their fidelity to the truths that they communicate.

As Benedict Anderson has suggested, the novel is an ideal vehicle for the presentation of argument in a secularized milieu, more congenial to the sensibilities of educated contemporary readers than allegory or parable. As "a device for the presentation of simultaneity in 'homogenous, empty time,' or a complex gloss on the word 'meanwhile'" (25), the novel invokes an "imagined community" that embeds and helps to explain its characters even as it generates conflicts among them.[12] Just as what binds millions of Americans into a single nation is less their shared intimacy or their commitment to a single set of beliefs than their simultaneous existence in a historically defined place, characters in novels interact and argue with each other without the harmonizing force of a single worldview—even when the author's own beliefs are evident. For this reason a theorist of genre such as Mikhail Bakhtin can view the novel as essentially dialogic and "unfinalizable" (68). I am happy to agree if "unfinalizable" means that beliefs expressed in novels are essentially contestable rather than "equally valid"—a distinction that Bakhtin's admirers do not always seem to recognize.

Even more than from Walsh, Anderson, or Bakhtin, however, I take my critical bearings from Booth, who never lost sight of the banal but radical fact that works of fiction, like all language, are communications between human beings. Communication in good faith requires an effort to understand that cannot be evaded by appeals to the "text itself" (as in many twentieth-century formalisms), to the ostensibly self-undermining properties of language (as in received accounts of deconstruction), or to some form of biological, historical, or ideological determinism. The bracketing of

---

12. The phrase "homogenous, empty time" is Walter Benjamin's.

authorial intention may perhaps be warranted when a reader focuses narrowly upon aesthetic judgment, though even then I have my doubts. But the mere fact that we exclude our own writing from such proscriptions, believing our persuasive efforts to be freely undertaken and worthwhile, suggests that we ought to extend the same courtesy to fiction writers. Unless one is willing to commit to a programmatic and contradictory antihumanism when confronting writing with persuasive intention (and it is striking how inconsistent even those who claim to do so become when push comes to shove—witness the later career of Michel Foucault), one must begin by taking writers at their word, respecting their efforts to communicate on their own terms, and acknowledging whatever clarifications they offer in commentary on their own work. As Booth makes clear in *The Company We Keep*, one's "coductions," in which one judges the intentions and merits of individual authors and works, will be "implicitly a comparison between the always complex experience we have had in its presence and what we have known before" (71). Such a stance does not rule out the possibility that a given piece of writing may be inept, its purposes incoherent or dishonest, or its author a victim of false consciousness. But the burden of proof for such claims is on readers; it cannot be waved away by recourse to general theories about language, subjectivity, or ideology whose premises are in principle unfalsifiable.

The writers examined here take for granted that in a world of secular, homogenous, and empty time, many in their intended audiences will not subscribe to their beliefs. And indeed, as writers of self-consciously literary fiction, they appeal to an educated audience more likely than the general population to live secular lives and to believe in the desirability (if not the inevitability) of secularization. They do not conclude, however, that the effort to persuade through fiction is futile. Instead, they present their beliefs forthrightly, in all their urgent contestability. Perhaps none is as explicit and thorough in the presentation of her beliefs as O'Connor, whose letters and essays, collected in *The Habit of Being* and *Mystery and Manners*, provide for many of her critics the definitive statement of how her fiction is to be interpreted. But even for those who are less explicit and whose concerns range afield from the strictly theological (such as Updike, Spark, and Gordon), the positive content of their Christian beliefs, rooted in the specific history, liturgies, and dogmas of Christianity, can be determined.

The specificity of these practices and beliefs ultimately derive from the centrality of revelation to Christianity—the claim that what is to be believed has been revealed by God through prophets; the inspiration of sacred scripture; and divine interventions in history such as the selection of Abraham and his descendants as a Chosen People, the Exodus of the Israelites from Egypt, or the incarnation, crucifixion, and resurrection of Jesus. Protestants and Catholics have traditionally agreed that whether reason contradicts or complements Christian orthodoxy, it cannot provide entirely sufficient grounds for Christian belief; only the authority of revelation can.[13] The importance of revelation to these six writers' fictive projects—often only implicitly expressed, but essential nonetheless—is rhetorically a double-edged sword. On the one hand, the ability to state one's beliefs in positive, succinct form constitutes a rhetorical strength. Against the thinness of many secular systems of belief and ethics—which, in my view, minimize the necessity of conflict by taking too much for granted that human beings want to be well disposed toward each other—a belief in revelation produces forthright, irreducibly contestable propositions.[14] (Either Jesus is the son of God who takes away the sins of the world, or he wasn't, and no amount of tolerance for Christian or non-Christian beliefs changes the fact that the question of who Jesus is/was is a truth claim, not an aesthetic preference.) On the other hand, if belief is founded upon revelation, then persuasion becomes much harder when the intended audience is not already open to the possibility that belief does not necessarily contradict reason. Even if many would agree in theory with Paul Giles's reminder that "[p]ure skepticism can never be attained, any more than pure reason or pure innocence can," such a reminder might do little more than suggest to secularist

13. When Martin Luther famously proclaimed that "Reason is the Devil's greatest whore," he seems to have meant that reason, while useful for the purposes of human knowledge, is a positive obstacle to knowledge of God, for it encourages the belief that one may achieve salvation entirely through one's own efforts. Catholicism has traditionally had a less hostile opinion of the relationship between reason and faith, but its official teaching maintains that while reason may suffice to justify theism, it cannot suffice to justify belief in the dogmas of Christianity. As the most recent *Catechism of the Catholic Church* puts it: "What moves us to believe is not the fact that revealed truths appear as true and intelligible in the light of our natural reason: we believe 'because of the authority of God himself who reveals them, who can neither deceive nor be deceived.'" And again: "Though faith is above reason, there can never be any real discrepancy between faith and reason. Since the same God who reveals mysteries and infuses faith has bestowed the light of reason on the human mind, God cannot deny himself, nor can truth ever contradict truth" (48, 49).

14. Many contemporary versions of pragmatism and cosmopolitanism, I would argue, fall under this category. Their emphasis on practice doesn't, of course, deny that beliefs motivate people, but it greatly underestimates the degree to which beliefs matter. Kwame Anthony Appiah, for instance, points out that "we can live in harmony without agreeing on underlying values" and that "we can find ourselves in conflict when we do agree on values" (78). He is of course correct, but to make this argument presupposes that the primary good *should* be harmony. There is much to be said for such a live-and-let-live attitude; it is even compatible with much of the ethical thrust of Christianity. It cannot be, however, the *sine qua non* for Christians, because it does not admit the primacy of revelation. The Misfit's claim (in O'Connor's "A Good Man Is Hard to Find") that Jesus "thown [sic] everything off balance" (27) is worth remembering here. Balance and harmony are not necessarily Christian virtues, as Slavoj Žižek has reminded us (*Fragile* 122–23).

readers what Giles calls "the discrepancy" between the "lucidity" of the "rational mind" and "every form of religious conditioning or assertion of religious truth" (19). Christian orthodox writers addressing a wider public therefore seldom rely on exhortations to the revealed word of God alone; they must employ other arguments, and various traditions within Christianity on the relationship between revelation and reason make possible a range of rhetorical approaches.[15] The difficulty, it would seem, is how to employ strategies that do not initially *depend* on an appeal to revelation, yet do not ultimately *contradict* its primacy.

A related difficulty has to do with historical context—or, put differently, the tension between the particularity of an act of persuasion and the universality of the claims asserted. A writer who proclaims the truth of Christianity might tailor rhetorical strategies to particular audiences—one thinks of Paul, a Jew among Jews and a Greek among Greeks, or of Augustine, accepting that Christians have something to learn from classical rhetoric as long as they don't cross the line into sophistry—but insofar as he considers his beliefs to be true and therefore universal, there can be no exclusions of anyone on principle. Yet because an intended audience is historically, geographically, or rhetorically delimited, there is always the risk that the appeal to that audience will undermine the belief's integrity. This risk is compounded when the vehicle for persuasion is a work of fiction and therefore bound up with culturally variable narratives and histories. The "transcendental signified" of any belief system is ahistorical, while the individual narratives that are the raw materials of fiction are temporal. Christianity, which affirms both an eternal, transcendent God and the teleology of God's involvement with human beings (most strikingly in the Incarnation), must negotiate both the temporal and the atemporal, accounting for its own enmeshment in the stream of human history. Yet the more writers invoke the particularities of their time and place, or resort to auto-

---

15. In presenting his own position on these matters, Giles mostly avoids definite statements about the validity of religious claims but reveals his own secular commitment to "demystification" clearly enough. *American Catholic Arts and Fictions* seeks "to reveal how a secularized form of religious consciousness has become implanted within twentieth-century American art" (21), in ways that often elude detection. The "lucidity" of the "rational mind" thus proves itself through the deconstruction of claims to authority. At best, Giles suggests, Catholicism performs its own demystifying function when it confronts other (primarily political) claims of authority: "The culture of Catholicism deconstructs the more celebrated American ideologies . . . to reveal them as provisional systems; Catholic arts and fictions in turn deconstruct the theological and philosophical bases of Catholicism . . . but the critical impulse of deconstruction in turn illuminates the fictional status of all these aesthetic creations, reconstituting them as inventions of the human imagination at particular times and places within history" (183). That it might provide access to a truth that is more than "provisional" and "aesthetic" is not seriously considered.

biographical explanations for their own beliefs, the more idiosyncratic their beliefs might seem.

Perhaps the first Christian writer to ponder the rhetorical problems involved in writing about belief within a secular context was Blaise Pascal. Earlier proselytizers, such as Paul and Augustine, could assume that their intended audience already shared a sense of the sacred (hence the enormous energy Augustine expends in *The City of God* arguing against the gods of pagan Rome, and in other works against Christian heresies). Pascal, however, reflects on the difficulties of arguments about belief when one's audience includes agnostics. He proposes a strategy for how to craft arguments that do not begin with revelation but do not preclude it: "[W]e must begin by showing that religion is not contrary to reason; that it is venerable, to inspire respect for it; then we must make it lovable, to make good men hope it is true; finally, we must prove it is true" (205).

If the truth of Christianity is guaranteed by its divine revelation, then it follows that making this revelation explicit would be the final step of an argument on its behalf—that a potential convert could make this leap only after having been persuaded of its reasonableness and desirability. This task would be far more difficult than the first, as Pascal perceived it to be even long before Marx, Darwin, or Freud. For Pascal understands the earlier tasks of persuasion, however necessary, as steps that must finally be *aufgehoben* (to use the anachronistic Hegelian term) in the "foolish" assent to Christian revelation:

> Our religion is wise and foolish. Wise, because it is the most learned and the most founded on miracles, prophecies, etc. Foolish, because it is not all this which makes us belong to it. This makes us, indeed, condemn those who do not belong to it; but it does not cause belief in those who belong to it. . . . And so Saint Paul, who came with wisdom and signs, says that he has come neither with wisdom nor with signs; for he came to convert. But those who come only to convince can say that they come with wisdom and signs. (277)

The distinction between "convincing" and "converting" that Pascal identifies here marks the acid test of religious persuasion, and it is difficult to reconcile the first passage I quoted (with its methodical progression of argumentative steps) with the exasperation toward argument implicit in the second passage. How, then, does one move from convincing to converting, and what rhetorical strategies does one employ in this effort?

For all six of the writers discussed below, *irony* is crucial to bridging the gap. "Irony" here should not be understood primarily as a steely-eyed fatalism that flirts with tragedy, corrodes any positive values, or leads only to a perpetually renewed (and frequently bogus) humility in the face of ethical and epistemological confusion. Rather, it is above all an invitation—to use Booth's helpful metaphor, an invitation to leap toward a new view "that is intended as wiser, wittier, more compassionate, subtler, truer, more moral, or at least less obviously vulnerable to further irony" than one's former view (*Rhetoric of Irony* 10). Some, such as O'Connor, assume the hostility of their audience and take for granted that the invitation will wound—that one must become a victim before (or at the same time as) one is admitted to the newer perspective. Others, such as Spark and Updike, make of the invitation a form of complicity between author and reader, wagering that much will depend on whether they have guessed their intended audience's predispositions and desires correctly. Yet for all of these writers, irony proves stable—it does not initiate an infinite regress in which no truths or bedrock values can be plausibly asserted or defended. What Booth states of irony in general is true of all six writers' approach to it, though their methods and degrees of intended "victimization" are very different: "[W]e need no very extensive survey of ironic examples to discover . . . that the building of amiable communities is often far more important than the exclusion of naïve victims. . . . The author I infer behind the false words is my kind of man, because . . . he grants me a kind of wisdom; he assumes that he does not have to spell out the shared and secret truths on which my reconstruction is to be built" (28). This double movement—on the one hand, an exclusion that may involve an appeal to elitism (an appeal particularly evident in Spark); on the other, the building up of an affirmative and potentially unlimited community of the like-minded—is, of course, intrinsic to Christianity itself, for the God who divides the sheep from the goats and emphasizes the narrowness of the straight path nevertheless wills the salvation of all human beings (1 Timothy 2:3–4). When such irony succeeds as an appeal, it probably does so in part because it accommodates both the exclusions of any actual community and the universality (that is, the truth) of that community's beliefs.

There is also, however, a more existential dimension to the irony that these six writers use—a sense that only an ironic approach can account for the messiness of the world and thus reach a contemporary audience effectively. Even a cursory glance at Western history during the twentieth century suggests not only the enormous importance that irony assumed as an aesthetic concept but also the tendency to invoke it as a coping mechanism for the traumas of modernity. Arguments against Christianity, after all, found much apparent support in the horrors of the early to mid-twentieth century—two world wars, the Nazi attempt to annihilate the Jews, the atrocities that took place in Stalin's Soviet Union, and the dropping of atomic bombs on cities in Japan—which raised the question of theodicy in unprecedented ways. Indeed, it has always been plausible to construct an account of modernism in the arts that places doubt about God and the social orders that he had allegedly blessed at center stage. Seminal modernist moments, texts, and themes would thus include Stephen Daedalus's revolt against Catholicism in Joyce's *A Portrait of the Artist as a Young Man*, Freud's deep and intractable pessimism about religion in *Civilization and Its Discontents*, the inaccessibility of divine law in Kafka's *The Trial*, and Brett Ashley's affirmation in Hemingway's *The Sun Also Rises* that "not to be a bitch" is "what we have instead of God" (245).

On the other hand—and partially in response to these developments—it is equally plausible to see modernism as a return to the primacy of belief after a long trek through the wilderness of positivist science and its monstrous offspring, global capitalism. Nietzsche, however scornful toward Christianity his work may have been, was in this camp, looking forward to a revival of self-conscious paganism that would reject the bourgeois capitalism and slavish, atavistic religions of the Last Men. D. H. Lawrence elaborated similar ideas in his novel *The Plumed Serpent*, suggesting that the modern world might rediscover more primordial and vital beliefs in the religion of the Aztecs. The key figure here, however, was T. S. Eliot, who also marks a decisive rupture within the "believing" wing of modernism. After beginning his career along vaguely Nietzschean lines, enthusiastically applauding Stravinsky's *Le sacre du printemps* and appealing to comparative mythology in *The Waste Land*, Eliot threw his allegiance to Christianity, shocking many of his admirers in 1927 with his declaration that he was now "classicist in literature, royalist in politics, and Anglo-Catholic in religion" (ix). By virtue of his visibility alone, Eliot probably did more than anyone else to make Christian orthodoxy compelling to anxious moderns— yet he appealed to irony no less than did those moderns who rejected Christianity. His literary career both paralleled and helped to influence a revival of religious writing, especially among Catholic writers. Indeed, were I to conduct a comprehensive survey of major Western writers during the age of high modernism (say, from 1910 to 1955) who either advocate orthodox Christian beliefs or engage seriously with them, I would have to deal not only with Eliot but also with G. K. Chesterton, Charles Péguy, Georges Bernanos, Graham Greene, François Mauriac, Czeslaw Milosz, Caroline Gordon, Allen Tate, Evelyn Waugh, W. H. Auden, C. S. Lewis, J. F. Powers, Robert Lowell, Nikos Kazantzakis, and Albert Camus.

Yet while O'Connor, Percy, Spark, and Updike first emerge in a period defined by aesthetic modernism, the bulk of their work was published during and after the 1960s, when the banners of postmodernism (whether defined primarily in aesthetic or epistemological terms) begin to fly. In the most common understanding of the term, postmodernism is even more committed to irony than modernism was: irony drives the "incredulity toward metanarratives" that Lyotard spoke of, undermining all metaphysics, but generating, instead of the angst, despair, or religious faith that were its most frequent effects under modernism, a breezy joy, a vague sense of liberation. Given such a definition of postmodernism, Christian orthodoxy becomes less plausible, even as the specific aspects of modernity that once seemed to challenge it recede or lose their initially traumatizing character. Perhaps it should not be surprising that writers who remain committed to Christian orthodoxy in such times increasingly present themselves as embattled and self-consciously contrarian.

Yet I do not view the ascendancy of postmodernism as a catastrophe, and I do not measure the rhetorical efficacy of Christian writers in postmodern conditions primarily by their degree of crankiness. Instead, I maintain that this usual understanding of postmodernism is wrong—or, at the very least, unwilling to embrace its implications fully. As Peter Augustine Lawler has suggested, postmodernism is best understood as "human reflection on the failure of the modern project to eradicate human mystery and misery and to bring history to an end" (1). The antifoundationalism that many conflate with postmodernism is, on the other hand, "really hypermodernism, or the exaggeration to the point of caricature of the modern impulse to self-creation" (2). I align myself not just with Lawler but with a group of thinkers from Romano Guardini to Ralph Wood who hold that "postmodernism" affords a propitious opportunity to speak and hear Christian orthodoxy, and to do so in relative freedom both from the cultural accretions that often distorted its message in the past (leading to, for instance, such phenomena as German *Kulturprotestantismus*) and from the increasingly discredited "modern" imperative to master and remake the world and human beings. Guardini's evocation of the conditions obtaining at "the end of the modern world"—a passage which was excerpted by Percy in the epigraph to his 1966 novel *The Last Gentleman*—remains powerful and, I believe, persuasive:

> Everywhere within the modern world [the Christian] found ideas and values whose Christian origin was clear, but which were declared the common property of all. How could he trust a situation like that? But the new age will do away with these ambivalences; the new age will declare that the secularized facets of Christianity are sentimentalities. This declaration will clear the air. The world to come will be filled with animosity and dan-

ger, but it will be a world open and clean. This danger within the new world will also have its cleansing effect upon the new Christian attitude, which in a special way must possess both trust and courage.

The character and the conduct of coming Christian life will reveal itself especially through its old dogmatic roots. Christianity will once again need to prove itself deliberately as a faith which is not self-evident; it will be forced to distinguish itself more sharply from a dominantly non-Christian ethos. . . . The absolute experiencing of dogma will, I believe, make men feel more sharply the direction of life and the meaning of existence itself. (105–6)

What Guardini calls "the new Christian attitude" centers upon the claim, accessible only through revelation, that God's salvific work is gratuitous and—as Ralph Wood often reminds us—scandalous, in the original sense of the word.[16] It can be reduced neither to a secularized ethics nor to a do-it-yourself spirituality. Against the backdrop of a discredited modernity, the electrifying character of Christian tidings is all the more evident. And those who wrestle with it honestly—including those who, like Gordon and Robinson, cannot fully embrace orthodox doctrine and practice—testify to its power. The irony proper to such tidings is not only affirmative in Booth's sense of creating a community—it is also so in the joyful conviction that the world, however imbued with evil it may be, is already redeemed.

In constructing this book, I have faced two recurring difficulties. On the one hand, there are the unavoidable problems of space and focus: because several of the writers discussed here have had extremely prolific careers (the published works of Spark and Updike, for instance, span roughly half a century), I have not been able to engage with all of their work in detail. On the other hand, because previous critics have read these writers through varied theological lenses, I am also wary of repeating familiar interpretations. I have tried to evade these difficulties not only by hewing closely to my focus on the rhetorical strategies of each writer, drawing comparisons and contrasts when appropriate, but also by focusing on works that are both representative of an author's career as a whole and, in my view, unjustly neglected. The chapter on Updike, for instance, examines *Couples* and the Rabbit Angstrom tetralogy only in passing but proffers extended close readings of *The Poorhouse Fair* and *In the Beauty of the Lilies*. In the case

---

16. "Scandalous" derives from the Greek word *skandalon*, a snare or stumbling block. Guardini suggests that the cooptation of Christian "ideas and values" by secular Western culture has obscured the scandalous character of Christianity, its claim to be a truth that is nonetheless not "self-evident," a truth that will have to be proven "deliberately," despite its implausibility, but which can be confirmed only in the "absolute experiencing of dogma."

of writers whose corpus is smaller, such as O'Connor, I have simply chosen the works that seem to me best suited to highlight the authors' distinct rhetorical appeals.

Chapter 1 begins by considering the fundamental impasse that has always governed interpretation of Flannery O'Connor's work. Because O'Connor was so explicit both about her intended audience of secularists and about her fictional aims, critics of her work have been divided into those who see her as a prophet and those who, rejecting her religious vision, seek either to redeem her work for twentieth-century liberalism or to castigate its alleged cruelty and antihumanism. After considering my own exasperation before this impasse, I argue that the impasse will persist, for it reveals that belief itself—whether in Christianity or in some other set of commitments—is inescapable, and that O'Connor's facility in foregrounding this fact is perhaps her most compelling strength as a writer. I then suggest that O'Connor intends her obsessive violence in large part as an index of human freedom, which her own Catholic version of Christian orthodoxy affirms. Precisely because intimations of freedom in a literary work must seem counterintuitive and self-contradictory—a fictional character, after all, is by definition not free—violence connotes freedom because it suggests a breaking of the chains of realist necessity and plausibility. The "freest" act of all thus becomes the acceptance of God's grace, in spite of the considerable obstacles to its accomplishment. Taking up three of O'Connor's most celebrated stories, "A Good Man Is Hard to Find," "The Artificial Nigger," and "Judgement [sic] Day," I contend that O'Connor more successfully dramatizes this nexus of violence, human freedom, and Christian belief in the first and the third of these stories than in the second.

Chapter 2 examines Muriel Spark, a convert to Catholicism and in some respects the most sophisticated of these writers. I argue that in contrast to O'Connor, who assumed the hostility of her audience, Spark declares herself to be writing for "really intelligent people" and tailors her rhetorical strategies as appeals to her readers' aesthetic sensitivity—an approach informed by her own reading in John Henry Newman and by her tendency to portray artist figures whose own work is figured as analogous to divine creation. Though Spark's particular approach runs the risks of theological distortion and unabashed elitism, I argue that often its cold, self-assured whimsicality often proves compelling, particularly in works such as *The Comforters, The Girls of Slender Means, The Abbess of Crewe, Loitering with Intent,* and *Reality and Dreams.*

Chapter 3 examines the contradiction that many have seen in the work of John Updike—an unfashionable and stern commitment to Protestant theology on the one hand and an obsessive attention to sexual delight on the other, both filtered through a sense of American exceptionalism. Through sustained readings of *The Poorhouse Fair* and *In the Beauty of the Lilies* and briefer considerations of *Couples, Roger's Version,* and *Terrorist,* I argue that what resolves this apparent contradiction is a commitment to narcissism. Updike perilously casts the doctrines of Christianity as appeals to the essential narcissism of the twentieth-century white American male, gambling that readers will find their own narcissism reflected and confirmed. In his first novel, *The Poorhouse Fair,* Updike accommodates this narcissism even as he (in light of his later work) uncharacteristically suggests that orthodox belief and moral conduct ought to go together. As his career progresses, however, Updike comes to divide the two and even to suggest that orthodoxy affords a greater frisson to one's sins. By the time he publishes *In the Beauty of the Lilies,* he has come not to take disbelief seriously but rather to regard it as a species of thwarted belief that springs from the same narcissistic desires that motivate faith.

Chapter 4 focuses on the later career of Walker Percy. Like Spark a convert to Catholicism, Percy argues for the truth of Catholic Christianity but takes as his point of departure what he regards as the near-universal condition of boredom in modernity. In my earlier book, *Fears and Fascinations: Representing Catholicism in the American South,* I argued that in his first three novels, Percy proposes that Catholicism can restore meaning to people made desperate by their boredom, but shows, against his intentions, how easily this Catholicism can become an essentially aesthetic marker of "lifestyle." Here I continue and refine this argument, considering the fictive works of Percy's later career—his novels *Lancelot, The Second Coming,* and *The Thanatos Syndrome,* and the narrative "A Space Odyssey" embedded in *Lost in the Cosmos.* These novels display a new stridency, and I argue that they represent an attempt to leave behind the ambiguities of the earlier books, even, perhaps, through a sacrifice of aesthetic complexity. At the same time, when these texts are at their most compelling, they continue to emphasize that only death brings closure to human lives, that any change in belief is possible until that point, and that the chief difficulty that Christians face is that of keeping faith in a world in which boredom is never permanently eradicated.

Finally, in chapter 5, I examine the work of Mary Gordon, a Catholic, and Marilynne Robinson, a Congregationalist. Both writers emerge in a context defined by recent turmoil in their respective traditions—the events and effects of the Second Vatican Council for Gordon; the decline of mainline American Protestantism and of the habits of civic responsibility that it nourished for Robinson. I do not challenge these writers' self-description as Christian, but I do argue that their treatment of Christian orthodoxy is more accurately described as a use of Christian orthodoxy than an argument in favor of it. Gordon's novels—particularly *Final Payments, The Company of Women, Spending,* and *Pearl*—evoke the vanishing milieu of ethnic working-class Catholicism in the Northeast, yet tend to argue that the value both of Catholicism itself and of the culture it produced is largely aesthetic. Theologically, Gordon invokes the "spirit of Vatican II," but her deepest commitments, to art and to sexual pleasure, both intersect with and oppose this spirit in ways that seem even more self-serving than Updike's avowedly narcissistic appeal. Turning attention to Robinson's intelligent and feisty appeal to a liberal Calvinist tradition in her essays, I argue that she places the doctrines of Christian orthodoxy in the service of a democratic humanism that she considers threatened by the triumphs of a materialist worldview and global capitalism. In her novels *Gilead* and *Home,* on the other hand, Robinson portrays Calvinism, as practiced in a small Iowa town in 1956, as the norm against which modern anomie is measured and found wanting—an approach that depends in part on an insular nostalgia that is in some tension with her avowed universalism. In both the novels and the essays, Robinson succeeds in making Christian orthodoxy attractive to her readers but does so in a way that emphasizes cultural critique instead of truth—and in doing so empties it of much of its specificity.

Throughout this book, as I develop my judgments of these writers' rhetorical appeals, my primary intention is less to convert people than to convey something of the remarkable power and integrity of Christian orthodoxy, to insist that such unabashed claims to tell the truth deserve a respectful hearing. Ralph Wood's salutary reminder that "Christians are not converted and sustained in their faith chiefly through art and culture, but through the community of worship and witness called the church" (*Comedy* 282) marks the limits of my inquiry, for I am maintaining neither that "correct" readings of these writers' fiction *should* result in conversion, nor that the work of these writers might provide—as per Hungerford's argument—an aesthetically rewarding surrogate for Christian belief. Nevertheless, I feel comfortable here following Augustine's cues in *On Christian Doctrine*—subsuming (as Wayne Booth does) fiction to rhetoric and likening these writers' specific fictive narratives to a kind of oratory. The celebrated claim attributed to Karl Barth—"Belief cannot argue with unbelief; it can only preach to it"—need not necessarily contradict my purpose, for surely one can distinguish between more and less effective preaching.

My overarching claim is that despite the difficulties negotiated by these six writers, Christian orthodoxy still has the potential to persuade or to trouble, even among educated audiences most committed to secular principles. Indeed, I suspect—as Kierkegaard argued and Guardini reaffirmed—

that this is truer, in a world deeply marked by Hungerford's postmodern belief, than it might have been in a more uniformly constituted Christendom. This is my own Boothian coduction, derived not only from my own experience of reading these works and finding my own faith both challenged and strengthened but also from the way my readings of these texts intersect with recent trends in the sphere of what used to be called "critical theory." I am particularly encouraged by the fact that even a number of contemporary Marxist philosophers, such as Alain Badiou and Slavoj Žižek, have claimed the banner of "belief" in an effort to resuscitate their moribund political projects.[17] The potential power of Christian orthodoxy, in other words, is evident even to those who would appropriate it for anti-Christian ends and distort its insistence on truth. If I am able to convey something of this power even to those who are nominally Christian but who are, to a far greater degree, citizens of the contemporary secular West, then this book will have fulfilled its purpose.

---

17. See especially Badiou's *Saint Paul: The Foundations of Universalism* and Žižek's *On Belief.*

1

Flannery O'Connor, the Irreducibility of Belief, and the Problem of Audience

I. On Homeric Battlefields:
A Confession and a Credo

Any consideration of the rhetoric of Christian orthodoxy in late modern fiction cannot avoid Flannery O'Connor, for no other Christian writer of the period has been as explicit about her avowed purpose and her intended audience. Her commentary on her fiction has been quoted perhaps more often than the fiction itself, and her statements have, through repetition, acquired a magisterial ring. "Let me make no bones about it: I write from the standpoint of Christian orthodoxy. . . . I write with a solid belief in *all* the Christian dogmas" (*Habit* 147; emphasis in text). "My audience are the people who think that God is dead" (*Habit* 92). "The novelist with Christian concerns will find in modern life distortions which are repugnant to him, and his problem will be to make these appear as distortions to an audience which is used to seeing them as natural; and he may well be forced to take ever more violent means to get his vision across to this hostile audience" ("Fiction Writer" 33–34). Precisely because O'Connor's intentions are indubitable, much of the debate surrounding her work has been shaped by the degree to which her critics are already in sympathy with her project. The distinguished company of readers who share O'Connor's theological premises, viewing her as a prophet who lashes the fallen world with the painful truth that Jesus died to save humankind, is matched by the distinguished company of readers, going at least as far back as John Hawkes, who hold that O'Connor is unknowingly of the Devil's party. And these two contending sides are joined today by historicist critics from Jon Lance Bacon to Patricia Yaeger, who see neither salvation nor nihilism in her work but only the distorted reflections of the racist, sexist, class-obsessed, and Cold War–damaged culture that was the South of her lifetime. The situation has not changed much since 1992, when Frederick Crews complained that "there is never a shortage of volunteers to replace the original antagonists" (156) in the fundamental debates over O'Connor's work. Some readers ask, "Should we take O'Connor's Catholicism seriously or stow it away in a box marked 'false consciousness' or 'irrelevant window dressing'"? Others ask, "Should we condemn O'Connor for remaining silent before the racial injustices of her time, or praise her for registering some slight or partial resistance to them?"

These questions cannot be answered solely on the basis of O'Connor's literary corpus. Although academic readers pride themselves on having escaped the limitations of the New Criticism, and although they repeat the notion that there is no disinterested point of view so often that it has become a bromide, the protocols of scholarly discourse still require readers to act as if their arguments were latent in texts themselves and only incidentally positions in which they happen to believe. When readers approach O'Connor, however, such protocols get them nowhere, for at this late date, it should be clear that *all* of these contending positions are amply supported by textual evidence. There is no good reason to doubt the sincerity or the orthodoxy of O'Connor's beliefs, and readers who know how these beliefs informed her fictional practice must acknowledge her consistency in applying them. There is no necessary contradiction, for instance, in the claim that the grandmother's murder in "A Good Man Is Hard to Find," or Mrs. May's goring on the horn of the scrub bull in "Greenleaf," might simultaneously function as the salvation of these women. Those who blanch at the ferocity of O'Connor's vision and dispute that so violent and uncompromising a stance can be authentically Christian need to read more both about the dogmas and the history of Christianity.

On the other hand, if O'Connor wrote "for those who believe that God is dead," seeking to shock them into a life-changing awareness of the Incarnation, then the response of individual readers suggests that she failed at least as often as she succeeded. Early critics of her work such as Josephine Hendin and Martha Stephens, who found O'Connor's fundamental premises (though not necessarily her fiction) repugnant, were neither stupid nor ignorant of her intentions, and while such readers might conceivably be guilty of the intellectual hubris that O'Connor loved to skewer, one cannot charge them with a willful misreading of the text. Their own beliefs may be wrong, but their arguments are based on an examination of O'Connor's fiction in good faith through the light of these beliefs.

Moreover, anyone who has taught O'Connor repeatedly knows that uninitiated students typically adore her work and are deft at generating interpretations, but they almost never arrive at those that O'Connor intended. My avowedly secular students, upon hearing of O'Connor's religious orthodoxy, are puzzled and sometimes intrigued by what they perceive as the exoticism of her position, but they then shrug and pursue their own interpretations, not converted, not feeling the slightest need to argue with her. My Christian students, on the other hand—unless they have been taught O'Connor by a previous teacher—are usually shocked. I almost always receive papers arguing either that O'Connor's vision cannot possibly be Christian or that her efforts to persuade are at best counterintuitive, at worst perverse, because in a contemporary United States shaped largely by what Christian Smith and Melinda Lundquist Denton call "Moral Therapeutic Deism" (118—my students do not use this term, but their descriptions make clear that they have something like it in mind), she makes Christianity look depraved and unattractive. The first of these arguments is untenable; the second, however, is difficult to dispute. There is a corpse with three bullet holes at the end of "A Good Man Is Hard to Find," a body killed by a man obsessed with Jesus. O'Connor tells us, famously, not to pay attention to it but to "the action of grace" and the "lines of spiritual motion" ("On Her Own Work" 113). Unfortunately, only the body is in the text; whatever grace and lines of spiritual motion there may be exist only in O'Connor's intentions, in the responses of readers to them, and in the coductions that readers might formulate in ongoing conversations about them. To interpret the murder either as a highly entertaining horror, as secular readers might, or as a sign that the grandmother has been saved by one of God's more inscrutable dispensations of grace, is to go outside the text, to refer to structures of belief rather than to simple, unproblematic evidence. The debate centers not on the interpretation of the text, but on the proper context to choose for the interpretation of the text—and as such, it is irresolvable.

The same is true of the debate surrounding O'Connor's relationship to racial justice. On the one hand, some readers have found much to praise in O'Connor's representation of black characters—Alice Walker notes her "distance . . . from the inner workings of her black characters" and praises her for the humility that made such distance possible (52), while Crews echoes many readers' sense that "the black characters in her fiction generally do come off better than the whites—more humane, more intuitively sensible, and of course markedly less susceptible to the status anxiety and self-aggrandizement that she loved to pillory" (157–58). There is also, of course, O'Connor's orthodox conviction, expressed most ringingly in "The Artificial Nigger" and in "Revelation," that everyone, black and white, can be saved. On the other hand, there is little in O'Connor's fiction to indicate clear, unambiguous support for the civil rights movement, much distaste for those who participated directly in it, and much to suggest that such merely political matters are insignificant when viewed *sub specie aeternitatis*. Again, the debate is not about the interpretation of the text, since readers on both sides point to the same passages and interpret them plausibly; it is about the priority of contexts of interpretation. What matters most—representational depth, declarations in support of racial justice, or the state of individual souls? Without a textually grounded way to adjudicate these competing claims, the debate remains irresolvable.

Faced with these impasses, my own impulse has always been to change the subject. Though as a Catholic I share O'Connor's theology, I have always felt a certain resistance to her work, even when I have found it most compelling. In my own writing on O'Connor, I have read "Parker's Back" as a critique of visuality that can be illuminated by the work of Lacan and Luce Irigaray; I have invoked Jane Jacobs's theories of urbanism to account for the function of community in "A Stroke of Good Fortune" and "The Artificial Nigger"; and I have suggested that literary naturalism, especially in its theories of sexual determinism, might be a profitable lens through which to read *Wise Blood*. In pursuing these readings, my motivation has been to say something fresh, to draw attention to hitherto unnoticed aspects of O'Connor's texts and, above all, to avoid the boredom of endless repetition. And yet I cannot escape the conviction that these readings, although not necessarily invalid—after all, they point to textual evidence and offer logical argument to make their cases, as any reading must—are ultimately beside the point. None of these readings challenges the fundamental debates about O'Connor's work; each can easily be pressed into the service of one side or the other. One can, for instance, endorse a Catholic reading of O'Connor *and* think that O'Connor's stance toward vision has more in common with Lacan's than with Descartes's; there is no necessary contradiction here. One can reject O'Connor's Christian commitments *and* believe that *Wise Blood* is best understood as a naturalist novel. My attention to differences has not made a difference.

In *The Shape of the Signifier: 1967 to the End of History*, Walter Benn Michaels suggests that what I have been trying to do—to multiply possible readings of O'Connor's work, to let a thousand flowers bloom—reflects a larger trend within academic writing, a move away from "disagreement" and toward "difference." The most obvious expressions of this trend are the rise of multiculturalism and the absolute commitment among many theorists and critics to the primacy of the subject position. As Michaels puts it, when readers commit to subject position—that is, to identity—as the key element that determines how they read a text, they commit to a protocol in which "there can be no conflicts of interpretation, not because there can be no conflict but because there can be no interpretation. All conflict has been turned into conflict between those who speak one language and those who speak another or between those who wish to eliminate difference and those who wish to preserve it, and the act of interpreting what someone says has been reconfigured either as the act of saying the same thing or as the act of saying something else" (64). While I have not proposed my readings of O'Connor as an expression of my own identity (in the manner of the "As a [fill in the blank with an identitarian category], I maintain" readings that one sometimes encounters), I have valued them precisely because I saw them as introducing an element of difference into an arena marked by endless disagreement. To speak of disagreement is to speak about belief, about questions of what is true and what is false; to speak of difference is to speak about identity or taste, neither of which is truly subject to debate.

And yet, Michaels suggests, to speak of difference instead of disagreement cannot, in the end, be anything other than a dodge, for the distinction between difference and disagreement is also a clash of beliefs, not a choice—as my writing on O'Connor has sometimes implied—between beliefs and something else. The claim that difference *qua* difference matters is, after all, a truth claim, and it is just as contestable as the claims that either O'Connor's religious vision or her vexing position on southern race relations should be the starting point for whatever critics say about her. And as a truth claim, it is necessarily exclusionary, despite its rhetoric of openness to multiplicity. It is, however, a claim that refuses to defend itself against direct challenges, and that smugly takes its refusal as a sign of unwarranted moral superiority.

I read Michaels's indictment of the way academics argue—or, more precisely, refuse to argue—and I find myself justly condemned. The enjoyment I have derived from my readings of O'Connor has taken the form of one-upmanship, of a sense that while others go on vulgarly shouting at each other about Christianity or about racial justice, I have perceived, as Wallace Stevens might put it, "ghostlier demarcations, keener sounds" (106). I have been like the representative intellectual that Slavoj Žižek posits in the following passage from *The Puppet and the Dwarf*, one of his recent books on the Judeo-Christian tradition:

[W]hen, today, one directly asks an intellectual: "OK, let's cut the crap and get down to basics: do you believe in some form of the divine or not?," the first answer is an embarrassed withdrawal, as if the question is too intimate, too probing; this withdrawal is then usually explained in more "theoretical" terms: "That is the wrong question to ask! It is not simply a matter of believing or not, but, rather, a matter of certain radical experience, of the ability to open oneself to a certain unheard-of dimension, of the way our openness to radical Otherness allows us to adopt a specific ethical stance, to experience a shattering form of enjoyment. . . ." What we are getting today is a kind of "suspended" belief, a belief that can thrive only as not fully (publicly) admitted, as a private obscene secret. Against this attitude, one should insist even more emphatically that the 'vulgar' question 'Do you really believe or not?' matters—more than ever, perhaps. (5–6)

Žižek is correct here. Although his recent work has been rightly criticized by those who perceive its opportunism—his stated thesis, after all, is that Christianity and his own brand of atheistic dialectical materialism belong, so to speak, on the same side of the barricades—this opportunism does not invalidate his more fundamental claim: that everyone is a *believer* of one kind or another, and that what divides believers in disagreement from believers in difference is merely that the first group takes both its beliefs and its antagonists seriously while the second group tries to disavow its beliefs or to prevent their emergence as points of contention. After all, one can argue with a belief; one cannot argue with a subject position. And one can respond to claims of radical openness to experience only by suggesting that the speaker is less radically open than he or she believes— which leaves unexamined the premise that radical openness is supremely desirable or even possible. To invoke such terms in the course of an argument is, in effect, to declare them off limits, to decline engagement with those who see interpretation as a function of something other than a mere reflection of identity, and to call one's seriousness into question.

In a time when the general public knows little about the work of literary scholars, and derives much of what it does know from the inevitable stories in the media after each MLA Convention that portray it as a circus, Žižek's lesson demands attention. The commitment to difference among literary scholars is also, above all, a commitment to novelty, and as such, it reinforces the consumerist imperatives both of capitalist society and the profession. It is becoming difficult to avoid the conclusion that scholars value difference *qua* difference primarily because they need to go on publishing new things, and that their disdain for repetition differs little from the disdain of the consumer who, having purchased last year's model, now needs this year's lest he or she feel outclassed by hipper, more beautiful people.

For this reason, scholars in the field of O'Connor studies may have much to offer their colleagues in the profession as a whole. The record of O'Connor criticism shows that for all the different topics that one might focus on in her work, it is impossible to avoid coming back to or being coopted by a few fundamental debates about significant matters. The profession would probably be healthier and its value more evident if all academic debate were like debate about O'Connor, if scholars were less consumed with the pursuit of novelty and publication and more concerned with the proposal and defense of core beliefs in their interpretations. As Fredric Jameson observed long ago in *The Political Unconscious*:

> [O]ur object of study is less the text itself than the interpretations through which we attempt to confront and to appropriate it. Interpretation is here construed as an essentially allegorical act, which consists in rewriting a given text in terms of a particular interpretive master code. [. . .] I happen to feel that no interpretation can be effectively disqualified on its own terms by a simple enumeration of inaccuracies or omissions, or by a list of unanswered questions. Interpretation is not an isolated act, but takes place within a Homeric battlefield, on which a host of interpretive options are either openly or implicitly in conflict. (9–10, 13)

O'Connor criticism certainly has been a "Homeric battlefield," in which a few interpretive master codes have slugged it out. Secular, religious, and historicizing critics have jumped into the fray, and whatever their arguments, they have expressed their basic commitment to their beliefs in ways that remind me of the altogether admirable sentiment of Rufus Johnson in "The Lame Shall Enter First": "Even if I didn't believe it, it would still be true" (477). In other words, they have not shrunk from emphasizing the universality of their claims, the logical conclusion that claims that are true or false must be true or false for everyone, and that every genuine debate—as opposed to proliferations of difference—is a clash of competing universalisms.

Henry T. Edmonson III has recently argued that O'Connor's work urges a "return to good and evil" and a rejection of modern attempts (beginning with Nietzsche) to transcend these categories. His argument is correct, and it ought to be acknowledged as such even by those readers who reject the Thomist framework that he draws upon to define good and evil. It is correct not only because O'Connor did indeed seek to make readers freshly aware of the distinction between good and evil (this is simply a fact about her intentions) but also because *everyone* who argues in good faith for the truth of his or her beliefs necessarily universalizes, necessarily combats those who reject them. Everyone, in other words, committed to the search for truth necessarily invokes definitions of good and evil. Even Nietzsche's claim to have transcended good and evil entails its own good and its own evil.

Many readers will find such a conclusion unsettling, because they have become accustomed to thinking of epistemic uncertainty and limitless tolerance as the highest virtues, as the indispensable preconditions for peace and justice. Many might point out that the world's most conspicuously militant universalism in recent years—a strand of Islamic fundamentalism with a very concrete notion of *jihad*—has turned to terrorism, religious warfare, and other forms of violent provocation in order to advance its cause. Does not my argument here suggest that firmly held convictions make violence inevitable, because in a pluralistic world, there is no other way to make one triumph over others?

I certainly hope that violence is not inevitable, and the banal fact that people sometimes do change their most firmly held convictions without having suffered coercion supports that conclusion. Yet even if violence is not inevitable, conflict most certainly is, because even the attempt to reject certitude in the name of tolerance grounds itself in a universalist notion of the good, however it strives to deny that fact. What is needed is a better account of how persuasion works, how conflicts about beliefs may end without recourse to violence. How does one interpretation of a work of fiction prove more convincing than another, especially when it is not, as Jameson suggests, a question of asking which interpretation has the fewest inaccuracies, omissions, or unanswered questions, but of asking one to subscribe to a completely different worldview? How does one universalism triumph over another, particularly when the debate is couched not in the conventions of philosophy but in the essentially rhetorical mode of fiction—a mode given as much to the cultivation of "mystery" (to use one of O'Connor's favorite words) as to rational argument?

In what follows, I will attempt a provisional answer to these questions in O'Connor's work, though it certainly falls short of a general theory of persuasion. Perhaps if I could answer these questions more generally, I would feel less exasperated. Until then I am, like too many others in this historical moment, too easily bored, too ready to pursue novelty for its own sake, too peevishly frustrated by the fact that debates about the true and the good are, however important, however inescapable, also (for the foreseeable future, at least) irresolvable. The debates go on, world without end, and all scholars in O'Connor studies—myself included—had better learn not merely to accept that fact but to embrace it.

II. Freedom, Grace, and Persuasion in "A Good Man Is Hard to Find"

Given O'Connor's stated intentions, what rhetorical strategies does she employ, and how do scholars formulate criteria to measure whether these succeed? I would like to begin with the observation that O'Connor typically cultivates identifications between her readers and particular characters. When these characters condemn other characters, readers are therefore invited to endorse the condemnation. At the climax of her stories, however, readers experience a violent reversal: they discover either that they are not so different from those whom they condemned, or (what is more often the case) that those with whom they identify are horribly flawed. For O'Connor, it follows that these characters need divine grace, and so do we. When Thomas Merton, eulogizing O'Connor, compared her to Sophocles (42), I believe that he had this structure of reversal and recognition (*peripeteia* and *anagnorisis*) in mind, which Aristotle has associated with tragedy. Some readers, upon perceiving this shock, accept the tidings she brings, while others (perhaps most) reject them. Although in practice it may be difficult to separate this decision from the question of whether readers have understood her intentions correctly, the two judgments are in principle distinct. One can believe that one fully understands O'Connor's intentions, even admire her skill in revealing them without resorting to overt didacticism, yet not be persuaded either of their truth or of their relevance to one's own life. One can also, to be sure, agree with O'Connor's moral judgments about her characters without agreeing that such judgments entail the necessity of Christian belief.[1] In short, one can reject the identification with her characters upon which such persuasion seems to depend.

---

1. In *A Rhetoric of Irony*, Wayne Booth made this argument about O'Connor's story "Everything That Rises Must Converge," though I believe that what he says is applicable to much of her fiction: "[T]his story can be experienced by anyone who catches the essential contrast among the three systems of norms, Julian's, his mother's, and the cluster of traditional, conventional values we share with the author. Though it may seem thinner to those for whom Julian's self-absorption and cruelty are judged in secular terms than for a Catholic who sees him as in mortal sin, the structure of experience will be the same for both: everyone will be forced to reject all or most of what the words seem to say. At every point we must decide on one out of many possible reconstructions, on the basis of a set of unshakable but silent beliefs that we are expected to share (however fleetingly) with the author. No one who fails to discern and feel some sympathy for these beliefs—only a few of them specifically Roman Catholic—is likely to make very much of the story" (168–69). No doubt this response would exasperate O'Connor, but she might admit that in "Everything That Rises Must Converge," where belief in Christianity is not explicitly addressed and where the civil rights movement's challenge to white southern racism forms a more immediate context for moral judgment than O'Connor's Catholicism, readers are more likely to agree with her moral judgments without perceiving the need to pursue a "thicker" reading grounded in Catholic doctrine.

If freedom is possible for her readers, and O'Connor's arguments invest much in the reader's identification with her characters, then it follows that such identification is most successful when readers attribute freedom to these characters. The author's note to the second edition of *Wise Blood* confirms this suspicion, though it also acknowledges the difficulties that readers may have in perceiving Hazel Motes's freedom: "Does one's integrity ever lie in what he is not able to do? I think that usually it does, for free will does not mean one will, but many wills conflicting in one man. Freedom cannot be conceived simply. It is a mystery . . . ." (no pg. number). Yet freedom, mysterious enough in living human beings, becomes altogether illusory when attributed to fictional characters. As René Girard once put it, mocking the putatively gratuitous freedom of protagonists in existentialist novels, "if the novelist is free it is hard to see how his characters would be" (256). But this answer falsifies the experience of reading, for while characters in a work of fiction may not be free—one will never, after all, open up "A Good Man Is Hard to Find" and discover that this time, The Misfit has shot himself or taken up beachcombing on a Caribbean island—readers' judgments of characters will prove incoherent if they do not attribute freedom to them. To identify with a character is thus to project my own consciousness of freedom into that character, so that decisions undertaken or fates suffered resonate with my sense that against that other choices are possible, that I might have chosen differently.[2]

When readers identify with characters in this way, they hypothesize not only about whether such identifications were intended by the author but also about how narrative conventions shape them. Any understanding of freedom in a text emerges against a prior understanding of what models of freedom have been made comprehensible within that text's tradition. The Catholic standpoint from which O'Connor begins presents special challenges, for its relationship to the mainstream of fiction in English and to the dominant understanding of freedom in that tradition is singularly vexed.

According to the received account of literary historians from Ian Watt to F. R. and Q. D. Leavis, the novel in English is an essentially Protestant genre, in that its commitments to literary realism, individualism, and above all character (in the dual sense of particularized personality and mature moral agency) reflect a Protestant understanding of human freedom and flourishing.[3] Over time, as Marina MacKay has suggested, this account

---

2. It is in this sense that I understand Bakthin's claims about the "unfinalizability" of the novel. Unfinalizability refers not to the freedom of the characters—for there is no such freedom—but to the inexhaustibility of readers' potential judgments of fiction.

3. Many theories about the nature of fiction in English take the novel, not the short story, as their starting point, and it might be objected that because the two are distinct genres,

of the English novel has tended to equate the exemplary virtues of Protestantism with those of political liberalism, so that even an agnostic such as George Eliot is plausibly described as a Protestant novelist. On the one hand, such novels celebrate what MacKay calls the "evangelical spirit of the nineteenth century" that "people are capable of changing" (228) for the better; on the other hand, the freedom they depict is admirable only insofar as it is reasonable and conducive to social harmony—that is, when characters privilege "'knowledge' . . . over mystery and 'accommodation' over principle" (217). The explicit anti-Catholicism of many British novels—for instance, the association of Catholicism with the gothic terrors and alleged oppressions of continental Europe—suggests that in this tradition, the Church can only be an enemy of freedom, out to corrupt the will and intellect of unwary Protestants.

Although this account, as MacKay puts it, "den[ies] . . . the primacy of the Spanish, Catholic *Don Quixote* in the inception of the novel, and den[ies], furthermore, that Catholic Europe contributed to the subsequent development of the form" (216), it has rarely been challenged. How might a history of the novel appear if readers were to acknowledge these Catholic influences? They might well reverse MacKay's terms and conclude that a Catholic vision of the novel might privilege mystery over knowledge and principle over accommodation. It might present models of the self not easily reconcilable with liberalism, models in which change is unpredictable, performative, paradoxical—and in which the "realized individual character is, in fact, the least free of all" (231). And it might suggest that the richest fictions are not necessarily novels such as *Middlemarch*, in which characters develop over a long span of time in a highly particularized world, but shorter forms that register the shock of freedom more strongly. Here, perhaps, is a possible explanation for why O'Connor's short stories are usually considered more accomplished than her novels.

It follows then, that precisely because O'Connor identifies herself as Catholic yet works within a tradition historically marked as Protestant, her efforts will take counterintuitive forms and challenge notions of freedom that are dominant in Protestant and post-Protestant milieux. In a sense, then, I am reaffirming O'Connor's oft-repeated statement that "to the hard of hearing you shout, and for the almost-blind you draw large and startling

---

this Leavisite account of the novel as essentially Protestant need not apply to O'Connor. It seems pertinent, though, that O'Connor does not seem to distinguish between the novel and the short story insofar as her own rhetorical strategies are concerned. Her two novels, *Wise Blood* and *The Violent Bear It Away,* display the same patterns of identification, reversal, and recognition that I described above, though most critics agree (as do I) that many of her short stories are superior as works of art.

figures" ("Fiction Writer" 34), with the qualification that it may be just as much the literary context of fiction in English as the unbelief of the twentieth century that contributes to such sensory disabilities. But shouting and drawing large and startling figures pose their own risks, for a Catholic understanding of such things must neither deny freedom nor minimize its essential mystery.

"A Good Man Is Hard to Find" perhaps provides the best illustration of this problem in O'Connor's fiction. O'Connor has of course been criticized for imposing her own interpretation of her work on readers, and her comments on this story, in which she simultaneously justifies and deemphasizes her use of violence, are often cited as evidence. But what has often gone unremarked is the distinction that O'Connor draws between the effect of violence upon her characters and its effect on readers. "I have found," she writes, "that violence is strangely capable of returning my characters to reality and preparing them to accept their moment of grace. Their heads are so hard that almost nothing else will do the work" ("On Her Own Work" 112). This is, I would argue, one of the cagiest moments in O'Connor's writing. Even as she underscores the function of violence in her work, she obscures her agency in inflicting it. She has not set out to dispense violence to her characters; she has only "found" that violence achieves the desired effect—and thus casts her characters as autonomous agents whose own stubbornness has driven her to this expedient. Yet while violence seems necessary for her characters, it has the potential to mislead readers. Hence her admonition that readers should "be on the lookout for such things as the action of grace in the Grandmother's soul, and not for the dead bodies" ("On Her Own Work" 113). So even though both characters and readers are potentially recalcitrant, characters are more certain to benefit from violence, not only because they cannot escape it but because there seems to be no danger of their misunderstanding what it portends. Readers, however, are freer but for this very reason more prone to error, and they too must be assaulted, but with commentary instead of direct violence. Here there seems to be a familiar standoff, one suggested long ago by partisans of reader-friendly criticism such as Roland Barthes: the freer a reader is, the more that freedom seems to be measured by resistance to authorial intention.

In what sense, then, can the grandmother—the third party in this transaction—be considered "free"? Readers' understanding of her proceeds initially through the familiar processing of realist fiction. They observe what she says and does, discern her thoughts, and absorb significant information about her—the name of her cat, her fear of highway patrolmen, her pride in her manner of dress. If readers believe that they understand her, it is because they recognize her as plausible within her time and place—a ridiculous old woman whose identity has been largely shaped by the discourse of southern ladyhood. The more plausible she seems, the more likely it would seem that she will develop according to a model of liberal selfhood if she is to win readers' approval—overcoming her vanities, her racism, and her selfishness through a painstakingly drawn sequence of experience and enlightenment.

Yet this does not happen. At the crux of the story, having failed to persuade The Misfit to spare her life, readers are told that her head "cleared for an instant," that she "saw the man's face twisted close to her own as if he were going to cry and murmured, 'Why you're one of my babies. You're one of my own children'" (29). She then touches him and is killed immediately afterward. In this passage, any sense of her thoughts and motivation falls away. The clearness of her head suggests that readers should trust her action here, but the content of this clearness is not specified. The fact that The Misfit seems close to tears might also be significant, but this perception is itself ambiguous—does it belong to the grandmother or the author? It is not certain that the grandmother experiences a rush of love or pity for The Misfit, plausible though such a reading may be. Nor is it certain that she feigns love or pity in a final attempt to save her life, though this reading is also plausible. Neither reading is *compelled* by the text as, for example, the earlier judgment of the grandmother's vanity is. If the grandmother acts freely here—and O'Connor invites this judgment when she refers to the grandmother's "special kind of triumph" ("On Her Own Work" 111)—her freedom is suggested most clearly by readers' ignorance of her motives. O'Connor does tell readers, in her commentary, that such freedom is associated with a moment of grace—but it would seem that she cannot, without turning it into an illustration of determinism, account for it. Hence the caginess I mentioned earlier, her reluctance to identify herself as the source of violence against her characters. This too, after all, would diminish the intended sense of the characters' freedom—it would make violence the ultimate cause, rather than the felicitous revelation, of this freedom.

In "Some Aspects of the Grotesque in Southern Fiction," O'Connor speaks of the writer for whom "the meaning of a story does not begin except at a depth where adequate motivation and adequate psychology and the various determinations have been exhausted. Such a writer will be interested in what we don't understand rather than in what we do. He will be interested in possibility rather than probability" (41–42). As David Sandner has argued, here O'Connor "anticipates that her grandmother can only be 'adequately' read as . . . [a] deluded figure . . . imagining at her last moment what was not there, what cannot be; she anticipates that her criticism can be discounted as well, that it asks for something that need not be deduced from the text as a necessary reading of its determining elements" (177). Indeed, everything that readers have learned about the grandmother, through their processing of realist conventions, might lead them astray, for readers seek clues to her "adequate" motivation in what came before. Any account of such motivation would lock the grandmother into a chain of cause and effect that the story neither confirms nor denies.

I tentatively conclude that O'Connor highlights an inherent tension between mimesis and freedom, and that in affirming freedom at crucial moments, she complicates Aristotle's judgment in the *Poetics* that "the use of impossible probabilities is preferable to that of unpersuasive possibilities" (61).[4] It is always "possible" to act freely, especially if one understands that one's truest freedom lies in accepting God's gift of grace. But is it probable that one will do so—especially if one has been shaped by a formerly Protestant and now liberal culture that tends to view will as untrammeled? O'Connor thinks, with much justification, that such probabilities are "unpersuasive," though not "impossible." When she warns her readers not to misread the violence in the story, she might well be exhorting, "don't worry about being persuaded. Be free instead, for only in openness to grace does proper freedom exist." The grace that allows for a conversion experience need not be tied to any human event, not even to the reading of a story about it. But O'Connor cannot simply give up the effort to persuade, even to preach—the Great Commission (Matthew 28:18–20) demands it, after all. If readers can be convinced of the grandmother's freedom even before death, perhaps they can be shocked into awareness of their own. But it is precisely readers' commitment to a false model of freedom that blinds them, and leads O'Connor to the more overt—and, for many readers, less persuasive—effort of her commentary, which has provoked far more critical resistance than her fiction itself has.

---

4. The distinctions here, admittedly, are subtle. Wendy Piper rightly notes that in the *Poetics*, "[t]he two elements of 'probability' and 'surprise' are interdependent; it is upon their synthesis that the emotional import of *peripeteia* and *anagnorisis* . . . depends and the moral and metaphysical weight of the tragedy, the sense of 'wonder,' is based" (164). The central issue seems to be whether the kind of tragic recognition and reversal of which Aristotle speaks affirms a conception of human freedom or of determinism. O'Connor contrasts her emphasis on freedom with a "great tragic naturalism" that she respects but believes is achieved despite "the limitations of [a] narrow vision" ("Some Aspects" 41). I read her as rejecting the "probabilities" asserted by determinist theorists of all kinds—which in some versions become invariable laws—in favor of the improbable possibilities of freedom and grace.

III. O'Connor Relaxes:
"The Artificial Nigger"

While "A Good Man Is Hard to Find" has probably not converted many readers, its presentation of what is at stake in questions of belief is admirably stark, neither minimizing the essential scandal of the Christian narrative nor shrinking from the fact that readers must make a free commitment to it or reject it. There is no third option. The grandmother's own attempt to construct an alternative based on moral consensus (and save her own skin) rather than on the irreducibility of doctrinal belief collapses, like most of her dialogue, into platitude: "I just know you're a good man" (25). O'Connor's stories, however, are not always so precisely delineated, and I turn now to "The Artificial Nigger" as a counterexample. My argument here is more openly personal, because I have long been struck by the divergence between my own religious beliefs and my assessment of the story, which dissents from the widespread judgment that it is one of her strongest. Because critics who find O'Connor's rhetorical strategies persuasive often already share her beliefs, I suspect that this divergence between my beliefs and a judgment to which these beliefs might predispose me sheds light on the more general question of when religious persuasion in fiction proves successful.

As a Roman Catholic, I believe in the same dogmas in which O'Connor believed. Moreover, I believe that Mr. Head, like all human beings, is vain, sinful, and in need of redemption. He is not a monster—or, to be more precise, he is a monster in the most ordinary way, for his nature, like ours, is proud and fallen. His recognition of his sinfulness, followed by the reconciliation with Nelson that occurs under the aegis of the story's grotesque statue, is therefore a crucial awakening. Indeed, O'Connor is unambiguous about what Mr. Head learns or rediscovers: "He realized that he was forgiven for sins from the beginning of time, when he had conceived in his own heart the sin of Adam, until the present, when he had denied poor Nelson. He saw that no sin was too monstrous for him to claim as his own, and since God loved in proportion as he forgave, he felt ready at that instant to enter Paradise" (270). This passage evinces not only a greater theological explicitness than is typically found in O'Connor's fiction but also an unusually lofty and affirmative tone. Indeed, it is uncomfortably close to what O'Connor scornfully called "Instant Uplift" ("Novelist" 165), and yet one cannot complain that it is more obscure for being so. It is not in and of itself vapid, because the theology that underpins it isn't. To an unusual degree in O'Connor's fiction (as opposed to her essays), the final paragraphs make her intentions unmistakable.

Yet despite this clarity of purpose, I remain unconvinced of the story's effectiveness, for I do not believe that Mr. Head experiences a genuine conversion. I have been surprised to discover that O'Connor considered this her favorite story (*Habit* 101, 209), irked by its popularity, and somewhat relieved to find Frederick Crews call the end of the story "one of the few trite, dramatically unearned, propagandistic passages in all of O'Connor's mature fiction" (160). To be sure, the word "unearned" here suggests that Crews has in mind the distinction between "showing" and "telling" in fiction, as well as the evaluative assumption that accompanies it and remains beloved of instructors in creative writing: showing is good, and telling, especially homiletic telling, is bad. But as Wayne Booth observed in *The Rhetoric of Fiction*, this maxim breaks down as soon as one scrutinizes it: one can cite endless examples of effective "telling" and ineffective "showing" in fictional narratives, so that the distinction between the two often betrays a "radical inadequacy" (16). What determines success is not the proportion of showing to telling, but the skill with which both showing and telling are adapted to the work's rhetorical ends. My sense of why Crews's judgment of the story is nevertheless correct begins with a key statement in the passage I quoted above—Mr. Head's realization that "no sin was too monstrous to claim as his own"—which concretizes the story's rhetorical weakness.

What prompts Mr. Head to this realization is his denial of his son Nelson. Faced with a crowd of angry women who threaten to call the police because Nelson has accidentally broken one woman's ankle, afraid because "[h]e had never in his life been accosted by a policeman," Mr. Head proclaims, "This is not my boy . . . I never seen him before" (265). Nelson responds with horror, accusing his father silently but effectively. Even the women fall silent and allow Mr. Head to leave, "as if they were so repulsed by a man who would deny his own image and likeness that they could not bear to lay hands on him" (265). Clearly O'Connor intends for everyone to recognize what the narrator calls Mr. Head's "true depravity" (270). His denial, in other words, must be singularly horrifying, but nevertheless in a way that signifies universal—and universally recognized—rather than individual depravity.

The problem, however, occurs in the leap between acknowledging that Mr. Head is guilty of a sin here and concluding that "no sin was too monstrous to claim as his own." Does his action really reveal his capacity for murder, or rape, or torture? Or does it merely show that he is proud, easily frightened, and ignobly willing to betray to save his own skin? Moreover, even his betrayal could have been far worse: he never actually abandons Nelson; he feels instant remorse, and he tries, in his fumbling way, to reconcile with Nelson even before he encounters the statue—by offering to get him a Coca-Cola and, later, to share water with him. His denial of Nelson is certainly sinful, certainly despicable. But to invest it with an aura of speech-depriving horror that stops the women's half-righteous indignation in its tracks, is simply not convincing.

Mr. Head's epiphany makes sense only if he is *already* within a Christian framework of belief, for the "true depravity" of *all* human beings, the taint of original sin, is an *a priori* belief, not something that can be syllogistically deduced from the existence of individual crimes. I believe it to be true because Christianity teaches it, not because human beings have always unleashed horrors upon each other—although the fact of such horrors certainly makes it easier to believe. Even though nearly everyone grants that a capacity for wrongdoing is universal, most people admit degrees of culpability (even the Church distinguishes between mortal and venial sin) and do not necessarily conclude, for instance, that one who tells a lie could just as easily have committed pedophilia or genocide. The "monstrosity" of Mr. Head's action lies in the overweening pride that it reveals, and to interpret this pride *as* a monstrous sin requires familiarity with a tradition in which pride can be just as vile as murder—which places pride, for instance, as the first of the Seven Deadly Sins. If I find the women's reaction unconvincing, it is in part because I do not live in a culture in which pride compels universal fear and loathing. In fact, my hunch is that most contemporary readers of the story despise Mr. Head long before he betrays Nelson, for his racism, his unwarranted arrogance, and his naïveté about urban life, and that his betrayal instead provokes their first real compassion for him, precisely because its motivation—pride and fear—is so understandable, so easy to identify with. Such a response is not admirable—I would even say that it displays its own pride in its smug, implicit assumption that racism is something of which only other people are guilty, and in its automatic contempt toward white, rural Southerners. But I do believe that such a response works against what O'Connor intends here.

Once one realizes that Mr. Head's epiphany makes little sense unless he is already some kind of Christian, it becomes easier to account for what Richard Giannone has called the "dissonance" between "the elevated language [of the narrator]" and "the rhetorical capacity of the plainspoken hick" (*Hermit Novelist* 125). Mr. Head would not express himself in this way, but he has, no doubt, been taught, for instance, that he has "conceived in his heart of the sin of Adam," and that "God loved in proportion as he forgave." He may well perceive, in the isolation and misery that he feels just before he encounters the grotesque statue, "what man would be like without salvation" (268). All of these claims resonate within Christian teaching, and they suggest that Mr. Head's belief has always been more genuine than that of the merely nominal Christians who appear more often in O'Connor's work, such as Mrs. MacIntyre from "The Displaced Person" or Mrs. May from "Greenleaf." Other critics have made this point as well. Martha Stephens, for instance, compares him to the twelve-year-old protagonist of "A Temple of the Holy Ghost." Both she and Mr. Head must learn a lesson in humility, but as Stephens puts it, because they are already believers, "any sins of [theirs] . . . are going to be quite indulgently dealt with, [their] lesson in humility quite tenderly viewed" (165). While I do not share Stephens's sarcasm, I think that she is on to something. Many readers know O'Connor's claim that "to the hard of hearing you shout, and for the almost-blind you draw large and startling figures." Yet they tend to forget what immediately precedes this statement: "When you can assume that your audience holds the same beliefs that you do, you can relax a little and use more normal means of talking to it" ("Fiction Writer" 34). Mr. Head, perhaps because he shares these beliefs, will not require so violent a lesson. Accordingly, one should describe what happens to him not as a conversion, but what one might call in Protestant terminology a rededication. Or, to use a Catholic formulation that O'Connor probably knew, Mr. Head experiences a movement from what John Henry Newman calls "notional assent" of Christianity to "real assent."[5] For this reason, however crucial such a change may be, it is not dramatically satisfying, because the distance to be traversed is not so great—certainly not the distance, as O'Connor once opined to Ben Griffith, "from the Garden of Eden to the Gates of Paradise" (*Habit* 78).[6]

What about the grotesque statue itself? The narrator underscores that it is not a mere symbol of reconciliation, but its active agent: "They could both feel it dissolving their differences like an action of mercy" (269). That O'Connor subscribes to a sacramental view of existence in which ordinary objects can become visible vehicles of God's invisible grace, is a critical commonplace, but the statue functions more literally as something like

---

5. "In its Notional Assents as well as in its inferences, the mind contemplates its own creations instead of things; in Real, it is directed towards things, represented by the impressions which they have left on the imagination" (*Grammar of Assent* 57). Moreover, "[Real assents] are of a personal character, each individual having his own, and being known by them. It is otherwise with notions; notional apprehension is in itself an ordinary act of our common nature. All of us have the power of abstraction, and can be taught either to make or to enter into the same abstractions" (*Grammar of Assent* 63).

6. To be sure, Mr. Head does feel, in his agony, "what man would be like without salvation" (268). The use of the conditional here, of course, suggests that the statement is contrary to fact: human beings are already (potentially) saved, through the accomplished death and resurrection of Jesus. Even in the depths of his agony, in other words, Mr. Head does not reject the basic claims of Christian orthodoxy.

the sacrament of reconciliation, for it appears only after both Mr. Head and Nelson have indicated a desire to be reconciled, however imperfect their contrition might be. Mr. Head's desire takes the form of his overtures toward Nelson (the Coca-Cola and the water); Nelson's takes the form of allowing himself to catch up slowly with his grandfather—within three pages, Nelson moves from "[t]wenty feet behind him" (266) to "within fifteen feet" (267) to "about ten feet away" (268). The statue effects the reconciliation in response to an implicitly expressed desire for it. How?

One might reply that the arbitrariness, even the "artificiality" of the statue, is part of the point, that God bestows his grace where he will, and that to ask "How?" is an arrogant presumption. Inasmuch as the statue has inevitable political implications, however—implications that O'Connor acknowledged when she called the statue "a terrible symbol of what the South has done to itself" (*Habit* 140)—the story cries out for a reading that will connect the statue's function as agent of grace to commentary about the suffering of African Americans and the moral responsibility for it. Mr. Head sees in the statue an image of universal agony—he learns from this experience that mercy "grew out of agony, which is not denied to any man and which is given in strange ways to children" (269). But it is understandable that readers might flinch at the quick leap to the universality of suffering here, as if what Mr. Head and Nelson have endured is comparable to the systematic oppression of African Americans that the statue makes visible. (To his credit, Mr. Head, having reflected on his suffering, immediately recognizes its paltriness, for he understands that agony "was all a man cold carry into death to give his Maker and he suddenly burned with shame that he had so little of it to take with him" [269].)

Moreover, the reconciliation does not lead to anything like racial enlightenment on Mr. Head's part, as other critics have acknowledged—indeed, the retreat to their rural home, punctuated with Nelson's "I'll never go back again" (270)—suggests a refusal to continue the challenge that the story has proposed, a challenge to test one's faith through continued interaction with the suffering of others. Whereas the language that refers to Mr. Head's individual salvation is clear and unambiguous, that which might suggest a recognition of his racism is vague—compare, for instance, "He saw now that no sin was too monstrous to claim as his own" with the story's most obscure sentence, "They stood gazing at the artificial Negro as if they were faced with some great mystery, some monument to another's victory that brought them together in their common defeat" (269). The best reading of this sentence I have seen is Christina Bieber Lake's: "Like Ozymandias in the sand, this 'monument to another's victory,' now completely effaced, shows how thin a victory it had really been. When Mr. Head sees it, it changes him—or, more accurately, helps him name the changes he has already experienced. Instead of seeing his identity as defined against the other, frozen in a cold rationality, he stands now with the suffering community in identification and sympathy" (106).

I do, however, have a quibble with Lake's interpretation. Whose victory is referred to here? It is "another's" victory, contrasted with Mr. Head and Nelson's defeat, presumably the victory of a racist society over those whom it oppresses. Yet to the extent that Mr. Head is complicit in the oppression of African Americans that the statue reveals, this victory has, until now, also been his own. Do readers therefore read a renunciation of racism here, since logically, identification with the suffering community must entail identification with African Americans as well? Does the contrast between "another's" victory and "their" defeat imply that Mr. Head, too, has, unknowingly, been a victim of racism—but a victim who can take comfort in the fragility of the victory? I see no evidence that Mr. Head's epiphany about the universality of suffering and pride entails specific *identification* with others, as opposed to recognition of a common humanity. Indeed, because the fact of suffering is existential and its specific causes not addressed, one might even suspect that Mr. Head now considers the amelioration of suffering undesirable. If is true that having so little agony to take to one's Maker at death is a source of shame, why not allow things to remain as they are? The more suffering that African Americans endure, the better off they will be when they face God; perhaps even the better off others will be, if we are to take seriously O'Connor's claim that the story suggests "the redemptive quality of the Negro's suffering for us all" (*Habit* 78).

I conclude that even though O'Connor envisaged her audience as the people who think that God is dead, "The Artificial Nigger" is best understood as a fable for Christians. Mr. Head serves as a kind of double for the Christian reader whose assent to Christian doctrine is mostly notional and who requires a shock to recognize anew his pride and his dependence on Jesus' sacrifice. I wonder, however, whether O'Connor's use of the racist statue is meant to extend Mr. Head's epiphany further into the minds of her readers. It is easy to perceive how ridiculous Mr. Head's pride makes him, long before he denies Nelson; but perhaps it is harder for a Christian, southern, white reader of the 1950s to extend the lesson that Mr. Head learns into a recognition that racism has distorted southern society and imperiled souls. I do not believe that Mr. Head learns this specific lesson, but the vagueness of O'Connor's language at this crucial point allows readers to draw it, if they will.

It is interesting that none of O'Connor's manuscript drafts of "The Artificial Nigger" contain the kind of extended commentary on reconciliation and salvation that the published story includes. There is also more doubt about just what has been learned. In all the versions of the story, Mr. Head and Nelson realize that they have been reconciled, but in one version neither one realizes that the statue had anything to do with it; in one version Nelson understands this but Mr. Head doesn't, and in yet another version Mr. Head does but Nelson doesn't.[7] Clearly O'Connor believed that the more explicit she was about the means and implications of the reconciliation, the more her readers would grasp the essential point. But in order for her to do this, it was necessary to make Mr. Head's Christianity more evident and thus to lessen the distance that he had to travel to his final revelation. Judged according to her own stated criteria, then—as an attempt to shock an unbelieving audience into the truth that Jesus died to save us— "The Artificial Nigger" seems less convincing.

IV. The City in "Judgement Day"

A similar situation prevails in "Judgement Day," which O'Connor completed in the last month of her life. Yet the results, I would argue, are very different. Like "The Artificial Nigger," "Judgement Day" depicts a protagonist who must leave his contented rural isolation, confront the crowds and the even more profound isolation of urban life, and discover through the usual process of recognition and reversal his own flaws. Like Mr. Head, who hates and fears Atlanta, Tanner regards New York as a place of filth and horrifically indiscriminate human mingling, with air "fit for cats and garbage," where "all stripes of foreigner, all of them twisted in the tongue" live together in "pigeon-hutch[es]"—in short, "no place for a sane man" (531, 541). He also shares with Mr. Head a measure of O'Connor's sympathy and some evidence of already being a Christian when he undergoes his experience, which might lead readers of "The Artificial Nigger" to expect him to receive a similarly gentle treatment from his author. Stuck in New York City at the home of his daughter, Tanner is determined to return home, either dead or alive. The conflation of his beloved home with heaven is obvious, and the fact that his daughter finally buries him in his native earth—after originally burying him in the city and then suffering from a guilty conscience—suggests the triumph of his rural vision over the urban wasteland.

---

7. O'Connor's drafts of "The Artificial Nigger" are located in the Flannery O'Connor Collection at the Library and Instructional Technology Center, Georgia College, Milledgeville, Georgia, files 157b, 157c, and 158.

Such a reading of the story dovetails with a widespread perception that in O'Connor's fictional world, cities are little more than foci of evil—places, on the one hand, where "interleckchuls" promote a superficial cosmopolitanism that is no substitute for genuine community, and on the other hand, where industrial capitalism's relentless activity, instrumentalization of human relationships, and destruction of the natural environment conspire to create a hell on earth. Yet even though O'Connor's own professed distaste for cities tends to confirm this reading, in practice, urban life in her work appears more complicated and more potentially beneficial—above all, because the sheer number of encounters with other people that are possible can force epiphanies (as they do for Mr. Head) that splendid rural isolation cannot.[8] Indeed, "Judgement Day" builds upon "The Artificial Nigger"—and is, in my judgment, a better story—precisely because it does not let its protagonist off so easily, but rather reveals that in his movement toward something approaching racial enlightenment, unpleasant encounters with others may exact a necessary cost.

If "Judgement Day" were merely about a longing for the country that is eventually satisfied, it would not be significantly better than "The Geranium," the much earlier version of the story that O'Connor had included in her M.F.A. thesis.[9] As Marshall Bruce Gentry points out, "The Geranium" "comes close to [a] sentimental longing for the South" more reminiscent of Carson McCullers (88). The story ends with Tanner's earlier incarnation, Dudley, reduced to tears and bewilderment by the condescension of a black man who calls him "old-timer" (13) and by the destruction of a geranium that he used to observe in an apartment window opposite his. Nothing complicates the story's sentimental pathos. In "Judgement Day," however, Tanner is eventually murdered—and, perhaps, simultaneously delivered to salvation—by an African American actor who lives in the apartment next door. If one is to read the ending of the story as a triumph for Tanner, as most critics have done, one must acknowledge that his exile in the city has been necessary. Just as in "The Artificial Nigger" the Heads were forced to confront both urban Atlanta and the presence of African-Americans in order to find redemption, in "Judgement Day" Tanner seems to require a confrontation with the city, with a black man, and with violence.

---

8. See my "The City Reconsidered: Problems and Possibilities of Urban Community in 'A Stroke of Good Fortune' and 'The Artificial Nigger'" for a fuller account of the benefits of cities in her work.

9. "The Geranium" is also O'Connor's first published story, which first appeared in print in 1946 but was not collected in a book until *The Complete Stories* appeared in 1971. For a representative discussion of the revisions that O'Connor made to the story through the years, including the intermediate versions entitled "An Exile in the East" and "Getting Home," see Giannone, *Mystery of Love* (233–39).

But why is this particular violence necessary? After all, what distinguishes Tanner even from Mr. Head is his lack of stubbornness. Unlike most hard-headed O'Connor characters, to whom change comes only as the result of divine violence, Tanner shows every sign of having learned several important lessons in the absence of violence. Though he is hardly perfect, he has made undeniable progress in overcoming his two most obvious (and interrelated) failings—his pride and his racism—well before he comes to New York.

In the extended flashback that comprises most of the story, readers learn that once, Tanner had owned land in Georgia and had been foreman to a crew of black workers, whom he had kept in check by brandishing a knife and threatening to kill them periodically. Though Tanner has never actually killed a black man, because he fears going to hell, his dominance depends upon the threat of violence and is fueled by a poisonous racism. Tanner constantly carves small wooden figures with his knife, in an effort to conceal the involuntary shaking of his hands caused by kidney illness. Even what might seem a sign of weakness, however, becomes transformed into a reflection of Tanner's power: "The Negroes picked [the figures] up and took them home; there was not much time between them and darkest Africa" (537). This passage's free indirect discourse, which blurs the distinction between Tanner's point of view and the narrator's, suggests that his carvings, even though the product of a physical weakness, function like fetishes, cast off by a powerful, disdainful god to superstitious worshipers, though it is unclear whether this is an accurate description of the African Americans' mindset or a fantasy of Tanner's.

Tanner experiences his first moral advance through his encounter with Coleman, a black man who had appeared on the scene one day, keeping his distance from the workers, watching them, and, provocatively, doing nothing. When Tanner confronts Coleman, the possibility of violence is in the air, and both men, the narrator hints, acknowledge to themselves the satisfaction they would feel were they to kill each other. But when Tanner finds himself carving a pair of false glasses without realizing it, he passes them along to Coleman, clearly intending to mock him: "'Put these on,' he said. 'I hate to see anybody can't see good'" (538). To both men's surprise, the event defuses the situation: "[Tanner] saw the exact instant in the muddy liquor-swollen eyes when the pleasure of having a knife in this white man's gut was balanced against something else, he could not tell what" (538). The result is that Tanner and Coleman become friends, even to the extent of sharing the same home thirty years later. Although Tanner rationalizes that since Coleman had "ma[d]e a monkey out of [him]," the only alternative would have been to kill him—"[a]nd he was not going to hell for killing a nigger" (539)—his bluster belies the fact that he has just acknowledged Coleman's humanity. The fact that their subsequent relationship conforms to racist protocols—as Tanner says, Coleman "cooks . . . cuts my firewood and empties my slops" (535)—does not lessen the horror that Tanner's daughter feels when she discovers that they share the same space.

Tanner's second, more enduring moral advance occurs after he moves to New York—a move necessitated because he has lost his land, become destitute, and taken shelter with Coleman in a shack on land owned by a prosperous local black man, Dr. Foley. A clear embodiment of the increased social and economic opportunities that African Americans were beginning to achieve in the 1960s, Dr. Foley taunts Tanner by observing that "[t]he day coming . . . when the white folks IS going to be working for the colored" (540). In lieu of rent, Foley demands that Tanner share with him the profits from the whiskey still that now gives Tanner his livelihood. Unable to face such humiliation, Tanner contacts his daughter, who, appalled by his situation, takes him north. Here, too, however, Tanner has learned his lesson, as a result of suffering, and conquered his pride: "If he had known it was a question of this—sitting here looking out of this window all day in this no-place, or just running a still for a nigger, he would have run the still for the nigger. He would have been a nigger's white nigger any day" (540).

In light of Tanner's progress against his pride and racism, it is not surprising that critics have generally liked him. Frederick Asals calls him "the most sympathetically handled adult protagonist in all her stories," the only one "in whom control and surrender, will and imagination, are reconciled and made one" (141). For Giannone, he is a "spiritual combatant" (*Hermit Novelist* 260), whose unhappy existence in New York parallels a hermit's expiatory time in the desert, and who goes to his deserved reward after undergoing purification. And for Gentry, Tanner is morally admirable but aesthetically flawed because O'Connor herself likes him too much and identifies too closely with him (88). But these assessments lead back to the previous question: if Tanner is capable of moral growth, if he grows without occasions of violence, then what function does the violence serve?

The most compelling attempt to answer this question to date is Ralph Wood's. Wood connects Tanner's fate to O'Connor's celebrated concern with manners, particularly insofar as they affect the changing racial politics of the South. Aligning O'Connor with such theorists of social mores as Alexis de Tocqueville and Jean Bethke Elshtain, Wood argues that "Judgement Day" presents O'Connor's conviction that "a democracy, perhaps more than any other polity, requires manners" because "[e]xactly to the extent that ancient inequalities have been overcome, there is an even greater demand for social restraint, for privacy, for the individual space one grants to others because one knows one's own need for it" (*Flannery O'Connor* 127). Since the civil rights movement has abolished many "ancient inequalities," those that remain will become even greater foci for resentment unless, as O'Connor maintained, whites and blacks can construct a new framework for living together based on mutual charity. Such charity will necessarily involve the wearing of masks. Rather than seeing masks as mere hypocrisy that prevent people from expressing their innermost convictions honestly, Wood argues that for O'Connor, masks are necessary for civilization itself. In their absence, society devolves either into a state of Hobbesian warfare or into an enforced egalitarianism that abolishes the distinction between the public and private and in doing so turns totalitarian.

From Wood's perspective, Tanner's moral progress is incomplete, because despite his friendship with Coleman, he has never quite relinquished the old mask of racial superiority for a newer "mask" that combines charity with unabashed affirmation of the truth. When Tanner meets the African American next door, he assumes that the man is from south Alabama and must be homesick. He tries to strike up an acquaintance with him, calling him "Preacher" (the only honorific he knows for black people) and suggesting that the two might go fishing together. The man reacts with rage, calling Tanner a "wool-hat red-neck son-of-a-bitch peckerwood old bastard" and for good measure asserting that "[t]here ain't no Jesus and there ain't no God"—though of course his double negative affirms the opposite of what he intends. Tanner immediately retorts, "And you ain't black! . . . And I ain't white" (545). The actor then assaults him, causing a stroke. Later, when Tanner is trying to escape the apartment and head southward, he meets the man a second time and repeats his mistake. This time, the man kills him and desecrates his body, forcing his head and arms through a banister so that he resembles a man in stocks. The upshot seems to be that while for most O'Connor characters, salvation and the presence of violence go together, Tanner has achieved his salvation *before* he is actually killed, in the moment when he simultaneously rejects the actor's blasphemy and (unwittingly) affirms the irrelevance of racial distinctions. His triumph is so perfect that O'Connor can dispense with further preaching or pointed commentary (Wood, *Flannery O'Connor* 141).

Wood's reading, compelling as it is, does not observe that Tanner repeats the mistake of calling the actor "Preacher." Even if this mistake can be attributed to the mental confusion that has plagued Tanner since his stroke (indeed, he initially mistakes the man for Coleman), this hardly suggests that he has completely overcome the racial condescension that Wood had criticized in the earlier encounter. Moreover, while Tanner has come to associate his rural home with heaven—his dream of returning in a coffin, only to burst through it and surprise Coleman and Hooten with the joyful cry, "Judgement Day! You idiots didn't know it was Judgement day, did you?" (549), reveals as much—it is difficult to see how he could have put into practice his new awareness of the meaninglessness of racial distinctions in the South. The story does not give him the opportunity to succeed or to fail: even if the actor who kills him reveals that in "this Yankee Babylon . . . people run over each other in their unrestrained and hell-bent rush" (Wood, *Flannery O'Connor* 140), even this violence fulfills Tanner's desires more quickly, and more efficiently, than a return home would. That Tanner's daughter sends his body home to be buried in Georgia is icing on the cake.

If it is misleading to see Tanner's violent death simply as a martyrdom or a just reward for his moral and spiritual progress, it is equally misleading to interpret it as a blow for racial justice, as Alice Walker, for instance, suggests when she states that the final version of "Judgement Day" reveals O'Connor's belief in "justice for the individual" (53). Indeed, Tanner's fate is constructed so that readers of fundamentally differing commitments can derive satisfaction from it: those appalled by his racism and contemptuous of the rural southern milieu that formed him can see poetic justice in his death at the hands of a black man in New York; those impressed by the moral progress that he makes can view his death (and the relocation of his body to Georgia), as a triumph, citing O'Connor's injunction to pay attention to lines of spiritual motion, not to dead bodies. Tanner's Christian belief, like Mr. Head's in "The Artificial Nigger," never seems in question—even his fear of going to hell were he to kill bespeaks it—yet his trials in the city and even his death are necessary to the narrative, providing a closure that retrospectively endows Tanner's life with meaning *and* with a graver sense of what might be at stake than in "The Artificial Nigger."

Many critics have argued that as O'Connor's career progressed, she left behind a tendency toward dualism that marred some of her earliest work, a tendency that belied her insistence elsewhere on the sacramental nature of God's creation.[10] It is easy to see why "Judgement Day" might be enlisted in support of this claim: the signature violence remains—and,

10. Ralph Wood, for instance, has argued that "O'Connor's public statements are often quasi-dualistic, and that her fiction at times suspends characters between the virtually equal powers of God and Satan" (*Comedy* 100). He prefers the more comic late stories, "The Enduring Chill," "Revelation," and "Judgement Day" itself, as instances of a more theologically accurate and more "splendid comic vision" (*Comedy* 106)—though he also criticizes "The Enduring Chill" for its "horrific ending" (*Comedy* 125).

indeed, remains dramatically necessary—but the sense that Tanner is suspended between God and Satan, the sense that gives "A Good Man Is Hard to Find" its unforgettable starkness, is attenuated in favor of a more nuanced portrayal of good and evil mixed up with each other, evil serving as the unwitting means of good, good triumphing despite its relative feebleness. Moreover, O'Connor's avowed belief in human freedom finds a more powerful confirmation here than in the heavy-handed affirmations of "The Artificial Nigger," or even in the undercurrent expressed in "A Good Man Is Hard to Find" that freedom may be possible but typically reveals itself in its very improbability. Tanner seems freer than the previous stories' protagonists—perhaps because he has already committed himself to the Christianity that the grandmother must discover and to which Mr. Head must rededicate himself, while readers of the story, perceiving both its greater nuance and its insistence nonetheless on meaningful closure, may also detect less browbeating from the author. The fundamental debate concerning the truth of O'Connor's theological claims and her effectiveness in making them will not cease, nor should it, and my own judgments of the relative merits of these three stories will not swing the balance in any direction. Even at her worst, however—in the pious insularity of "The Artificial Nigger"—O'Connor demands respect, and at her best, she proves to be the most gifted and incisive of postwar fiction writers committed to orthodox Christian doctrine and practice.

2

Catholicism for "Really Intelligent People"

The Rhetoric of Muriel Spark

My own kind would be really intelligent people, more or less intellectuals. I'm weary for them if I'm cut off too long.

—Muriel Spark, interview with Martin McQuillan (219)

I. On the Superior Pleasures of Catholicism

When Muriel Spark died in 2006, after a career that spanned five decades, obituaries duly identified her as a Catholic writer, and the most perceptive of them followed earlier critics in noting her affinities with Flannery O'Connor.[1] Both writers avow a religious dimension in their work; both have a marked hatred for sentimentality; and both are known for violence and shock—not only in the fates that often befall their characters but also in their frequent use of narrators who violate conventional readerly expec-

---

1. Roger Kimball, for instance, observes that in Spark's work, "There is a moral but no catechism. In this respect, if in few others, her work recalls the Gothic realism of the American novelist and master of the short story Flannery O'Connor. For both writers, the operation of grace is generally a funny but decidedly astringent affair" (2). Though he approaches Spark from a different angle, arguing rather too breezily that "in principle there is no disagreement between Spark and Derrida" (171), Willy Maley's essay from four years before reaches a similar judgment: "[I]n her Catholicism, Gothicism, formalism, and dispassionate rendering of the struggle between good and evil, Spark resembles in many ways Flannery O'Connor. . . ." (178).

tations by passing intrusive judgment on the characters. Perhaps for these very reasons, both have achieved their greatest success in shorter fictional forms—for O'Connor, the short story; for Spark, the novel considered, as Rodney Stenning Edgecombe argues, as an expanded epigram, "with all the specious finality or, conversely, the elegant incompleteness that characterizes the form" (2). Not surprisingly, both have also been loved and hated for similar reasons. Until recently, admirers tended to view their fiction as caustically witty arguments for theological truths and their use of violence as a means of presenting such truths without pious cliché. Detractors, often positioning themselves against the writers' religious beliefs, have found their purposes antihumanist and repellent, and their lack of sympathetic identification with their characters—often presented through authoritarian narrators—aesthetically crippling. Richard Mayne's characterization of Spark's method is characteristic: "Always, behind the tale, there lurks an alert didactic narrator . . . [with] a mother-knows-best dead-certainty that holds Mrs. Spark's novels in what her actress' ghost-writer would call a vise-like grip." (49).

Any comparison between the two writers, however, reveals not only the obvious differences of setting and tone (O'Connor's backwoods Georgia contrasted with Spark's urban Edinburgh or cosmopolitan Italy, or O'Connor's realism-cum-grotesquerie with Spark's austere echoes of the *nouveau roman*) but also an asymmetry in critical interest—which even so blunt an instrument as the MLA International Bibliography reveals.[2] Despite a much larger body of work, Spark has provoked far less commentary than O'Connor. Though this asymmetry may simply reflect O'Connor's greater stature as a writer, a more immediately plausible reason for it is the greater certainty among readers of what is at stake in reading O'Connor. It is impossible, as I argued in chapter 1, to avoid confronting O'Connor's own justification for her work. And the gravity of what is at stake—salvation or damnation—demands attention, even from readers who wish that critics would find something else to talk about.

Spark's own statements about her religion and art, however, are fewer and far more guarded. Though she has consistently maintained that her Catholicism is essential to her writing voice, she has provided neither theological context nor approved readings of her work, asserting (not entirely credibly), "I don't set out to be a Catholic apologist in any form" (McQuillan interview 217). In interviews, she has expressed exasperation with the stupidity of other Catholics, the priesthood, and the liturgy, and while she

---

2. A keyword search for "Flannery O'Connor" on 13 June 2011 yielded 1,206 sources; one on the same date for "Muriel Spark" yielded only 245.

has not taken on the public role of a dissenting Catholic, she has acknowledged her own departures from Catholic teaching with blithe indifference. Even her famous reference to Catholic belief as "a norm from which one can depart" ("My Conversion" 26) for satirical purposes hardly suggests the same commitment to core Christian propositions that one sees in O'Connor. And while references to Catholicism abound in Spark's novels (in this, her work is far more overtly "Catholic" than O'Connor's), their significance is more obscure, lacking the portentous intrusions of the divine into everyday life that characterize O'Connor's fiction.

Only in the first nine years of Spark's career as a novelist, in the works stretching from *The Comforters* (1957) to *The Mandelbaum Gate* (1965), is it possible to identify continuous, though often qualified, support for Catholic beliefs—and indeed, both Spark's religious admirers and her detractors tend to emphasize these novels. As with O'Connor, the degree of interest in these early novels seems to correspond to a sense of what is theologically at stake. Yet even among them, only *Memento Mori* (1959), *The Bachelors* (1960), and possibly *The Girls of Slender Means* (1963) move beyond a glancingly favorable presentation of Catholicism to present anything like O'Connor's repeated argument that Christianity is true and that nothing is more important than recognizing its truth. What Frank Baldanza observed about Spark's work in 1965 remains apt many novels later: "[S]he has not treated themes that make any direct confrontation with Roman Catholic dogma [. . . .] the practice of a religious discipline [in her novels] is not very widespread, and where it does exist, it seems to make relatively little difference one way or the other in terms of the moral or immoral acts of her characters" (191, 194).

Moreover, beginning with *The Public Image* (1968), the references to Catholicism no longer suggest general approval. Many of these references seem to be arbitrary, not fully integrated into the text, and repeated for no apparent reason from novel to novel, as if Spark were merely brandishing a trademark. The religious framework that had seemed crucial to understanding the earlier novels now often reads as another aspect of what Bernard Harrison calls the "studied inconsequentiality" (131) of Spark's style:

> Nothing is ever fully explained or given depth. When, at crucial points, the puzzled reader demands explicit enlightenment, he is invariably fobbed off with an authorial giggle or a significant silence. Or novels suddenly peter out into scraps and fragments of action and conversation, as at the end of *Jean Brodie* or *The Comforters,* and the reader is left to work out for himself why these particular fragments have been shored against the ruin of what had appeared until then, at least in long stretches, to be

almost a conventional plot [. . .] On this view, surface and fashionable enigma have finally won out: there is nothing to be seen but what is to be seen, and that is precious little, though terribly stylish. (133)

Such a perception of Spark's work, certainly plausible enough, probably explains why she has fewer orthodox defenders than O'Connor.

It also certainly explains why many of Spark's more recent fans, committed to a mystique of transgression and often drawing upon poststructuralist theory, are impatient with talk of her Catholicism. Bryan Cheyette, for instance, argues that "her playful and anarchic fiction . . . disrupts the certainties of her supposedly stable identity as a 'Catholic writer'" (ix). He does not deny that religious conversion is important in Spark's work, but he decries attempts to impose a "conversionist orthodoxy" (11) on readings of it, because such an orthodoxy "unproblematically splits the self into old and new, before and after, inner and outer. Conversion, in these terms, is turned into a form of determinism and becomes a rather too facile act of redemption" (7). Martin McQuillan, on the other hand, grants that Spark is a Catholic writer but then defines Catholicism so broadly as to be meaningless. "[E]ven the documents of the Catholic church are not Catholic," he maintains, because, as writing, they necessarily undermine "essential and stable meanings, which presuppose and seek an authoritative center." On the other hand, given the sheer historical influence of Christianity (and monotheism more generally), "[i]t is impossible to be European today and not be 'Catholic,' it is impossible to live in the world today and not to be, in some way, 'Abrahamic'" (4, 5).[3] Against both critics, I maintain that after several decades of such moves, few things are more "facile" than ritual proclamations against binary oppositions and appeals to the endless proliferation of meaning, whether attributed to a particular writer or to language itself. Indeed, there is an implicit (and false) binary in such arguments—one that pits putatively authoritarian dogma against putatively free interpretive play.

In this chapter I will argue that Spark's presentation of religious belief is best seen neither as a seamless argument for orthodoxy nor as a testament to the anarchy of writing but as a rhetorical strategy adapted to the population with whom she has most often identified—namely, "really intelligent people, more or less intellectuals." Spark does not, of course, provide a rigorous, Gramscian definition of "intellectual," but the positive connotations that she evokes are familiar enough: intellectuals belong to

---

3. Still more amusingly, McQuillan maintains that "heaven, death, hell, and judgement" are "ideas not currently en vogue in the Catholic church" (5)—as if references to them had been quietly expunged from documents and liturgies.

an intelligent, creative, and ethically sensitive minority, capable of greater logical reasoning and finer aesthetic discrimination than the general public, but also more attuned to the connections between language and power.[4] The relationship between "intellectuals" in this broad sense and religion in the late twentieth century is uneasy, for although, as Terry Eagleton has observed, religion "is capable of operating at every social level: if there is a doctrinal inflection of it for the intellectual elite, there is also a pietistic brand of it for the masses" (*Literary Theory* 20), it is nevertheless evident that many twentieth-century intellectuals, committed to a narrative that links secularization with modernity, have tended to regard religion either as a lifestyle accessory (and so an essentially private and aesthetic concern) or as a crutch for those too afraid or unintelligent to trust their own powers of reasoning. As a Catholic writer, Spark, like O'Connor, is concerned with making religious belief credible to an intellectual audience presumed not to share it. Yet whereas O'Connor assumes the hostility of this audience, deriding intellectuals and obsessively staging the spectacle of *bien-pensant* hubris laid low, Spark dramatizes her complicity with it. The reader who can appreciate Spark's cold, whimsical art, seeing in it what she once called "the liberation of our minds from the comfortable cells of lofty sentiment" ("Desegregation" 36), is invited to regard Catholicism in the same light, as a system that affords superior aesthetic delights—if, that is, one can see beyond the tribal vulgarities of one's fellow Catholics. That it also happens to be true is presented offhandedly, as a kind of fringe benefit.

This rhetorical appeal also suggests a reason for the discrepancy in critical commentary on Spark and O'Connor. To insist too strongly on what is at stake in belief or unbelief, as O'Connor does, would negate Spark's particular appeal, for such a move would cast the intended reader as someone weak enough to require either the threat of hell or a sentimentally lov-

---

4. Geoffrey Galt Harpham suggests that "[f]or the past century, the dominant grounding idea for intellectual culture as a whole has been the thought of language. . . . This kind of emphasis on language itself is characteristically modern. A 'premodern' orientation, we might say, is signaled by a faith in the primacy of concepts on the one hand and the possibility of an unmediated observation of material fact on the other. . . . The modernist moment is achieved when immediacy in either direction is renounced as an illusion, when the limits of language are seen as the limits of the world, and linguistic mediation itself becomes the object of observation" (4). Though Harpham is speaking primarily of twentieth-century philosophers of language, his observation is equally applicable to twentieth-century "intellectuals" in the broader sense I have defined above, for it speaks to the association of the "intellectual" with aesthetic discrimination and pleasure (a novel, after all, is not an "unmediated" material fact) and to the self-consciousness and anxiety about agency and meaning that such aesthetic facility often promotes. I am tempted to extrapolate from Harpham and to define an intellectual as one who regards language "in itself" as an ultimate reality but cannot decide whether it is the source and expression of freedom (aesthetic play) or the key mechanism that perpetuates determinism (ideology).

ing God. Hence the apparent inconsequentiality of many of Spark's references to religion: the worthy reader, it would seem, finds aesthetic richness precisely in this lack of consequence. Moreover, this particular aesthetic is bound up with an interest in the peculiar pleasures of determinism, as novel after novel dispenses arbitrary fates to its characters, inviting readers to rejoice in their lack of freedom and to shift their own identification between free narrator and unfree characters continually. The pleasures of such a dialectic of bondage and freedom are real, but they are also characteristic of intellectuals who have acceded to different versions of linguistic determinism—and who, unable to assert a grounded faith in freedom, turn to the delights of subversion as the next best thing.[5] Indeed, readers of Spark who ground themselves in poststructuralist theory, such as Fotini E. Apostolou, tend to reduce her work to "an endless spiral of seduction and death, where one enters a structure that envelops him/her in order to create a construct that will imprison others, who will, in their turn, desire to be enticed by this construct in order to enter and change it" (xvi).

Though Spark does indeed appeal to such pleasures, she provides a more orthodox frame within which to understand them—one that reflects her own conversion to Catholicism under the influence of John Henry Newman. Known for his intellectual rigor, his highly aesthetic use of rhetoric in the *Apologia Pro Vita Sua*, his devotion to the beauties as well as the theology of the Eucharist and the liturgy, and his theory of the "illative sense" that emphasizes the personal nature of the apprehension of truth, Newman combines the sense of intellectual and aesthetic richness that Spark relishes with an appeal to the determinism implicit in any appeal to the irreducibly personal. Viewed through Newman's theory, Spark's playful investigations of the relationship between writing and determinism suggest that the apprehension of religious truth comes more easily and is more rewarding

---

5. Michel Foucault and Judith Butler are representative figures here—indeed, it might be said that they make unusually explicit the anxiety about the relationship between language and power that is characteristic of twentieth-century intellectuals more generally and try to defuse it by suggesting that subversion is the only possible recourse in a linguistically determined world. The later work of Foucault (especially the volumes of *The History of Sexuality*) repeats the double gesture of invoking the omnipresence of power and discourse on the one hand and cataloguing the possibilities of self-cultivation within such a determinist framework on the other. Butler's entire oeuvre is a continual turning of the screws of this problem, an attempt to account for the emergence of a subject's severely limited agency from within a totality that subordinates subjects even as it calls them into being. A major consequence of Foucault and Butler's work, as Martha Nussbaum has suggested, has been the eroticization of power and subversion. Though I cannot mount here a full-scale critique of such a position, suffice it to say that even if there were not good reasons to doubt the characterization of language as a "prison-house" (to allude to Fredric Jameson), the repeated description of such moves has become stupefyingly boring.

for those gifted enough to see its complexity—which is to say, those with an aesthetic and intellectual disposition. Indeed, it may be that one way to understand Spark is to see her as a kind of "bridge" figure between Newman and such contemporary theological developments as Radical Orthodoxy, which reaffirm the urgency of Christianity within postmodernity and have much to say about the intersection between Christianity and aesthetics—though such a comparison might too blithely suggest the interchangeability of art and theology.

In making this argument about Spark's rhetorical strategies against certain emphases in poststructuralist theory, I am in basic agreement with Wayne Booth's claim that in a work of fiction, "the author's judgment is always present, always evident to anyone who knows how to look for it" (*Rhetoric of Fiction* 20)—though I would add that Booth's matter-of-fact tone here understates the difficulty of such a task in a writer as cerebral as Spark. Booth's insight that "unreliable" fictions frequently "depend for their effects on ironic collusion between the author and his readers" (391) is true of nearly all of Spark's work, and it becomes especially so after 1965, but such collusion is achieved only through considerable labor on the part of the reader, which in turn tends to confirm readers who believe themselves to be "in" on her project in their own intellectual prowess. In what follows, I will demonstrate the successes and sketch some of the limitations of Spark's rhetorical strategies, tracing her portrayal of Catholicism as a system that provides superior intellectual and aesthetic delights even as it continues to foreground the problem of how to reconcile freedom with divine providence, the author's design with the expectation that characters in a novel be recognizably free. In most of the novels that I examine—*The Comforters, The Girls of Slender Means* (1964), *The Abbess of Crewe* (1974), *Loitering with Intent* (1981), and *Reality and Dreams* (1996)—Spark foregrounds characters who are aspiring or accomplished artists, as if to suggest that both the problems and the potential achievements of Catholic belief should be understood primarily in aesthetic terms and only secondarily in terms of truth.

II. Freeing Oneself from a Novel:
The Strange Case of *The Comforters*

At the center of Spark's aesthetic, as many have noted, is an analogy between an author's control over her work and God's omnipotence. The characters in a novel are, of course, not "free," but Spark is perhaps unusual in highlighting the moral problematic that this basic fact of the reading experience provokes—what Ruth Whittaker calls the tension between "the formal demands of her art and the mute claims of her characters for narratorial recognition of their humanity" (150). David Lodge has read *The Prime of Miss Jean Brodie* as a contest between "the Catholic God who allows for free will and the Calvinistic one who doesn't" ("Time-Shift" 76), but the novelist is necessarily like the Calvinist God, and any attempt to view a novel as relevant to real life therefore invites the problem of how to square the tendency to judge characters as if they were free agents with their actual lack of freedom. In chapter 1, I referred to Marina MacKay's argument that a Catholic genealogy of the novel, as opposed to the Leavisite assumption of the genre's Protestant underpinnings, might yield a different understanding of character and of one's judgment of it. Whereas "[c]haracter in life and the novel were conflated because Leavisite criticism tapped into the evangelical spirit of the nineteenth century" that "people are capable of changing" (228), a Catholic lens might well suggest that change is unpredictable, performative, and paradoxical—with the corollary that "the realized individual character is, in fact, the least free of all" (231). In this framing of the problem, the dichotomy is not between Calvinist and Catholic Author-Gods but between an illusory Protestant freedom and an illusory Catholic determinism. Perhaps the "determined" quality of a character in a novel in fact functions as the clearest sign of the character's freedom— if only because such characters frustrate readers' attempts to understand them.

This is, in fact, how MacKay reads Spark's novel *The Driver's Seat* (1970). Lise, the novel's protagonist, intends to be murdered and chooses her murderer. Her victimization is proleptically announced by the narrator early in the novel, but only near the end do readers discover that she has been pulling the strings all along, despite the fact that they know nothing of her motivations: "Spark gives autonomy to a character who consequently becomes depthless and unmotivated. The driver's seat is the death of character" (MacKay 232). As the narrator maintains of Lise, "Who knows her thoughts? Who can tell?" (53). A similar situation structures *Not to Disturb* (1971), whose plot Martin Stannard engagingly summarizes: "The servants of the Château Klopstock await the inevitable bloody deaths of their masters and prepare to profit from this by appropriating the contents of the house and by selling the story . . . Neither are we told how Lister and his crew know that murder is imminent, and know with such certainty that they have alerted journalists, written a scenario, and arranged for two pornographic film-makers to be on hand" (381–82). When the plot in which the servants wish to entrap their masters threatens to come apart, a quick and inventive rewriting occurs. In both novels, an author-figure—whether

Spark herself in *The Driver's Seat* or the servants in *Not to Disturb*—maintains and even flaunts control of plot, while the dominated characters remain stubbornly opaque.

Yet I would argue that Spark's most accomplished variation on this theme occurs in her first novel, *The Comforters*, which lacks the icy impersonality of these later works. *The Comforters* reads less like a *tour de force* but proves more penetrating as a moral inquiry, in part because of its thinly disguised autobiographical element, which works against the systematic foreclosing of moral judgment that *The Driver's Seat* and *Not to Disturb* attempt.[6] The central figure of the novel, Caroline Rose, is a recent convert to Catholicism and a writer (working on a study called *Form in the Modern Novel*) who has, after her conversion, given up sex with her boyfriend, Laurence Mathers. Convinced of the truth of Catholic dogma, she endures much irritation for it—less from the incomprehension of her friends and Laurence (who is himself a lapsed Catholic) than from the pettiness and tribalism of most of the Catholics she encounters, whom she regards as stupid, ugly, and "infatuated with a tragic image of themselves" (37). Shortly after Caroline is introduced, she flees from a retreat at the Pilgrim Centre of St. Philumena after unpleasant conversations with Mrs. Georgina Hogg, who disapprovingly says, "You're the sort that doesn't mix" (29), wears no brassiere under her cotton blouse, and describes her position at St. Philumena's as a miracle effected by the intervention of the Virgin Mary (32–33). Though disgusted by such pious believers, Caroline finds in the discrepancy between them and the truth of Catholic dogma confirmation of the Church's authenticity.[7] When Laurence tells her that she is

---

6. Willy Maley, in my judgment the best of Spark's critics who draw upon poststructuralist theory, has also made the best possible case for the merits of *Not to Disturb*, though he does not emphasize the freedom that lack of characterological depth might intimate. He finds, instead, an exposure of the "mutually assured destruction between aristocracy and peasantry, between the arrogant and the ignorant (however knowing in the ways of the world)" (183–84), and connects this exposure to Spark's often quoted claim that "[r]idicule is the only honourable weapon [artists] have left" ("Desegregation" 35). Thematically, Maley is on to something here, but I do not share his judgment that such deconstructive moves are "disturbing," nor do I detect any ridicule in them. Spark's recommendation of ridicule is voiced from a position of moral and aesthetic commitment that may call political commitments into question, but does not prove as self-undermining as a Derridean focus would imply. Because *Not to Disturb* provides no basis for judgment, it works against Spark's program of an art of ridicule.

7. It is possible to characterize Caroline's attitude here as "sacramental," as long as the sacramental is not conflated with the emotionally uplifting. Caroline is a kindred spirit of Sandy Stranger, the convert and nun in *The Prime of Miss Jean Brodie*, who achieves fame for writing a book called *The Transfiguration of the Commonplace* but whose expectations for ordinary happiness in the Church seem to be dashed nevertheless. Having betrayed Miss Brodie for her fascist sympathies, Sandy discovers in the Catholic Church "quite a number

"always bad-tempered after Mass," she responds that this is "one of the proofs of the Faith so far as I'm concerned," because "[t]he flesh despairs" (112) at such contact with her coreligionists. Her favorite fellow Catholic is her Uncle Ernest, a gay man who, like her, has renounced sexual relationships and taken a "critical but conforming" attitude toward Catholicism: "the True Church was awful but, unfortunately, one couldn't deny, true" (88–89). The novel makes clear that Caroline's fastidiousness is not itself a product of her conversion itself; it continues an established pattern of "nervous responses to food and sleep at the best of times" and frequent physical illnesses (70). For all her distaste with attitudes of martyrdom, she is accurately judged by Laurence as one who cultivates a "[m]artyrdom by misunderstanding" (232) and by the narrator as possessing a "rapacity for suffering" (37).

Appearing at first to be a straightforward realist narrative, *The Comforters* shifts decisively toward metafiction when Caroline begins hearing the sound of a typewriter, accompanied by voices that comment on her actions and even her thoughts. She concludes that "a writer on another plane of existence" is using her as a character in a novel (66). (The biblical allusion to the book of Job in the novel's title now comes into play: Caroline's "comforters" are those who would provide a coherent explanation for the voices—namely, that she is going mad—rather than permit her to confront the evident fact that there is no reason for her suffering.) As initial fear for her sanity gives way to a determination to resist this unknown author, the third-person narrator of *The Comforters* begins to express irritation with Caroline's meddling. When the narrator abruptly relates, "At this point in the narrative, it might be as well to state that the characters in this novel are all fictitious, and do not refer to any living persons whatsoever" (74), Caroline screams in reply (though her words are delayed for eight pages), "That's a damned lie. You're getting scared, I think. Why are you suddenly taking cover under that protestation?" (82). Later, when Caroline is in the hospital after suffering injuries in an automobile accident, the narrator complains that at this point in the narrative, "no experience of hers ought to be allowed to intrude," but because she sleeps badly, she remains awake

---

of Fascists much less agreeable than Miss Brodie" (123). When Sandy, now Sister Helena of the Transfiguration, receives visitors, her mannerisms suggest imprisonment—she "clutche[s] the bars of her grille as if she wanted to escape from the dim parlour beyond, for she was not composed like the other nuns" (33). Here Spark seems to mock Sandy's impatience, but she also mocks those who would read too much into this gesture and perhaps discredit Sandy's insights in doing so: "[E]veryone likes to visit a nun, it provides a spiritual sensation, a catharsis to go home with, especially if the nun clutches the bars of the grille" (118–19). See also Benilde Montgomery's reading of the novel, which perceptively links Sandy's sense of doctrinal development to Newman's.

and "turn[s] her mind to the art of the novel, wondering and cogitating, those long hours, and exerting an undue, unreckoned, influence on the narrative from which she is supposed to be absent from the time" (154, 155). Caroline resists the narrator in other ways as well, complaining that Georgina Hogg is "[n]ot a real-life character . . . only a gargoyle" (157), and that other key events of the plot, such as Laurence's grandmother's position as leader of a gang of diamond smugglers, are too implausible to be convincing as fiction. When the narrator reports that Georgina Hogg stops wearing brassieres because it is "like damming up the sea" to restrain her breasts, Caroline responds, "Bad taste . . . Revolting taste," which prompts a further, defensive remark: 'Bad taste'—typical comment of Caroline Rose. Wasn't it she in the first place who had noticed with revulsion the transparent blouse of Mrs. Hogg . . .? It was Caroline herself who introduced into the story the question of Mrs. Hogg's bosom" (157).

Caroline explains her resistance to the unknown author in explicitly theological terms: "I intend to stand aside and see if the novel has any real form apart from this artificial plot. I happen to be a Christian" (117). Since her faith teaches that human beings are in fact free, she must determine whether her actions and the actions of the other characters correspond to freely undertaken decisions rather than an implausible novelistic logic if she is to maintain her faith. Such an attitude is consistent with her dismissive response to Mrs. Hogg's talk of miracles and demands for social "mixing": against such popular piety and appeals to a determinist Providence, she will use her reason to test her faith, apparently secure in the knowledge that faith will prevail. The narrator responds, "All very well for her to resolve upon holding up the action. Easy for her to criticize," and immediately arranges an automobile crash (118), as if to prove her wrong. It is precisely in the hospital, however, when Caroline is "supposed" to be out of the narrative, that she begins to escape the narrator's complete control precisely by meditating on the art of the novel. Though her "sense of being written into the novel" remains "painful," she also begins to glimpse her eventual deliverance from it: "[N]ow she was impatient for the story to come to an end, knowing that the narrative could never become coherent to her until she was at last outside it, and at the same time consummately inside it" (206). Evidently, fiction is both a means of domination over helpless characters and a medium that can teach readers something about their own freedom. How to reconcile this apparent paradox?

The final resolution of the plot, which confirms Caroline's continued entrapment yet gestures toward a sense in which she might also be free, is anticipated when Laurence asks, "How is your book going?" and she responds, "I think it is nearing the end." Laurence, who means her book *Form in the Modern Novel,* is surprised, "for only a few days since she had announced that the work was slow in progress" (190). When Laurence presses her to clarify, she says, "I look forward to the end of the book . . . in a manner of speaking to get some peace"—here clearly referring to the book "about" her. Immediately afterward, she asks, "Do you remember the passage in Proust where he discusses the ambiguous use of the word book . . .?" (194). Though she does not specify which passage from Proust she has in mind, this allusion is enough to alter a reader's sense of how *The Comforters* configures the freedom of its characters.

As Dorrit Cohn has painstakingly argued in *The Distinction of Fiction*, Proust's *Remembrance of Things Past* possesses a "generic ambiguity" (58) that makes it difficult for readers to read it confidently either as a novel or as an autobiography. Though Cohn concludes that the work is a novel, she admits that a "genuinely fictional reading" of it is extremely difficult to achieve, both because "the sheer mass of essayistic, philosophical discourse in the *Recherche* discourages the mental construction of a narrator who is not identified with the author" and because "criteria of narrative content and narrative mode are too weak, as compared to contractual criteria, to enforce a bona fide fictional reading" (78). By referring to "Proust" rather than to "Proust's narrator" or even to "Marcel," Caroline tacitly endorses an autobiographical reading of the text, and though she does not specify which passage from the work she has in mind, thematically there is a strong case made for this one on the "*livre intérieur*" from the final third:

> As for the interior book of unknown symbols (symbols carved in relief they might have been, which my attention, as it explored my unconscious, groped for and stumbled against and followed the contours of, like a diver exploring the ocean bed), if I tried to read them no one could help me with any rules, for to read them was an act of creation in which no one can do our work for us or even collaborate with us. How many for this reason turn aside from writing! . . . But excuses have no place in art and intentions count for nothing: at every moment the artist has to listen to his instinct, and it is this that makes art the most real of all things, the most austere school of life, the true last judgment. This book, more laborious to decipher than any other, is also the only one which has been dictated to us by reality, the only one of which the "impression" has been printed in us by reality itself. . . . The book whose hieroglyphs are patterns not traced by us is the only book that really belongs to us. . . . What we have not had to decipher, to elucidate by our own efforts, what was clear before we looked at it, is not ours. . . . I had arrived then at the conclusion that in fashioning a work of art we are by no means free, that we do not choose how we shall make it but that it pre-exists us and therefore we are obliged, since it is both necessary and hidden, to do what we should have to do if it were a

law of nature, that is to say to discover it. . . . In this conclusion I was confirmed by the thought of the falseness of so-called realist art, which would
not be so untruthful if we had not in life acquired the habit of giving to
what we feel a form of expression which differs so much from, and which
we nevertheless after a little time take to be, reality itself. (III 913–15)

The simultaneous avowal and disavowal of conscious artistry in this
passage, the claim that the "interior book," the true book, is achieved only
by pursuing one's impressions as if to trace "a law of nature," suggests
Caroline's own resolution of her predicament: she will become a novelist herself, following not realistic conventions (significantly, she has been
struggling with the chapter in *Form in the Modern Novel* on realism [59]),
but by listening to "unconscious" suggestions and learning to distinguish
what is true in them. The strongest implication is that while Caroline has
not ceased to be a character in the work, she has also become its author.
Though this suspicion is not confirmed by what Cohn calls "contractual
criteria" (for instance, the narrator never uses the pronoun "I" in a way
that would establish her co-identity with Caroline), Laurence's discovery
of "an enormous sheaf" for Caroline's novel in the final pages suggests its
plausibility, as does his reaction to the notes: "You misrepresent all of us"
(232).

Spark does not, to be sure, identify Caroline with herself in the ambiguous way that Proust applies the name "Marcel" to his narrator, but the
biographical parallels between her and Caroline extend even to Caroline's
hearing voices. In January 1954, Spark began having hallucinations as she
worked on a study of T. S. Eliot: "[T]he letters of the words I was reading
became confused. They formed anagrams and crosswords. . . . I thought at
first that there was a code built into Eliot's work and tried to decipher it"
(*Curriculum* 204). The hallucinations proved to be an effect of Spark's taking
Dexedrine as an appetite suppressant, and as she recovered from the drug's
effects, she resolved "to write a novel about my recent brief but extremely
intense word-game experience" (*Curriculum* 205), though she recast the
visual hallucinations as auditory. Moreover, Spark responded to the discovery of her hallucinations as Caroline does, coming to believe that despite
their literal falsity, they provided valuable information about herself. As she
put it in a letter of 26 March 1954 to Derek Stanford, "Now I feel released
from a very real bondage & can make use of the experience. The real deliverance is the feeling that I can discover things about myself independent
of the 'code'—things that I didn't intuitively find among the anagrams but
which I hope will come to light in my mind & in fact have already done
so" (qtd. in Stannard 157). Here, too, the parallel with the Proust passage—
in which "no one could help" the writer "with any rules" because reading

"the interior book of unknown symbols" is an act of "creation" rather than "collaboration"—is suggestive.[8]

I have dwelled on these parallels not to argue that *The Comforters* is merely a disguised autobiography but to suggest that in its reworking of obviously autobiographical material, it provides a revealing point of entry into Spark's larger argument about the relations among religious belief, aesthetic pleasure, human freedom, and the moral ambiguity of authorship. Laurence reflects that "[r]eligion had so changed Caroline," for it made her insist that he would "have to be involved personally" to understand her, and the "know-all assumption of the words" had "infuriate[ed] him" (233). He does, it would seem, understand her desire to know the truth and to turn this knowledge into a form of control, for since his childhood, he has delighted in spying on people and reading their private letters (4), though when the shoe is on the other foot, he reacts with rage (78) before, apparently, resigning himself to being "the character called Laurence Manders" (231). The implication seems to be that Caroline's belief in Catholicism affords her greater freedom to see the truth and to benefit from it—her "personal" involvement absolves her of the charge of merely playing God, for it ensures that she does have a genuine relationship with the truth, a relationship that confirms her vocation as a writer. As Spark put it in "My Conversion," "Nobody can deny I speak with my own voice as a writer now, whereas before my conversion I couldn't do it because I was never sure what I was, the ideas teemed but I couldn't sort them out, I was talking and writing with other people's voices all the time" (26). Conversion, then, is a vehicle to personal and artistic freedom, but one needs to tread carefully, for there is inevitably a moral hazard in the writer's trade—predestining the fates of characters as if one were God. By staging a novel in which a Catholic convert character fights for her own freedom and becomes, as it were, her own author, Spark hints—but does not confirm—that a properly religious but suitably intellectual faith alone enables such a liberation, especially if it not accompanied by illusions about its capacity to make human beings nicer.

III. Spark's Misfit:
The Girls of Slender Means

If *The Comforters* associates religious faith with pursuit of the truth, artistic ambition, and the extension of one's freedom, *The Girls of Slender Means*,

---

8. It is, admittedly, tempting to read Spark's experience as an illustration of Harold Bloom's "anxiety of influence," in which she fights off Eliot, her overdetermined precursor, by creatively misreading what had been his secret, threatening code.

her novel set in London during the final days of the Second World War, seems more analogous to O'Connor's work, for it uses violence as an occasion for grace and portrays genuine freedom as an elusive, improbable occurrence. The belated explosion of a bomb outside the May of Teck Club, a girls' hostel, sets the building on fire. As the firemen attempt to rescue those trapped on the top floor, Nicholas Farringdon, a feckless anarchist poet who has frequented the club because he has an idealized image of the girls who live there, witnesses two events in quick succession. First, his lover Selina manages to escape, but as she does so she steals another girl's Schiaparelli dress that she had coveted. Secondly, Joanna, the daughter of an Anglican curate known for her elocution and her devotion to unworldly romantic ideals, falls to her death as the building collapses. As a result of this shocking juxtaposition—the equivalent of The Misfit's encounter with the grandmother—Nicholas converts to Catholicism, becomes a priest, and dies in Haiti as a martyr.

In addition to sharing this basic plot structure with O'Connor, Spark reveals herself to be even less committed to the individualized character portrait than O'Connor. Despite the splendidly realized period ambience and sparkling dialogue of *The Girls of Slender Means*, Spark ruthlessly reduces her characters to types in ways that foreshadow the cipherlike human beings of *Not to Disturb*, yet simultaneously critiques prevailing stereotypes of the period for their sentimentality. At a moment when the "general axiom" is that "[a]ll the nice people in England were poor" (1), the poverty of the May of Teck girls should speak in their favor, but Spark deftly undercuts such a conclusion: "few people alive at the time were more delightful, more ingenious, more movingly lovely, and, as it might happen, more savage, than the girls of slender means" (4). The girls themselves are not unique in their corruption: as crowds assemble on VJ night to await the appearance of the royal family, Nicholas witnesses a sailor stab a woman to death, undetected. When he cannot draw attention to the murder because of the thickness and preoccupation of the crowd, Nicholas contents himself with shoving a forged letter in praise of his manuscript (intended to impress a publisher) down the sailor's blouse, because "it was a gesture. That is the way things were at the time" (183). Collectively obsessed with "love and money" (27), individually the girls and their boyfriends are reduced to a few broad strokes and "gestures": Joanna is idealistic and naïve, Selina stupid and "extremely slim" (36), Jane "fat but intellectually glamorous by virtue of the fact that she worked for a publisher" (33), and Nicholas himself a familiar, pretentious type of artist. The repeated taglines and *idées fixes* that might seem to convey individuality in fact do just the opposite, so that the predictability of everyone forms a background against which Nicolas's conversion, the genuinely free or genuinely providential act, registers more strongly.

Yet despite these similarities, Spark's novel also provides revealing contrasts to O'Connor's method. Whereas "A Good Man Is Hard to Find" moves chronologically toward the encounter between the grandmother and The Misfit, whose gravity it is impossible to doubt, Spark does not foreground the conversion when it occurs but treats it from the beginning of her novel as a *fait accompli*. The novel oscillates between the events of 1945 and brief proleptic passages referring to an unspecified future date, and even in the first chapter presents Nicholas's conversion and martyrdom, well before introducing him as a character. Later, the reader discovers that it was indeed his observation of Selina's theft that prompted the conversion, but this information is revealed offhandedly, long before the moment happens: "He had not yet slept on the roof with Selina on the hot summer nights . . . and he had not yet witnessed that action of savagery so extreme that it forced him involuntarily to make an entirely unaccustomed gesture, the signing of the cross upon himself" (73). Interestingly, Nicholas seems less certain than the narrator that this is the moment of conversion, for, as the narrator reports, "Later, reflecting on this lightning scene, he could not trust his memory as to whether he then involuntarily signed himself with the cross. It seemed to him, in recollection, that he did" (161). But to avoid any doubt that he considers his conversion provoked by Selina's action, whether he remembers crossing himself or not, the narrator reveals that he has left in the manuscript of *The Sabbath Notebooks*, his collection of *pensées*, "a note that a vision of evil may be as effective to conversion as a vision of good" (180).

This departure from traditional chronology, which Spark has explained by saying, "I don't think chronology is causality" (Interview with Sara Frankel 451), in fact implies a more determinist vision of conversion than O'Connor's. Readers see the author's design from the beginning, which time cannot alter, and so are partially inoculated against the shock of the event. Moreover, they know Nicholas's thoughts about what he witnesses far more clearly than they know the grandmother's—not only because the narrator reports them, but also because the fact that he is not simultaneously the victim and the beneficiary of violence allows him to explain his conversion and so to confirm its necessity. The image with which the novel concludes—one of the remaining May of Teck girls, "sturdy and barelegged on the dark grass, occupied with her hair" (183)—is remembered by Nicholas years later in Haiti, and what Edgecombe calls this image's "epigrammatic closure" (60) indeed provides a fitting illustration of Spark's design.

How, then, should readers understand these differences between O'Connor's and Spark's texts? It would seem that Spark, more than O'Connor, has taken to heart Girard's claim that if an author is free, her characters cannot be. Because readers are never allowed to forget this lack of freedom in Spark's novel, they must locate her appeal to the reader instead as an ironic, intellectual savoring of the pleasures of determinism. O'Connor, however, in striving to make readers forget her design, and placing at the heart of even a story so heavy with chronological necessity and foreshadowing a space into which any possibility at all might flow, proves both more faithful to Catholic teaching and, as her greater popularity among ordinary readers and critics alike suggests, more accessible.

In subsequent novels, Spark would continue to explore the connections between artistic vision and the truths and benefits of religious faith. In general, the more central Spark's focus on a particular artist-figure, the greater his or her achievement and freedom. When she pursues a strategy of indirection and interrupted chronology, as in *The Girls of Slender Means,* she entraps her characters in a predestined structure and invites audiences to admire the turning of her screws: Nicholas's authorship and conversion, for instance, may associate him with the apprehension of intellectual truth, but it does not confirm his autonomy, as his life ends in a martyrdom reported second-hand rather than witnessed, whose significance is lost even to those who repeat the word. When Spark employs a more straightforward chronology and more consistent focalization through a single character, as in *The Abbess of Crewe* and *Loitering with Intent,* her portrayals of artists become both more loving and more fabulous. At the same time, these characters continue to reflect upon the problems of determinism, both in their own conception of themselves before God and in the way they use other people toward the achievement of their artistic goals. As Spark becomes more indulgent with her characters, her stance toward Catholic doctrine becomes more ambiguous, though references to it are never abandoned.

IV. Totality, Freedom, and Personalism:
The Influence of Newman

The opening sentence of Spark's late novel *Reality and Dreams* gestures toward these problems, both theological and narrative: "He often wondered if we were all characters in one of God's dreams" (7). By introducing the protagonist with a pronoun rather than a proper name, the novel implies the lack of individual agency associated with dreams. Yet despite such feelings, Tom Richards is not just a character in a novel (and so presumed to have "depth" and autonomy until proven otherwise) but also, as a film director, a fellow artist. And in fact he displays his own Artist-God complex nakedly, going to ridiculous lengths to control every aspect of his artistic production and dismissing others as "superfluous" (13). When the novel opens, he is in a drugged state of semiconsciousness, recovering in a hospital from a fall from a crane on the set of his current film, tentatively called *The Hamburger Girl*. Reflecting later upon the moments before the fall, he thinks, "Yes, I did feel like God up on that crane. It was wonderful to shout orders through the amplifier and like God watch the team down there group and re-group as bidden" (14). A reader of Flannery O'Connor might suspect that the fall functions as a deserved humiliation. When readers learn that in his drugged state, he had entertained the thought of murdering his wife, Claire, in order to inherit her fortune and to give it to the girl who inspired his film (a young woman glimpsed cooking hamburgers at a campsite kiosk in France), the problem of confusing life and art is established clearly.

At this point, one might refer this problem, as David Lodge does, back to the specific content of Catholicism and its emphasis on freedom. Even if Tom cannot demonstrate his "freedom" from the text in which he is inscribed, Catholic references in the novel might work toward an argument about extratextual human freedom. Here, however, readers confront the apparent arbitrariness of such references. Complaining to one of his friends, Ralph, that "[i]f Auden was alive, he would have come to see me in his shabby clothes," Tom continues to reminisce about writers he has known, turning the subject to Catholicism as he does so:

> "If Graham Greene were alive he would have looked in to see me, perhaps not in hospital but certainly here at home. Sex was his main subject, when you met him at least to start with. He had a mix-up of women and felt guilty the whole time. Without girls I think he couldn't have carried on. He needed it for his writing. Graham would have sent me a dozen bottles of rare wine or champagne. He would have come for an evening's talk and drink if he had known I was stuck in this bedroom. He would talk about sex always as if it was the forbidden fruit of the tree of knowledge. Sex and desire and the hazards thereof, such as divorce and venereal disease. I tried to get him on to religion but he was chary of that subject, Catholicism. He believed in it without swallowing everything, which is possible, and in fact more widely practised than one might think. In fact, he couldn't not believe, in spite of himself.
>
> "So much for his beliefs, but in some ways he had a bureaucratic conception of Catholic doctrine, but so do many Catholics including the pres-

ent Pope [John Paul II]. Greene never called me Tom, by the way. It was always 'Richards.' But he called Claire 'Claire' of course. Which reminds me of Allen Tate another Catholic who was keen on women. Have you heard of Tate?"

"No," said Ralph. "Unless you mean an American writer, I seem to remember. . . ."

"You remember right. He was an American poet, critic, and Anglophile. He went to see Pius XII in 1957. He told me how it went. Allen said, 'Your Holiness, the English and American Catholic Bishops are feeling uneasy about the Index of Forbidden Books. After the acts of censorship under totalitarianism the intelligent Catholic laity want more democratic freedom.'

"'Ah yes,' said Pius, '[Jacques] Maritain was here last week with that problem. Greene came about it recently. How many children,—nephews, do you have?'

"Allen told him how many.

"The Pope said, 'Here are four rosaries. The black ones are for boys, the white for girls.' End of audience."

"Was that the Pope before this?"

"No it was actually five Popes ago." (45–47)

This passage is funny, but establishing the target of the humor is surprisingly difficult. Who or what is being mocked here—"cafeteria" Catholics who profess to believe but are selective in their application of belief, such as Greene? (Certainly Greene and Tate *were* "keen on women.") Writers who think that promiscuity is essential to their art or take sex too seriously? A Church and Pope so cut off from the laity that the rote dispensing of rosaries passes for "dialogue"? Critics who invariably seek references to Catholicism in Spark's work, and of whose theories she has become "chary"? The naïveté of Catholic intellectuals such as Tate, whose interest in "democratic freedom" pales in significance next to the truths and of the Church and who deserve to be brushed aside in this way? Ecclesial corruption and infidelity to vows, perhaps hinted in the reference to "nephews"?[9] The ridiculousness of the now-abolished Index—yet another focus for arguments about the scope of freedom? The garrulity and peevishness of an old, ill, and nostalgic man? All of the above? And to what extent are readers to approve of Tom's judgments about Catholic matters—for instance, that it *is* possible "to believe without swallowing everything," or that John Paul II's conception of doctrine is "essentially bureaucratic"?

9. The reference to nephews alludes to Robert Browning's "The Bishop Orders His Tomb at Saint Praxed's Church," in which the dying bishop addresses his illegitimate sons as "nephews."

If readers refer, as they might in the case of O'Connor, to Spark's commentary on the people mentioned to help them answer these questions, the confusion only deepens. In this passage, Greene "couldn't *not* believe, in spite of himself," but in a 1987 interview Spark used this phrase to refer to herself—and, in the same passage, to distinguish her own kind of "Catholic writing" from Greene's: "Graham Greene is a different type of Catholic writer. . . . I have the impression that he's always on the verge of disbelief, and so he's constantly faced with a conflict. I don't have that conflict, because I can't *not* believe: I *couldn't* not believe" (Interview with Sara Frankel 446). Are readers to conclude that Spark has changed her mind about Greene, or that Tom's assessment of Greene's belief is unreliable? On the other hand, the notion that Greene "believed in it without swallowing everything" sounds remarkably like Spark's own position—her distaste for "popular Catholicism," with its "terrible bleeding hearts, the saints, the Pope, priests," her claim that she arrives at Mass only "after the sermons, because the sermons are so bad I couldn't possibly listen to them" (Interview with Sara Frankel 446)—and it even echoes the artist-figures from her fiction, such as Fleur, who resemble her. Of John Paul II, Spark once wrote, "I wouldn't take the Pope too seriously. He's a Pole first, a pope second, and maybe a Christian third" (qtd. in Neuhaus 74)—provoking hostility from at least one prominent Catholic intellectual.[10] And what of Maritain? When asked whether she accepted Maritain's claim that Catholics ought to be the best novelists, Spark once replied, "I think Maritain was full of a bit of air, actually," but did not clarify (Interview with Sara Frankel 447). The specificity of the references leads in numerous directions, but any authority that might attach to them individually seems to disperse. Thus far, complaints of the stylish triviality of it all seem justified.

Perhaps, then, readers should conceive of Spark's religious references in the broadest sense, so that mention of Greene or John Paul II functions only as a nod to the totality of Catholic belief and practice, as understood by Spark and as revealed to readers through her account of her conversion—the most concise description of which is found in *Curriculum Vitae* (1993), her autobiography:

> In 1953 I was absorbed by the theological writings of John Henry Newman through whose influence I finally became a Roman Catholic. I tried the Church of England first, as being more "natural" and near to home. But I felt uneasy. It was historically too new for me to take to. When I am

10. Richard John Neuhaus: "That's just vulgar nasty, the kind of thing said by minor celebrities who get interviewed and feel the need to say something smart. . . . I cannot imagine that three hundred years from now, or thirty years from now, anyone will wonder what Muriel Spark might have said about anything" (74–75).

asked about my conversion, why I became a Catholic, I can only say that the answer is both too easy and too difficult. The simple explanation is that I felt the Roman Catholic faith corresponded to what I had always felt and known and believed; there was no blinding revelation in my case. The more difficult explanation would involve the step by step building up of a conviction; as Newman himself pointed out, when asked about his conversion, it was not a thing one could propound "between the soup and the fish" at a dinner party. (202) [11]

Though I do not doubt Spark's sincerity here, her foregrounding of Newman should also be seen as a part of her own appeal to an intellectual audience—a conversion under the sign of an undoubted philosophical giant, who tackles the question of Catholicism's historical validity and philosophical soundness, carries more weight than one provoked by (to use an example from O'Connor's "Revelation") a vision in the sky.

Moreover, Newman's own account of belief provides a helpful frame around the problem of freedom and determinism in Spark's work. When Spark declares that she became a Catholic because it was what she already believed, she does not of course mean that she had unknowingly affirmed the existence of purgatory, the Immaculate Conception, or transubstantiation. It does, however, suggest that she understands her conversion as an instance of what Newman calls the "indefectibility of certitude" (*Grammar* 167). For Newman, certitude has "a definite and fixed place among our mental acts;—it follows upon examination and proof," and it always has "reference to propositions, one by one" (*Grammar* 179, 184). Furthermore, once certitude has been achieved, it does not change. Religious conversions, however much they resemble changes in certitude, should be understood as processes of development, in which a human being, tenaciously working through the logic and implications of a given certitude, arrives at a truer understanding of what it encompasses—as in his hypothetical example of three Protestants who change their religious convictions but not their certitudes. [12] Throughout this process, what Newman calls the "illative

---

11. In *The Comforters*, Caroline's account of her conversion to Georgina Hogg echoes Newman's account, though more haughtily. When asked "What made you a Catholic, then?" Caroline responds, "Many reasons . . . which are not too easy to define: and so I prefer not to discuss them" (29).

12. "Thus, of three Protestants, one becomes a Catholic, a second a Unitarian, and a third an unbeliever: how is this? The first becomes a Catholic, because he assented, as a Protestant, to the doctrine of our Lord's divinity, with a real assent and a genuine conviction, and because this certitude, taking possession of his mind, led him on to welcome the Catholic doctrines of the Real Presence and the Theotocos, till his Protestantism fell off from him, and he submitted himself to the Church. The second became a Unitarian, because, proceeding on

sense" operates, allowing readers to reason from partial evidence to general conclusions that carry just as much authority as if they had syllogistically proven every intermediate step. The convert who, having assented to the authority of Catholicism because she has pursued the implications of her certitude, may not understand or even be aware of many of the specific doctrines that such a belief entails, but this does not matter: having proclaimed a belief in the "'One Holy and Apostolic Church' . . . an article, which, inclusive of her infallibility, all . . . can easily master and accept with a real and operative assent," it follows that she can assent even to what she cannot understand, because she believes in the Church (*Grammar* 113).

But the implications of Newman's philosophical theology extend even further, for his "illative sense" is irreducibly personal. She who acts in accord with it is on the one hand merely obeying the law of her nature, and there is simply no gainsaying its existence or reliability: "We are what we are, and we use, not trust our faculties. To debate about trusting in a case like this, is parallel to the confusion implied in wishing I had had a choice if I would be created or no, or speculating what I should be like, if I were born of other parents" (*Grammar* 47). Yet there is a further criterion that confirms the certitudes of the illative sense: complexity. In an astonishing passage, Newman argues that the very complexity—even the apparent self-contradiction—of the Catholic Church proves its truth:

> There is a religious communion claiming a divine commission, and holding all other bodies around it heretical or infidel; it is a well-organized,

---

the principle that Scripture was the rule of faith and that a man's private judgment was its rule of interpretation, and finding that the doctrine of the Nicene and Athanasian Creeds did not follow by logical necessity from the text of Scripture, he said to himself, 'The word of God has been made of none [sic] effect by the traditions of men, and therefore nothing was left for him to profess what he considered primitive Christianity, and to become a Humanitarian. The third gradually subsided into infidelity, because he started with the Protestant dogma, cherished in the depths of his nature, that a priesthood was a corruption of the simplicity of the Gospel. . . . then came the question, what after all was the use of teachers of religion? why should anyone stand between him and his Maker? . . . [S]o he came to the conclusion that the true and only revelation of God to man is that which is written on the heart. This did for a time . . . [b]ut then it occurred to him that this moral law was there within the breast, whether there was a God or not, and that it was a roundabout way of enforcing that law, to say that it came from God, and simply unnecessary, considering it carried with it its own sacred and sovereign authority, as our feelings instinctively testified . . . so he dropped it, and became a *purus, putus* Atheist.

"Now the world will say that in these three cases old certitudes were lost, and new were gained; but it is not so: each of the three men started with just one certitude, as he would have himself professed, had he examined himself narrowly; and he carried it out and carried it with him into a new system of belief. He was true to that one conviction from first to last [. . .] He has indeed made serious additions to his initial ruling principle, but he has lost no conviction of which he was originally possessed" (*Grammar* 186–87).

well disciplined body; it is a sort of secret society, binding together its members by influences and by engagements which it is difficult for strangers to ascertain. It is spread over the known world; it may be weak or insignificant locally, but it is strong on the whole from its continuity; it may be smaller than all other religious bodies together, but it is larger than each separately. It is a natural enemy to governments external to itself; it is intolerant and engrossing, and tends to a new modeling of society; it breaks laws, it divides families. It is a gross superstition: it is charged with the foulest crimes; it is despised by the intellect of the day; it is frightful to the imagination of many. And there is but one communion such.

Place this description before Pliny or Julian; place it before Frederick the Second or Guizot. "Apparent dirae facies." Each knows at once, without asking a question, who is meant by it. One object, and only one, absorbs each item of the detail of the delineation. (*Development* 192–93)

This complexity, moreover, is grasped as a totality, and it is only once this totality is imaginatively apprehended that any kind of "local" effort to distinguish between its true and false aspects can make sense at all. As Stephen Prickett puts it,

For Newman . . . the true analogy of the Church is not a grain of mustard-seed, nor yet a vine, but a sentient human being—and preferably, indeed, one who had been educated at Oxford through the controversies of the 1820s and 1830s, and had held a fellowship at Oriel. . . . How are we, finally, to distinguish between the living body and the vain enchantments of simulacra? The true story and the false? Beyond the application of rule-of-thumb tests, the final answer appears to be by means of the imagination. This is the reason for the apparent circularity of the argument of the *Essay*. It is only after our imaginations have intuitively grasped the whole picture that such tests will serve to convince us. (175, 176)

It follows that the richer one's imaginative capacity, the "truer" one's perceptions and beliefs should be, and that the index of their "truth" would be their complexity. And it is no great leap to conclude that the very distinction between reality and dream—the opposition that frames Spark's novel—becomes meaningless viewed from the standpoint of this all-encompassing imaginative truth. Spark's own frequently quoted statement, "I don't claim that my novels are truth—I claim that they are fiction, out of which a kind of truth emerges" (qtd. in Kermode 30) takes on a greater resonance in light of Newman's framework. So does her insistence that "Nobody can deny I speak with my own voice as a writer now, because before my conversion I was never sure what I was" ("My Conversion" 26).

Although Newman is not mentioned in *Reality and Dreams*, his account of the self offers a model for how Tom's references to religion function in the text—as a display of imaginative, contradictory richness that mark him not just as a believer (and so in touch with the truth) but as the best *kind* of believer. Unlike the rote beliefs of those who have inherited their religion and feel little need to question it, Tom's self-consciousness and even his playfulness about it imply, to invoke Newman's language, a certitude reflected both in the authority with which he dispenses religious judgments and in his lack of seriousness about them. Even when Tom wonders whether he is a character in one of God's dreams, the narrator takes pains to emphasize the paradoxical *reality* of such an idea: "To an unbeliever this would have meant the casting of an insubstantiality within an already insubstantial context. Tom was a believer. He meant the very opposite. Our dreams, yes, are insubstantial; the dreams of God, no. They are real, frighteningly real. They bulge with flesh, they drip with blood. My own dreams, said Tom to himself, are shadows, my arguments—all shadows" (63–64). This reality, in turn, casts a different light on his artistic production, his own meager attempts to play God. As long as he recognizes the shadowy nature of his dreams, without confusing them with reality (he is appropriately horrified when he remembers after his operation his drug-induced plans to have Claire murdered, and contents himself with having an "element of this scenario" [20] in the film script), his artistry remains praiseworthy. If he occasionally requires correction—such as a fall from a crane—we are nevertheless not invited to exult in his humiliation or to experience pity and fear in identifying with him.

V. The Nun and the Autobiographer:
Figures of the Artist in *The Abbess of Crewe* and *Loitering with Intent*

The deftness of Spark's achievement in creating Tom becomes more evident if we compare him to two of his forebears—Alexandra, the Abbess of Crewe, and Fleur Talbot, the aspiring novelist of *Loitering with Intent*—whose very different personalities are combined and rendered more convincing in Tom. Though *The Abbess of Crewe* is among Spark's most spirited performances—taking inspiration from Alexander Pope's "The Rape of the Lock," the Watergate break-in, and the often comical spectacle of factionalism in the Catholic Church after the Second Vatican Council—Alexandra herself is so grandiose as to be alternately lovable and creepy. Determined to remake the Abbey in light of her megalomaniacal vision, Alexandra manipulates the scandal that occurs when a nun's thimble is stolen into a drama that the engrosses the global media, all the while building a regime of surveillance—even the poplars of the nuns' avenue are bugged—in her campaign against her rival, Sister Felicity. Alexandra's transformation of the abbey is intended to maximize good taste and to minimize vulgar piety. Detesting no less than Caroline Rose the drabness of ordinary Catholics, Alexandra does not share her conviction that truth should trump style. Not only does she respond to the chants of the Liturgy of the Hours not with prayer but with poetry by Marvell and Keats; she reveals, in an address to the nuns, her aristocratic indifference to religious belief: "A Lady may secretly believe in nothing; but a Bourgeoise [sic] invariably proclaims her belief, and believes in the wrong things. . . . A Lady is free; a Bourgeoise is never free from the desire for freedom" (79, 80). Even at the level of material comforts, these differences are enforced: Alexandria and her henchmen enjoy pâté and white wine, while the despised ordinary nuns, ostensibly to mortify themselves, subsist on nettles and tinned cat food.

Much of the humor of *The Abbess of Crewe* derives from the way such pronouncements, impossible to take at face value, nevertheless provoke a kind of admiration in readers for their zany singularity and for the oblique light they shed on the context of the Catholic Church beyond the abbey walls. Alexandra's innovations, for instance, satisfy neither traditionalists nor progressives in the tumultuous post–Vatican II context. As she puts it,

> "It is absurd in modern times that the nuns should have to get up twice in the middle of the night to sing the Matins and the Lauds. But modern times come into a historical context, and as far as I'm concerned history doesn't work. Here, in the Abbey of Crewe, we have discarded history. We have entered the sphere, dear Sisters, of mythology. My nuns love it. Who doesn't yearn to be part of a myth at whatever the price in comfort? The monastic system is in revolt throughout the rest of the world, thanks to historical development. Here, within the ambience of mythology, we have consummate satisfaction, we have peace." (20)

As Edgecombe aptly notes, "It is almost impossible to disentangle the skeins of sympathy and mockery in the tone here" (97). One of the attractions of Christianity has always been its promulgation of a standard by which to judge the world. Yet while the appeal to something that stands above the vagaries of "historical context" makes sense, the Christian narrative must remain "historical" rather than merely "mythic" if it is to retain its integrity. Even as she makes such astonishing claims, however, she proves shrewd enough to detect lapses in orthodoxy in other nuns. When the globe-trotting Sister Gertrude, modeled on Henry Kissinger, compromises Catholic doctrine in her efforts to preach to a group of "witch doctors" in the Congo, Alexandra pours scorn on her synthesizing, relativizing approach: "Sister Gertrude, believe me, is a philosopher at heart. There is a touch of Hegel, her compatriot, there" (20). In this way she manages to stand against both the historical relativism of post–Vatican II progressives and the "mythic" approach that would recommend results and "ambience" over dogma—a contradiction reconciled, if at all, only by the force of her singular charisma. Drawing from St. Paul and the heretical theology of Joachim of Fiore (with a possibly feminist twist) to justify her actions, Alexandra soars into antinomian ether:[13] "The ages of the Father and the Son are past. We have entered the age of the Holy Ghost. The wind bloweth where it listeth and it listeth most certainly on the Abbey of Crewe. I am a Benedictine with the Benedictines, a Jesuit with the Jesuits. I was elected Abbess and I stay the Abbess and I move as the Spirit moves me" (5).

Spark plays out such appealing yet appalling zaniness as far as it can possibly go before yielding to verisimilitude. No abbess in the Catholic Church would be permitted such blasphemous eccentricities, and at the end of the novel Alexandra is en route to Rome to answer the charges against her. Echoing Shakespeare's *Tempest,* the novel's final paragraph hints at Alexandra's almost-certain fate while indulging in one final paean to her glory: "Our revels now are ended. Be still, be watchful. She sails indeed on the fine day of her desire into waters exceptionally smooth, and stands on the upper deck, straight as a white ship's funnel, marveling how the wide sea billows from shore to shore like that cornfield of sublimity which never should be reaped nor was ever sown, orient and immortal wheat" (116). John Updike's judgment that "though the author cannot approve of the Abbess Alexandra, she does love her, love her as she hasn't loved a character in a decade" ("Top-Notch" 344) seems largely correct, and the proof is clinched when Alexandra, quoting Ezra Pound, declares her membership in Spark's fraternity of artists and intellectuals: "For I am homesick after mine own kind / And ordinary people touch me not" (59).[14] Alexandra surely exaggerates her artistic credentials to a degree that Spark herself, ever impressed by results instead of sentiments, would not—yet her fantasies are so beguiling that Spark is willing to give mostly free rein to them.

---

13. Joachim of Fiore's apocalyptic teaching of the "three ages" was condemned by the Church as heretical in 1263—a hint that Spark's appeal to a more "intellectual" Catholicism that equates divine inspiration with aesthetic production might indeed flirt with heresy.

14. For two frustrated attempts to account for the discrepancy that Updike notes between disapproval and love, see Whittaker (103) and Edgecombe (93–110).

If Alexandra impresses but in the end must be let go as too implausible even for Spark, Fleur Talbot, the protagonist of *Loitering with Intent*, has more substance. Like Caroline Rose, Fleur is modeled largely on Spark herself as she scrounges to survive the British postwar world of austerity and seeks to make it as a writer "right in the middle of the twentieth century" (197). Like *The Comforters*, *Loitering with Intent* probes the relationship between fiction and autobiography: Fleur looks back to the time when she worked temporarily as a secretary for a motley but undistinguished crew of minor aristocrats and snobs who called themselves the "Autobiographical Association" and wished to write their life stories for the benefit of posterity. The stories are obviously not worth telling, and Fleur amuses herself by revising the narratives so as to make them more interesting. In the interval since then, Fleur has become a successful writer of novels, but *Loitering with Intent* purports to be autobiography: "[I]t strikes me how much easier it is with characters in a novel than in real life. In a novel the author invents characters and arranges them in convenient order. Now that I come to write biographically I have to tell of whatever actually happened and whoever naturally turns up" (59). By playing with readers who know the book to be fiction (albeit of an admittedly autobiographical cast), Spark flaunts her facility with both genres, and Fleur herself offers a naked appeal to the vanity of the book's readers: "I always hope the readers of my novels are of good quality. I wouldn't like to think of anyone cheap reading my books" (216).

Such self-conscious and skilled generic crossings are also commented upon in the text in ways that look to Newman for inspiration and carry implications for the role of Catholic belief in the life of a writer. Like Caroline Rose, Fleur despises vulgar piety even as she believes in Catholic doctrines; but like the Abbess of Alexandria, she refuses to mortify herself in the service of such beliefs: "I too was a Catholic believer but not that sort, not that sort at all. And if it was true . . . that I was taking terrible risks with my immortal soul, I would have been incapable of caution on those grounds. I had an art to practise and a life to live, and faith abounding; and I simply didn't have the time or the mentality for guilds and indulgences, fasts and feasts and observances. I've never held it right to create more difficulties in matters of religion than already exist" (128–29). A partial justification for such attitudes may be gleaned from Fleur's admiration for two biographies that complement each other: Newman's *Apologia pro Vita Sua* and the *Life* of Benvenuto Cellini. Cellini's rollicking narrative hints at the full range of license permitted to the writer, while Newman, accepting complexity, particularity, and even apparent contradiction, nevertheless provides continuous grounding for this license in the securely personal relationship with God.

Bryan Cheyette has argued that in *Loitering with Intent*, Spark retreats from her earlier admiration of Newman. The key passage from the *Apologia* that Fleur cites deals with Newman's religious feelings as a boy, when he "mistrust[ed] . . . the reality of material phenomena" and "rest[ed] in the thought of two and two only supreme and luminously self-evident beings, myself and my Creator." Struck by this passage after she has recommended the *Apologia* to a member of the Autobiographical Association, Fleur comes to perceive an "awful madness" (95) in this apparent solipsism, though her initial resentment springs from the fact that her interlocutor likes the passage despite the fact that she, unlike Fleur, has not spent three and a half years studying Newman, "at the sacrifice of pleasures and happiness which would never come my way again" (95). Skipping over Fleur's petulance here, Cheyette comments: "While Newman unites his youthful and matured selves through his 'neurotic' (*Loitering* 96) relationship with God, Cellini is 'comically contradictory' (*Loitering* 124), recognizing a range of possible selves. Fleur, in the end, rejects the 'awful madness' (*Loitering* 95) inherent in Newman's homogenizing narrative" (108). This is a distortion of Newman's account of the self, which is capacious enough (as I have already suggested) to embrace the "comically contradictory." It is revealing that Cheyette's own language trips him up, for he at once criticizes Newman for "unit[ing] his youthful and matured selves" and lauds Spark for being "on the side of unification or desegregation" and seeing "a split self as untenable" (102). What's the difference? Moreover, he does not acknowledge that Fleur, retreating almost at once from her own petulance, concedes that her characterization of the *Apologia* as "a beautiful piece of poetic paranoia" is "over-simple, a distortion" (96). She then continues to refer to the text as "lovely" (195), and when she places a passage from it alongside Cellini's *Life* at the end of the novel, "admiring both" (196), the two autobiographies are revealed not as opposed to each other but as complementary. The phrase "from there by the grace of God I go on my way rejoicing" (217), which ends the novel, gives Cellini the last word but does not thereby diminish her admiration for Newman.

VI. Religion against Moralism in *Reality and Dreams*

Although I judge *Reality and Dreams* as a novel to be inferior to *Loitering with Intent*, its portrait of Tom provides in some respects the most convincing portrait of Spark's romance with "really intelligent people," the artists with whom she identifies and whose beliefs she recommends to her readers. Lacking the Abbess Alexandria's zaniness, Tom shares her conviction of self-worth; possessing the shrewdness and common sense of Fleur Talbot, Tom nonetheless shows that artists need not prove their credentials through poverty in postwar London. Like his compatriots, Tom has an imaginative literary sensibility (as his friendships with great writers and his frequent musings on T. S. Eliot's "The Love Song of J. Alfred Prufock" indicate) and an exalted, even grandiose conception of his creativity. In a novel in which redundancy (in American parlance, being laid off) is a major motif—and in which Tom is himself briefly made "redundant" when his injuries prevent him from directing his own film—he has no sympathy for those in this predicament, maintaining that "Nobody fires a man if he is exceptionally good, unless the whole outfit closes down" (21) and that artists are by definition *not* redundant: "No work of art can be replaced. A work of art is like living people" (23).[15] Like them, he is a religious believer, but one who is unrepentant about his sins (above all, his frequent adulteries), and whose own theological pronouncements, however confidently delivered, are questionable—as when he tells Dave, his deeply religious taxi driver and confidant, "The Bible doesn't teach Christian beliefs. It only illustrates them. The Bible came before Christianity by hundreds of years" (66).[16]

The catalog of admirable traits continues: Tom accepts the intermingling of spirit and matter in a way that might be called sacramental—as when he tells his masseur that the two are "[a]t least, interdependent" (55). He overcomes several obstacles to his work, including not just his injuries and a series of delays in filming, but also two attempts on his life. And as with the Abbess and Fleur, there is virtually no hint that the narrator disap-

---

15. In an interview with Martin McQuillan, Spark expanded on the theme of the redundancy in the novel: "The issue is to have a whole new philosophy of life where usefulness is questioned. . . . A lot of people do without having the problem of whether they're useful of not. If it's an economic problem, it can be solved by society being arranged in such a way that there's enough for everybody. What one does with one's time is said to be important because of this puritanical thing about having to work to be useful" (223). Here Spark associates work with Puritanism and utility in a way consistent with Tom's remarks on redundancy. Human beings are irreplaceable, but this is so because they are like works of art, not because they are useful. To have one's uselessness confirmed by being laid off is, both Tom and Spark suggest, no reason for despair. Those who do despair become easy targets for manipulative, puritanical do-gooders—at which point any possibility of sympathy for them ceases.

16. One obvious mark of Tom's kinship with the Abbess of Crewe is his repetition of her Joachite theology: "I want some sign of inspiration. Do you know what inspiration is? It is the descent of the Holy Spirit. I was talking to a Cardinal the other day. He said there was a theory that the ages of the Father and the Son were over and we were approaching the age of the Holy Spirit, or as we used to say, Ghost. The century is old, very old" (59). In both novels, however amusingly grandiose these pronouncements, there is little to suggest that they are intended ironically—that the Abbess and Tom are not, in fact, "inspired" in a sense that conflates the theological with the aesthetic.

proves of him. Even when the narrator appears to introduce doubt about him—"[W]ho was to say that he was the just arbiter of other people's character?"—she immediately qualifies it in ways that redound to his credit: "Simply because he was always ready to assume that part, and others only too ready to listen to him with dazzled conviction is not to say that Tom was always right (although generally there was something in what he said" (33). He is innately talented, aesthetically sensitive, and capable of weaving any complexity and uncertainty—even the limits on his own powers—into a satisfying whole. His preoccupation with J. Alfred Prufrock may suggest, as Anna Walczuk would have it, that he is "unable to find a definite verbal formula for everything that bothers and fascinates him in life" (96), but although he acknowledges such hesitations (and even releases *The Hamburger Girl* under the title *Unfinished Business*), he nevertheless succeeds, as Eliot does, in making such confusion into genuine art. He is, in short, just the kind of protagonist whom avowedly postmodern intellectuals, suspicious of theological discourse but deeply invested in their own status as right-thinking and creative individuals, would admire.

What makes his religious belief attractive to such an audience—as opposed to merely an eccentricity that can be taken or left—is not only the fun to be had with it but also its implicit opposition to moralism, embodied in the novel by his daughter, Marigold. Described early in the novel as (by Tom) an "unfrocked priest of a woman" (11) and later (by the narrator) as "worthy as any woman or man in the works of George Eliot, unlovely, graceless" (34) and still later as "[h]ideous" and "[a]lways negative" (87), Marigold functions throughout the novel as a malignant force, full of righteous but—as the narrator continually insists—unjustified anger. When she complains to Claire that Tom is cheating on her, she is astonished when Claire declares that the subject "bores" her and that she has no intention of divorcing him (62). She also likes to make sarcastic remarks about Tom's wealth, but the narrator immediately ironizes them: "You must not imagine Marigold was particularly deprived" (12). When Tom and Claire wonder whether they are responsible for Marigold's negativity, the narrator reassures us: "[T]hey were in no wise to blame. Marigold was simply a natural disaster" (90). And again: "How had Tom managed to conceive her? And Claire, so emotionally creative?" (34). "In no way could she be explained" (87).

As Tom reflects, what makes Marigold particularly unpleasant is the fact that "[s]ooner or later . . . [she] had to make it out to be a moral question" (54), irrespective of what "it" is. She describes moral deliberation as "see[ing] things *sub specie aeternitatis*" (making herself pedantic by adding, "Which means . . . 'under the light of eternity'" [37]), and when Tom is not actively appalled by her attitude, he finds it "too serious" (33). Much of her moral energy is directed against what she regards as the evils of redundancy, and she spends several memorable sequences pontificating not just against the cruelty of making people redundant, but also against luxury in general: "[N]obody should take on responsibilities which would demand more expenditure than would be gained from the dole and the income support schemes. . . . In other words, if all lived austerely, redundancy would bring no shock to the person or the family" (34). As Spark has suggested, Marigold's interest in redundancy is meant to be seen as unhealthy.[17] Eventually she disappears, leading Tom and Claire to worry that she might have been murdered, only to be discovered later disguised as a homeless man on a campsite in Gloucestershire, "living like this," as she explains, "in order to experience at first hand what it's like to be destitute. . . . Few realize what redundancy can lead to" (136). Although Claire, after speaking with her, is convinced that "she means every word" (137), the novel also implies that she is equally driven by a desire to make Tom feel guilty and to manipulate him—as when she briefly hides with a temporary and unnamed lover on the campsite in France that had inspired *The Hamburger Girl,* having had a (confirmed) hunch that Tom will search there for her (101). There is also the possibility—neither confirmed nor denied in the text—that while in hiding Marigold has persuaded Kevin Woodstock, a redundant television director with whose wife Tom has been having an affair, to assassinate Tom (the bullet instead hits Dave, nearly killing him). At no point is there any indication that Marigold shares her father's religious beliefs, which suggests that when religion disappears, an unattractive and even murderous moralism replaces it.

Marigold does, to be sure, display her own kind of creativity—passing as a homeless man, becoming a national figure, and writing *Out of Work in a Camper,* which becomes a bestseller. Tom, who initially finds her own attempt at filmmaking (on redundancy) laughable ("Tom and Claire hurled themselves about the sofa in their hilarity" [86]), later considers that her book gives her "a glamour which [he] could only admire" and concludes that she is "more ambitious" than he (141). Even so, he finds ways to make use of Marigold's talents for his own purposes, casting her as a "hermaphroditic Celt of the years c. 436" who foresees the future in his next film, *Watling Street* (140). In doing so, he again suggests the priority of the aes-

---

17. "That's one of the things I wanted to bring out in the book, this frustration people have about redundancy. There's this awful girl, Marigold, a sort of social worker, working up this feeling at the same time" ("The Same" 223). Spark implies that frustration at redundancy is unwarranted, and that those who exploit such feelings—whether from a sincere desire to help or not—cause more harm than good.

thetic over the moral, the imaginative over the factual, and angers her all over again: "It was often said privately that her disappearance had been a publicity stunt to work up interest in *Watling Street*. And when this was suggested publicly on a talk-show, she denied it vehemently. Her experiences were real sufferings, she explained" (141). "Real" they may have been, but even her newly acquired celebrity cannot hide the aesthetic flaws of their presentation, as Claire eventually suggests upon learning of her plans for a second book on redundancy: "I hope she gets a better ghostwriter this time" (147). Her murderousness, doubtful earlier in the novel, is confirmed when she encourages Jeanne (the actress who plays the hamburger girl, and who has her own grievances against Tom) to tamper with his crane a second time.

In the novel's final chapter, Tom tells his crew, "What we are doing . . . is real and not real. We are living in a world where dreams are reality and reality is dreams. In our world everything starts from a dream" (157). Working, like Spark, on a fiction from which a kind of truth emerges, Tom's aesthetic position has now earned a certain authority and can be seen, like Newman's, as a matter of imaginative, personal connection to truth. It almost seems a foregone conclusion that instead of killing Tom, Jeanne falls to her death from the crane, while Marigold flees to the United States. Tom, shaken by his latest brush with death, ends the novel with Claire's "strength and courage sustaining [him], here in the tract of no-man's land between dreams and reality, reality and dreams" (160).

VII. The Nature of Sparkian Irony

In recent years, it has become common to speak of Spark's novels as postmodern—no doubt because of their metafictive properties and their flouting of conventional readerly pleasures. Yet the most familiar definition of the postmodern—Jean-François Lyotard's "incredulity toward metanarratives" (xxiv), which finds an even more extreme embodiment in Richard Rorty's figure of the "liberal ironist" (*Contingency* xv)—does not convincingly apply to Spark, despite the attempts of some contemporary critics to invoke something like it in connection with her. Bryan Cheyette, for instance, argues that Spark places "a sense of history, tradition, and the avant-garde next to an irreverent and whimsical sense of the absurdity of all human philosophies" (10), that her work amounts to a continuous demystification of anything that would propose itself as true or binding.

I hope to have shown that for all the playfulness of *Reality and Dreams*, this novel does commit to certain nonnegotiable and binding values, explic-

itly aesthetic and implicitly religious. What saves these values from formula is not their nonnegotiability but their particular relation to irony,
which has little in common with the thought of Lyotard or Rorty. Stephen
Prickett observes that in such versions of postmodernism, "There is no hidden meaning to be implicitly drawn on, because there is . . . nothing to be
hidden. There can be no implicit conflict between various versions of reality; there can be no gap between what is asserted and what we all know to
be true; all is surface, there is no depth" (204). For Prickett, Rorty counts
as a "fundamentalist" (204) precisely because he "knows," in advance, that
there can be no relationship whatsoever between language and whatever
"bedrock reality" might exist outside of it (203). Such a position leaves
nothing meaningful to be said and has no use for persuasion in good faith;
it also misunderstands what literature is, because "a novel that is unre-
lated to any unrecognizable truth at all is boring, if not downright unread-
able" (205). A genuine ironist, by contrast, recognizes that the relationship
between words and things "is neither constant, nor contingent, but *essentially* unstable" (257). Spark suggests that perhaps only in God is a bridge
between narrative and thing possible—as in Tom Richards's notion that
God's dreams bulge and bleed—but artists and religious converts construct
their own imperfect bridges, "dreams" that nevertheless partake of (though
never coinciding with) "reality." There is an element of determinism in such
a vision, for those gifted with artistic vision or religious faith are best suited
to build these bridges. But within this determinist framework, such people are also genuinely free—free from aesthetic or moralizing convention,
and free to bring new and irreplaceable objects into the world that gesture
toward truth. They also live comfortably with contradiction.

For all the richness of Spark's Catholic irony, there are two obvious
risks that it runs. The first is that its appeal to an intellectual audience
might descend into what Booth calls "disguised expressions of snobbery
which would never be tolerated if expressed openly in commentary" (391).
The second is the distortion of Catholic doctrine in the service of such
an appeal. If there is a hint of unseemly arrogance in Spark's self-identi-
fication with "really intelligent people," there is also the danger that contradiction will become something not merely to be lived with but even
celebrated. There is no necessary contradiction, for instance, between
Tom's sincere religious belief and his adulteries in *Reality and Dreams*—
but while he does not (as he says that Greene did) avow that many sexual partners are essential for his work, he is forthright enough about the
usual pattern of his affairs to suggest that he feels no guilt about them. To
the extent that Spark's work does suggest that Catholic morality may be
neatly demarcated from Catholic belief and rendered optional—especially

among practicing artists—it does indeed distort Catholic doctrine and comes to resemble the "once saved, always saved" position of some Protestant denominations. If the orthodox position that adultery is under all circumstances sinful remains discernible as the norm from which Spark's vision departs—and in *Reality and Dreams* it is present in the figure of the "biblically religious married" taxi driver Dave, who enjoys Tom's "religious reflections" and finds himself "in full sympathetic understanding" with him (64)—it is nevertheless presented as essentially boring. A cynical reader might conclude that it is better for Dave to take the bullet that is intended for Tom—had Dave been killed, it would be no great loss and he would have his reward, but had Tom been killed, there would have been no more of his films. This is indeed, as Booth would fear, snobbery.

The question of whether such a presentation would appeal to Spark's intended audience, however, is a separate issue, and here her rhetorical skill seems certain and surprisingly timely. Indeed, as contemporary intellectuals have begun to observe that secularization may not be the irreversible and inevitable process that it once seemed, the pluralistic condition of postmodernity has become "a supreme opportunity" (Milbank 1) for some to assert the Christian story anew, in all its radical claim to truth. By combining the aesthetic strategies of postmodernism with the recognition that postmodern theories rooted in the centrality of language are increasingly untenable, Spark's fiction speaks to—though does not necessarily endorse—the arguments of recent thinkers as different as John Milbank, Geoffrey Galt Harpham, and Peter Augustine Lawler.[18] Moreover, her finessing of the freedom/determinism binary appeals to thinkers who have seen subversion instead of blows for freedom as the surest way to engage with (and perhaps even to enjoy) one's own embeddedness in a larger system. Catholicism in Spark comes across not as a system of moral injunctions but as an aesthetic of freedom, experienced as a complex personal discipline that colors all of life. If it also happens to be true, so much the better.

All of which suggests both why Spark's fiction is uniquely positioned to speak to current arguments about religion in the twenty-first century *and* why she lags behind O'Connor in popularity among critics and ordinary readers. O'Connor does not count as a "fundamentalist" in Prickett's sense of the word, but her commitment to the existential urgency of whether to

---

18. I have in mind here Milbank's project of "radical orthodoxy," Lawler's reinterpretation of postmodernism as a "return to realism," and Harpham's argument that there is no such thing as "language alone"—that is, that theories purporting to treat of language in itself surreptitiously smuggle in all kinds of unacknowledged or unavowable assumptions, usually about the nature of human beings.

believe, with its undoubted emotional punch, is simply more compelling even to most intellectual readers than Spark's more complex treatment of belief. From an orthodox standpoint, O'Connor's position is more solid— not only because it distorts Christianity less but also because God is on the record as not being particularly fond of intellectuals. That Spark has identified with them, elected to appeal to them, and even fallen into what a strict accounting of Christian doctrine would acknowledge as theological error in this appeal only confirms the difficulty of her task. That she has undertaken it at all is admirable, for "really intelligent people" are people too.

3

John Updike's Rhetoric of Christian American Narcissism

I. Barth, Tocqueville, and Emerson:
Updike's Appeals to the Self

In an unfavorable—and now legendary—review of *Toward the End of Time* (1997), David Foster Wallace refers to John Updike as one of the "Great Male Narcissists who've dominated postwar American fiction" (51). The label is apt, for many of the specific indictments that have been lodged against Updike in the course of his career—misogyny, satyriasis, quietism, racism, preciousness of style, distortion of Christian doctrine—converge upon the accusation of a pervasive narcissism. Whatever his ostensible subject, Updike's constant focus is his ineffable self, embracing contradiction and perpetually affirming, even in his weaknesses and anxieties, the wondrousness of his being. It may be a remarkable feat to win both the St. Edmund Campion Medal (awarded by the Catholic Book Club to a "distinguished Christian person of letters") and a "Lifetime Achievement Award" for "Bad Sex" in fiction—but somehow it seems less surprising in a man who titled his memoir *Self-Consciousness* and devoted far more space in it to his psoriasis than to his wives and children.[1]

---

1. The phrase "distinguished Christian person of letters," from the award description of the Campion Medal, is quoted by Updike in the remarks he delivered upon receiving the medal the medal on 11 September 1997 (*More Matter* 850). Updike won the Bad Sex in Fiction

To call Updike's fiction narcissistic is of course to criticize the author as well as the work, and indeed, to an unusual degree readers who dislike the work view the man as reprehensible. No doubt this has something to do with the fact that many of Updike's fiercest critics have been feminists who have interpreted the slogan "the personal is the political" as license for *ad hominem* attacks. Yet this cannot be a sufficient explanation, for in the case of many other twentieth-century male writers, "personal" attacks in the 1970s soon gave way to more sophisticated critiques that located sexism less in the malice of the author than in all-encompassing structures of discourse or ideology—while critiques of Updike have frequently retained their personal character.[2] Though I agree with feminist critics that Updike is as self-absorbed as his writing suggests, I do not agree with their implication that his work may therefore be dismissed as unconscious solipsism or gratuitous offense. (No *merely* solipsistic writer, after all, can sustain the interest—or even the opposition—that Updike has.) Wayne Booth's famous distinction between the implied and real author of a work of fiction, intended to forestall unproductive debates about the sincerity of authors when readers judge their work, may or may not be tenable—Richard Walsh, for instance, has mounted a vigorous critique of it—but whether readers regard the narrators of Updike's novels as real or implied standins for the man (as I am usually comfortable doing) or not, they can certainly identify a deliberate rhetoric of narcissism as central to his work.[3]

Lifetime Achievement Award, a distinction conferred by the Edinburgh-based *Literary Review*, in 2008.

2. Consider, for instance, Mary Gordon's judgment: "[Updike] has a real problem about women. He covers that up with a notion that he really does love women, but he doesn't. . . . For him, women are really corrupt in the flesh. He's a liar, stylistically and morally" (*Conversations* 66–67). Such a judgment seems on a continuum with the (admittedly anecdotal) judgments reported by David Foster Wallace as representative of "literary readers . . . under forty . . . a fair number [of whom] are female": Updike is "[j]ust a penis with a thesaurus," a "son of a bitch" who has never had "one unpublished thought," who "[m]akes misogyny seem literary" (52).

3. For Walsh, "fictions are narrated by their authors, or by their characters. . . . Extradiegetic heterodiegetic narrators (that is, "impersonal" and "authorial" narrators), who cannot be represented without thereby being rendered homodiegetic or intradiegetic, are in no way distinguishable from authors" (84). The "implied author" disappears entirely. What do we make of fictions by a writer such as Updike, whose characters, whether first-person narrators or not, are often versions of himself? I am not sure that "reliability" (or the lack thereof) is a sufficient criterion for distinguishing between Updike the author and one of his narrated characters, for many of the hallmarks of an "unreliable" narrator—such as inconsistency between thoughts and actions, or false consciousness—are revealed, once one has explored Updike's fictional project more closely, not to indicate unreliability at all. Updike's work, that is to say, is inconsistent in the same consistent ways. We may reject his premises or the judgments of his characters that they imply, but if my argument in this chapter is correct,

Updike's protagonists present themselves or are limned by their narrators both as representative selves of their historical moment—an effect typically achieved through the proliferation of realistic detail about the world they inhabit—and as quasi-shamanistic illuminators who bestow meaning on this world through their sustained attention to it. When they succeed in persuading readers of their sometimes outrageous claims, they do so because Updike has successfully exploited his readers' own narcissism. This is so not only when the territory is sex—where the possibilities for solipsism are obvious—but also, more audaciously, when Updike presses the claims of his Protestant Christianity.

For Updike, the necessity of Christianity is described in unabashedly narcissistic terms, as the means to thwart death, to go on "being a self forever." Updike has candidly identified himself as one "for whom nothingness . . . is an insuperable problem, an outrageous cancellation rendering every other concern, from mismatching socks to nuclear holocaust, negligible" (*Self-Consciousness* 228). He also implies that the division of humanity into those who fear nothingness and those who regard it with indifference is a phenomenon that fully comes into its own in the twentieth century, when not only grave and high-minded Victorian agnostics but also large numbers of professed Christians in the United States find belief difficult:

> During [my] adolescence, I reluctantly perceived of the Christian religion I had been born into that almost no one believed it, believed it really— not its ministers, nor its pillars like my father and his father before him. Though signs of belief (churches, public prayers, mottos on coins) existed everywhere, when you moved toward Christianity it disappeared, as fog solidly opaque in the distance thins to transparency when you walk into it. I decided I nevertheless *would* believe. I found a few authors, a very few— Chesterton, Eliot, Unamuno, Kierkegaard, Karl Barth—who helped me believe. Under the shelter (like the wicker chairs on the side porch) that I improvised from their pages I have lived my life. (*Self-Consciousness* 230)

This confession emphasizes not only the fiercely willed quality of Updike's belief, but also his sense that his predicament is historically representative. As an educated man of the twentieth century, unable to deny the strengths of a thoroughgoing materialism, he suggests that if Christian belief is salvageable, it must be buttressed by arguments both suitably intellectual (hence his need for the imprimatur of celebrated theologians and writers)

---

his authorial intentions, whether expressed through an extradiegetic heterodiegetic narrator or a character, are discernible.

and deeply felt—arguments that seem absent from the daily life of existing congregations. Yet what makes this desire for eternal life narcissistic is neither the desire itself nor the arguments that it marshals but the nature of the life imagined. As the Reverend Tom Marshfield puts it in *A Month of Sundays* (1975), humans possess "a craving not for transformation into a life beyond imagining but for our *ordinary life*, the mundane life we so driftingly and numbly live, to go on forever and forever. The only Paradise we can imagine is this Earth. The only life we desire is this one" (209). The corollary is announced by Alfred Clayton in *Memories of the Ford Administration* (1992): "We want life eternally, or else its joys are hopelessly poisoned" (215). Hence the continuity between the erotic and the religious in Updike's work: sex, like Christian belief, is a fist shaken in the face of death, an intimation of familiar corporeal splendors forever. What Freud calls primary narcissism—"the libidinal complement to the egoism of the instinct of self-preservation" (546)—corresponds more closely to Updike's sexual and religious yearnings alike than to the orthodox Christian hope for a transfigured life in the presence of God.

To be sure, Updike sometimes obscures the narcissism of his writing by casting it as testimony to the splendor of God's creation, in a manner that occasionally recalls O'Connor's notion of writing as sacramental: "The yearning for an afterlife is the opposite of selfish: it is love and praise for the world that we are privileged, in this complex interval of light, to witness and experience" (*Self-Consciousness* 217). Or, more explicitly:

> Imitation is praise. Description expresses love. I early arrived at these self-justifying inklings. Having accepted that old Shillington blessing, I have felt free to describe life as accurately as I could, with especial attention to human erosions and betrayals. What small faith I have has given me what artistic courage I have. My theory was that God already knows everything and cannot be shocked. And only truth is useful. Only truth can be built upon. From a higher, inhuman point of view, only truth, however harsh, is holy. (231)

Yet such sentiments are accompanied by a note of deliberate self-justification, a rhetorical ploy that admits to the compensatory nature of narcissism. Humans love the created world and yearn for an afterlife not because the world exists and is good but because they desire "an intended relation to the outer world," a "coherent matrix [that] has been prepared for this precious self of ours" (218). Even the truth-telling of writing is, in the end, about comfort: "The fabricated truth of poetry and fiction makes a shelter in which I feel safe, sheltered within interlaced plausibilities in the image of a real world for which I am not to blame. Such writing is in essence pure" (231). The confession of self-love and the conviction of "purity" follow so swiftly upon the theological affirmation that they cannot but be read as an invitation to fellow narcissists, a wager that readers will recognize their own desires in the work and enjoy with Updike the fellowship of complicity. Like David, the protagonist of his early story "Pigeon Feathers," Updike pays tribute to creation but does so because he believes that it confirms his own centrality: "[T]he God who had lavished such craft upon these worthless birds would not destroy His whole Creation by refusing to let David live forever" (150).

Updike's suturing of this narcissistic motive for Christian belief to a theology derived from Karl Barth is one of the most intriguing aspects of his work, for it distinguishes him both from the other major Christian fiction writers of the mid-twentieth century (most of whom were Roman or Anglo-Catholic) and from the half-secularized mainline American Protestantism of the late twentieth century. A schematic account of Updike's differences from mainline Protestantism might read like this: Barth, not Paul Tillich or John Shelby Spong; *sola fide,* not faith and works; a God transcendent and *absconditus,* not immanent and accessible; traditional dogma, including the insistence that some will be damned, not trendy appeals to social justice and feel-good universalism. Updike's sanctioning of unrestrained erotic pursuit is, of course, inconsistent with traditional Christian morality—as John Gardner once sarcastically put it, "Christ has redeemed us in advance, so let's fornicate" (98)—but it has its origins in Luther's injunction to "sin boldly" and in Barth's pugnacious claim that Satan's appeal is "to genuine morality, to the freedom of a knowledge which distinguishes and an activity which elects" (qtd. in Wood, *Redemption* 46) instead of to a simple, abiding trust in God. Such a position rejects ethics as sinful presumption and calls into question Updike's own assertion that his novels "are all meant to be moral debates with the reader," in which "[t]he question is usually, 'What is a good man? or 'What is goodness?'" ("One Big Interview" 502).[4] Only in Updike's earliest work—and above all in *The Poorhouse Fair* (1959)—are there protagonists in whom ethical action and orthodox belief form a coherent whole, and it seems significant that

---

4. It is instructive to contrast Updike's use of the word "good" here with his complaint elsewhere that Muriel Spark's novels "lacked a compelling portrait of the good, and that without that it was difficult to provide a convincing portrait of evil" (qtd. in Spark, Interview with Sara Frankel, 452). Once, when once asked about this judgment, Spark retorted, with much justice, "Well I think it depends on what you mean by a portrait of the good. . . . I don't know whether John Updike has given us a convincing portrait of the good, mind you; his characters are just in and out of bed all the time" (Interview with Sara Frankel 452–53).

the clearest of these exemplars, John Hook, is modeled on Updike's grand-father, whose serene connection to a premodern ethos is assumed. For anx-ious moderns such as Updike himself, it would seem, orthodoxy can be preserved only when ethics is renounced altogether, for ethics is by its very nature too worldly, too unconcerned with eternity—indeed, too feminine. It may be uncharitable to attribute the change in Updike's attitude, as Fred-erick Crews does, to "an overreaction to self-judgment on the single point of adultery" (173)—but it is true that the "charitable works and kindly feel-ings" that Barth denigrates as a retreat from true Christianity are indeed, in Updike's fiction, "the values invariably associated with the deserted or soon-to-be-deserted wife" (173).

The straight line between Updike's version of Christianity and the importance of adultery and divorce to his work reveals that for all its debt to European theologians, Updike's Christianity is also distinctly Ameri-can, for it conflates adherence to *sola fide* with an American ideal of inno-cence, as Mary Gordon, following Leslie Fiedler, once shrewdly noted.[5] Updike retains the notion of sin, which in orthodox Christianity maims all human beings, as the chief source of evil and confusion in the world. Yet in a development that that can be read either as a startling reversal of ortho-dox Christianity or as its necessary evolution in a secularized world, Chris-tian faith often appears not as the mark of God's redemption from sin but as the expression of a primordial innocence, a matter of narcissistic being rather than doing, that is somehow retained in the face of evil. Unlike the heroes of the nineteenth-century novels that Fiedler examines, for instance, Updike's run toward rather than away from sex, but the underlying fear remains: there is always, as Ralph Wood observes, "the fearsome coin-cidence and equation of opposites: sex equals life equals death" (*Comedy* 189). That they pursue sex nevertheless and sing in praise of it suggests that adultery is in part a testing ground for innocence, that one confirms one's innocence by plunging into carnality and emerging unscathed, ready, like Rabbit Angstrom, to run again. The materiality of sex, however enjoy-able, becomes a focus of contempt—as Rabbit puts it, "the mud of women, of making babies" (*Rabbit is Rich* 202)—but the essential and innocent self remains unengaged. Indeed, the distaste with procreation that accompanies such an attitude helps to explain the increasingly *outré* depictions of car-

---

5. "One of the things that I think is remarkable about the American idea of innocence is that it doesn't seem connected to behavior. So that, in other words, you can behave badly, you can even kill and still be called an innocent. And that, to me, is extraordinarily peculiar. That is, I think, a tremendously Protestant notion of innocence, that goodness is something you're born with and that you don't lose by behaving un-innocently. And I think this is very, very different from a European tradition." (Gordon, *Conversations* 75) Because Updike embraces such innocence, he is, for Gordon, "a kind of professional boy" (66).

nality in Updike's work (in Rabbit's case, from fellatio to anal sex to sleeping with his daughter-in-law—not, perhaps, comparable to the Marquis de Sade, but certainly "transgressive" enough to earn notoriety). The power of reproduction, figured as belonging to women, becomes a trap for men to escape or triumph over—either by conceiving of nonprocreative sexuality as fecund nevertheless, or, in the most chilling instances, as something close to celebrating sterility for its own sake.[6]

Indeed, in his most unguarded moments, Updike's reflections about innocence and death seem less an expression of Christianity than of a thinly disguised version of what Harold Bloom calls the Gnostic "American religion," delivered in an Emersonian accent.[7] The Calvinist mystery—that God is the ultimate author of evil, but human beings are nevertheless responsible for it—becomes transmuted into a kind of radical innocence that would equate creation with the fall and yearn for whatever spark of uncreated divinity might still be imprisoned within matter. Consider, for instance, this autobiographical account of watching a rainstorm from the safety of his porch as a boy:

> On our side porch, it was my humble job, when it rained, to turn the wicker furniture with its seats to the wall, and in these porous woven caves I would crouch, happy almost to tears, as the rain drummed on the porch rail and rattled the leaves of the grape arbor and touched my wicker shelter with a mist like the vain assault of an atomic army . . . [T]he experiencer is motionless, holding his breath as it were, and the things experienced are morally detached from him: there is nothing he can do, or ought to do, about the flow, the tumult. He is irresponsible, safe, and witnessing: the entire body, for those rapt moments, mimics the position of the essential self within its jungle of physiology and its moldering tangle of inheritance and circumstance. Early in his life the child I was sensed the guilt in

---

6. A few examples: The ludicrous poem "Fellatio" (1969) imagines that "each of these clean secretaries" "takes / a fountain into her mouth / and lets her insides, drenched into seed, / flower into landscapes" that include "small farms each / with a silver silo" (*Midpoint* 73). In *Rabbit Is Rich*, Rabbit Angstrom describes anal sex with Thelma in this way: "The grip is tight at the base but beyond, where a cunt is all velvety suction and caress, there is no sensation: a void, a pure black box, a casket of perfect nothingness. He is in that void" (417). Marshall Boswell associates this passage with references to homosexual ministers in Updike's work and argues that in both instances, we see the influence of Barth's notion of evil as "the power of the being which arises out of the weight of the divine 'No'" (qtd. in Boswell 165). That Roger Lambert cheerfully urges his niece Verna to have an abortion in *Roger's Version*, despite the fact that he is not the father of the child, may also be relevant here.

7. For this reason, I find it ironic that Bloom has consistently ranked Updike as a second-rate writer, "a minor novelist with a major style" (7). For a good exposition of Updike's Emersonian strain in the *Rabbit* novels, see David Jarraway.

things, inseparable from the pain, the competition: the sparrow dead on the lawn, the flies swatted on the porch, the impervious leer of the bully on the school playground. The burden of activity, of participation, must plainly be shouldered, and has its pleasures. But they are cruel pleasures. There was nothing cruel about crouching in a shelter and letting phenomena slide by: it was ecstasy. The essential self is innocent, and when it tastes its own innocence knows that it lives forever. If we keep utterly still, we can suffer no wear and tear, and will never die. (*Self-Consciousness* 34–35)

This passage, an extraordinarily pure distillation of Updike's rhetoric of narcissism, is surpassingly lovely but difficult to describe as Christian. Its Cartesian implication that the "essential self" is imprisoned in a "jungle of physiology" works against a sacramental understanding of matter and tends toward heterodox interpretations of the Incarnation, while the notion that this self is "innocent" as long as it does nothing contradicts the doctrine of original sin. We would die, of course, even if we could "keep utterly still," but the Christianity that we believe will save us from eternal death does not, in Updike's view, transfigure us in ways now unimaginable; it returns us to our individual childhood narcissisms, before we sensed "the guilt in things." The narcissistic appeal is thus inseparable from a capacity for American nostalgia, but the imagined lost golden age is usually, in Updike, the recent past, a time actually experienced by his characters and invested both with its glamour and with a wistful sense of failure by the very fact of their having lived through it.

As a fictive strategy of persuasion, a rhetoric of narcissism is fraught with danger. Unlike more forthright appeals to elitism (whether aesthetic and intellectual or ethical and religious), which gesture toward objective standards against which a claim to elite status can be measured, narcissism offers no justification for itself and thus always risks the response, "Who the hell do you think you are?" Yet in another sense, narcissistic appeals are more in keeping with the character of everyday life in secular, democratic societies, for in precisely this lack of justification they reflect what Alexis de Tocqueville called the democratic "passion for equality" (226). Noting that "[i]n democratic societies, each citizen is usually preoccupied with something quite insignificant: himself" (561), Tocqueville hypothesized that such preoccupation explains why an American who approaches poetry expects "some prodigious thing to behold" as "the price he demands to tear himself briefly away from the myriad small concerns that keep him busy and lend charm to his existence" (561). Tocqueville feared that such demands would produce a literature of the bizarre; he did not foresee that in the work of

Whitman and many of his successors, the tendency toward grandiosity would be applied to and conflated with the perceiving consciousness itself, with more felicitous, if uneven, results. He did, however, accurately perceive that such a literature springs from conditions of broad equality and gives rise not only to vaunting feelings of independence but also to fantasies of plenitude that mask or self-consciously transfigure the weakness of any given individual.

The egalitarian impulse behind Updike's rhetoric of narcissism helps to account, I believe, for the delight with which Updike adopts so-called politically incorrect positions—for it suggests that those who style themselves as progressives or leftists are similarly motivated and have no claim to a bogus ethical superiority. In *Self-Consciousness*, the *Rabbit* tetralogy, and the "Pennsylvania books" (such as *The Centaur*, *Of the Farm*, and the play *Buchanan Dying*), Updike identifies with the rural and small-town world of what has come to be called "Red America" and suggests that his own life among readers of *The New Yorker* has been a deliciously ironic exile. Christopher Lasch notes that many cosmopolitan Americans imagine this territory to be "technologically backward, politically reactionary, repressive in its sexual morality, middlebrow in its tastes, smug and complacent, dull and dowdy" (5–6), and both Updike and his characters have accepted many of these characterizations with a kind of whimsically defiant pride. (As D. Keith Mano once jeered: "Pennsylvania, my God. Only a magnificent eccentric could run up debts to Pennsylvania" [75]). Yet this egalitarian narcissism applies no less to characters and narrators from Updike's novels of suburban New England, such as *Couples* or *Roger's Version*. Neither the working-class- and *petit bourgeois* nationalism that led Rabbit (and Updike) himself to support the Vietnam War nor the cold self-indulgence of his affluent Tarboxers in *Couples* is subject to anything approaching a rigorous critique; both are equally the expression of narcissistic rather than elitist attitudes. If there is any justification for these attitudes, something that might allow readers to identify with and share them, it is to be found in the egalitarian, American milieu of the fiction itself, no matter where it is set—hence the affectionate profligacy of Updike's descriptions, which strive in Whitmanian fashion for an observer who assimilates and redeems the observed.

Christians and non-Christians alike have observed that one of the attractions of Christianity is its insistence that before God, human beings are, in Peter Augustine Lawler's words, "unique, free, and infinitely valuable" (33), irrespective of their intelligence, moral standing (if anything, conspicuous sinners have a certain advantage), taste, or degree of wealth. The conviction of their own value that Updike's protagonists generally possess seems to be derived from both their Christianity and their Ameri-canness, which for some characters appear to be conflated. (In Rabbit Ang-strom's words, "America is beyond power, it acts as in a dream, as a face of God" [*Rabbit Redux* 47]). While Updike and his more cerebral narrators may have required the permission of Barth or Tertullian to believe, he does not demand similar justification for Rabbit, nor does he intend that his readers despise the "unexamined" quality of Rabbit's faith or his visceral love for the United States. Updike's theology and patriotism are deeply personal: characters who quote Barth or meditate upon James Buchanan do so not out of a snobbish or sincere desire for intellectual rigor or amplitude, but simply because they are the kind of people who do this kind of thing. (Indeed, their intellectualism is itself mediocre.) Other characters, equally narcissistic and mediocre, do their own kinds of things. Most often, the stakes are weighted most heavily against those characters who reject not only the "infinite value" of Updike's heroes but also their own—those char-acters, that is, who refuse to wear their American innocence proudly, either because they are women or because their adherence to liberalism or secu-lar humanism entails a critique of American innocence. To be American, or, more precisely, to be privileged observer and participant of the American scene, is to be already redeemed—all one has to do is acknowledge the fact.

Paradoxically, Updike's egalitarianism produces an ethos both affec-tionate and misanthropic. On the one hand, everyone is eligible for the redemptive embrace of Updike's American Christianity; on the other hand, no innocent American owes anything to anyone but God, and in this iso-lation cruelty and solipsism spring eternal. Perhaps Updike's greater pop-ularity with educated general readers than with tenured critics springs in part from this egalitarianism, which makes intellectuals understand-ably distrustful. On the other hand, if Updike succeeds in making Chris-tian belief attractive, this may have something to do with the appealingly egalitarian, yet also complacent revelation that believers are not only just as susceptible to cruelty as anyone else, but also already forgiven for it and therefore (and here the claim becomes doctrinally problematic) immune to further charges of hypocrisy.

In this chapter, I will consider Updike's rhetoric of narcissism broadly over the course of his career, focusing primarily on his first novel, *The Poorhouse Fair* (1959), and his late historical novel, *In the Beauty of the Lil-ies* (1996), though I will also touch briefly on a number of his other texts, including *Couples* (1968), *Roger's Version* (1986), and *Terrorist* (2006). I do not develop an extended reading of the Rabbit novels, partly out of a desire not to step onto well-trodden ground or to repeat critical commonplaces, but also out of a conviction that the two novels at the center of this chapter have not yet received the attention that they deserve. I argue that these two novels can be viewed as poles between which Updike's rhetoric of narcissism moves, and the premise common to both is the waning of historic Christianity in the United States—a problem that extends back at least as far as to what Ann Douglas called "the feminization of American culture" in the early nineteenth century, but which is exacerbated by the remoteness of God in Updike's Barthean theology. In *The Poorhouse Fair*, Updike has not yet broken with the conviction that belief and right conduct should accompany each other, and in the novel's central debate between a believer and an atheist, the believer compels not so much because of his arguments—the atheist's are in fact stronger—but because of his personal integrity. The believer's ringing defense of Christian belief and evident charity toward his opponent, moreover, reveal that at the beginning of his career, Updike was willing to take the claims of atheism seriously and to combat those claims in the culture at large, even if the overwhelming fear of death as a motive for belief is still present. *In the Beauty of the Lilies*, on the other hand, suggests that because Updike finds it hard to take disbelief seriously—despite the fact that two of its protagonists are professed unbelievers—he also has difficulty portraying authentic belief convincingly. Across the whole of his career, Updike retains the image of a God who has withdrawn, but in his later work, his characters' reasons to believe or not to believe become equally narcissistic yet also more marked with a persistent sense of personal failure. Indeed, for all that Updike maintains his critique of liberal, feminized theology, his own protagonists increasingly seem too conscious of—indeed, too narcissistically delighted by—their own weaknesses to proffer a convincing alternative.

II. When the Wood Was Green:
Fears of Religious and National Decline in
The Poorhouse Fair

Readers who come to *The Poorhouse Fair* after having read Updike's more celebrated works are generally surprised: no sex, no thinly disguised ciphers for Updike himself, no extended discussions of Protestant theologians, no icy misanthropy lurking in the wings. Yet it is not necessarily misleading to call the novel, as George J. Searles has done, Updike's "thesis statement" (231), for at its center is a defense of traditional Christian belief. This defense partakes of several rhetorical strategies, of which an actual positive argument for God's existence (a fairly predictable argument from design) is the least prominent. More often, God is presented as the necessary precondition for love, patriotism, excellence, and—most uncharacteristically for Updike—goodness. At the same time, arguments against God, grounding themselves in a desire that the world should be other than it is, are revealed to spring from the same narcissistic impulses as belief in God, so that their ethical force is called into question. Published before "the sexual revolution" became a slogan, *The Poorhouse Fair* does not revel in the putative gap between ethics and Christian orthodoxy, as many of Updike's later works do. Yet it is continuous with them in its overt argument that religious faith and love of the sensuous particular are essential to the good life in general and to the continued existence of the United States in particular.

At the center of the novel is the debate between John Hook, a ninety-four year-old former schoolteacher, and Conner, the administrator of the poorhouse where he lives, about the existence of God and the afterlife. Structurally, the debate recalls similar verbal tussles in O'Connor's fiction—between Sheppard and Rufus Johnson in "The Lame Shall Enter First," or between Mason Tarwater and Rayburn in *The Violent Bear It Away*—and like O'Connor's characters, Hook and Conner are types: the one deeply religious, gentle, and slightly ridiculous but lovable; the other tormented but passionate in his atheism and torn between a heartfelt desire to do good and an even more powerful desire to be admired for his goodness. Yet despite Updike's clear sympathies for Hook's side in the argument, there is an apparent effort to be fair to Conner, evident in the greater portion of the novel devoted to Conner's thoughts and words, which are often sympathetically presented, though never without the narrator's irony.

The debate between Hook and Conner springs up when Amy Mortis, another resident of the poorhouse, speculates about what Heaven must be like. Conner responds with a rapturous picture of the future:

> "I see [Heaven] placed on this earth. There will be no disease. There will be no oppression, political or economic, because the administration of power will be in the hands of those who have no hunger for power, but who are, rather, dedicated to the cause of all humanity. . . . No longer suffering but beauty will be worshipped. Art will mirror no longer struggle but fulfillment. Each man will know himself—without delusions, without muddle, and within the limits of that self-knowledge will construct a sane and useful life. Work and love: parks: orchards. Understand me. The factors which for ages have warped the mind of man and stunted his body will be destroyed; man will grow like a tree in the open. There will be no waste. No pain and above all no *waste*. And this heaven *will* come to *this* earth, and come soon."

Mrs. Mortis asked, "Soon enough for us?"

"Not you personally perhaps. But for your children, and your grand-children."

"But for us ourselves?"

"No." The word hung huge in the living room, the "o" a hole that let in the cold of the void.

"Well, then," Mrs. Mortis spryly said, "to hell with it." (106–8)

In this first stage of the argument, before Hook joins it, Conner's vision is deflated by Mrs. Mortis's final remark, and everyone listening laughs with her in agreement. Mrs. Mortis voices here the characteristic Updikean narcissism: what good is a heaven confined to this life, from which vast numbers will be excluded simply because they die before technology and proper education make it available? Only eternal life would allow Conner's vision to be a true heaven, for only it would guarantee the infinite value of each human being, in his or her solitariness, without qualification. Conner appeals to an image of individual strength when he describes the future man as "like a tree in the open," but his heaven is nonetheless communal, with "work," "love," and—implicitly but nonetheless inescapably—sacrifice ("above all no *waste*") as essential to it. Mrs. Mortis's response refuses sacrifice for the happiness of future generations and reaffirms her earlier resentment toward Conner when he suggested that she might like to move her table: "You expect us to give up the old ways, and make this place a little copy of the world outside, the way it's going. I don't say you don't mean well, but it won't do. We're too old and too mean; we're too tired. Now if you say to me, you must move your belongings over beneath the tree, I'll do it, because I have no delusions as to whose mercy we're dependent upon" (43). Conner is astonished by the "blunt injustice" (43) of her words. Yet her selfishness binds her more closely to her fellow human beings, who laugh in identification with her, while Connor, feeling "the common exclusion from the run of human hearts that minutes before he had imagined as binding them" (108), is pained. The man who imagines future humanity in terms of communal work and belonging nevertheless perceives his own isolation from more fundamental forms of connection, such as the family. It is fitting that he hates beds—those most common foci of domestic and erotic relation—because they are "damp and possessive" (49).

Belittled by Mrs. Mortis, Conner continues the argument with Hook. Hook does not contradict Mrs. Mortis, but he turns the argument away from the desire for eternal life and toward the conviction that God exists and that faith in God requires right conduct. According to Hook, punishment necessarily follows sin and is even transferred between generations: "And who is to say how the ailments of my childhood may have been the fruit of my father's short-comings, or of his before him. . . . The book-keeping is far more strict than even that of a Boston banker. If the size of a mouth is passed down, why not the burden of wrongdoing?" (111). When Conner asks for evidence that God exists, Hook turns to the argument from design, professing delight in creation and skepticism that something could be generated from nothing without God. Conner counters with the existence of pain, ugliness, and stupidity, contending that "if the universe was made, it was made by an idiot, and an idiot crueler than Nero. . . . Life is a maniac raving in a sealed room" (113, 114). The two sides of the argument are familiar enough, drawing opposed conclusions from the same points of reference, and they quickly end in an impasse. Conner speaks of the terrible immensity of the stars in the nothingness of space, while Hook speaks of them as "points of light arranged at random, to give the night sky adorn-ment" (114). In the end, Conner wins the argument on logic, shaking Hook with his anecdote of a Peruvian Indian who, upon being given electric shock, had a hallucination of Christ speaking. But Hook wins rhetorically, charging Conner with a "bitterness" that "is the willful work of [his] own heart" (111) and concluding that "[t]here is no goodness, without belief. There is only busy-ness" (116). His perception that Conner is both bitter and full of busy-ness (the novel begins, in fact, with Hook's quite unneces-sary marking of the chairs in the poorhouse with personalized nameplates for each resident—an action that provokes anger in most of the residents and that Hook dismisses with the phrase "A child must tinker" [4])—does not, of course, prove the existence of God, but it does suggest that athe-ism is more often the result of personal bitterness than of logical arguments pursued in good faith.

Conner is wounded by Hook's accusations because he knows them to be true. For all that he desires to do good, he is even greedier for praise. Stirred by music, he indulges in fantasies that combine his desire to be wor-shiped for his achievements with visions of corporeal beauty and sexual fulfillment:

> In the language of melody speeches about man's aspirations and eventual victory could be made that explicit language would embarrass. He could not hear a dozen chords without crystals building in his head, images: naked limbs, the exact curve of the great muscle of a male thigh, cities, colored spires soaring. Man was good. There was a destination. Health could be bought. . . . He envisioned grown men and women, lightly clad, playing, on the brilliant sand of a seashore, children's games. A man threw

a golden ball, his tunic slowly swirling with the exertion; a girl caught it. . . . Another man caught the girl by the waist. She had a wide belt. He had her above his head; she bent way back, her throat curved against the blue above the distant domes. The man was Conner. Then there was Conner again, at his desk, speaking to grateful delegates, calm, flexible, humorous; the listeners laughed, admiringly. Conner shunned admiration, and gained it doublefold; the world was under his wing. Yet in visualizing this world which worshipped him, he returned to the triangles and rhomboids flashingly formed by the intersection of legs and torsos scissoring in sport, and the modulated angles of nude thoracic regions, brown breasts leaning one against another, among scarves of everlasting cloth, beneath the sun. (124–25)

Again, Conner is made both sympathetic and ridiculous. His discomfort with language is of course disadvantageous for a character in a novel, for the music and mental imagery that move him must be rendered verbally—and were he real, he would no doubt be embarrassed by Updike's description of his fantasies. His delight in the human form of course makes him a kindred spirit of humanists who trace their intellectual heritage to the Greeks, while the playful eroticism of the scene might be seen as tribute to Updike's praise of creation. Yet there is a disturbing undercurrent as well. Conner responds less to the particularity of human flesh than to its ability to be redescribed as geometric figures, as "triangles and rhomboids," so that his delight in it seems continuous with that of the cities with "colored spires soaring." The power to refigure human beings as manipulable shapes, in turn, is continuous with his own desire for power, both sexual and political, and with his conviction that intangible markers of well-being such as health may be purchased. Conner may dream of a world in which power is exercised by "those who have no hunger for it," but his own hunger for it raises the question of how one knows such a world could ever exist.

Indeed, Conner provides a textbook illustration of the tension inherent within many contemporary intellectuals' embrace of Darwin. On the one hand, the process of evolution, guided as it is by natural selection, cannot possibly be teleological, and viewed objectively, existence cannot have any meaning beyond what is groundlessly attributed to it. On the other hand, Conner's faith in an evolutionary telos—a thoroughly human world without oppression, greed, or the desire for power—is clung to despite this lack of grounding, and in this sense his view is just dependent upon faith as Hook's. Repeatedly Conner torments himself with the discrepancy between the glorious imagined future and the intolerableness of what is, and while he is capable of flashes of searing humility when he realizes how imperfectly he lives his ideals, more often he is "appalled by the conservatism zoological charts portrayed" and indulges eugenicist thoughts about his subhuman enemies: "He could picture the woman who had sent him the letter, her active pink nose, her dim fearful eyes, her pointed fingers crabbedly scraping across the paper—a tree-shrew, a rat that clings to bark. When would they all die and let the human day dawn?" (78). Conner is in this sense faithful to the project that Alain Badiou identifies as the crucial to the thought of the twentieth century, "the idea of changing man, of creating a new man . . . [which] always comes down to demanding that the old one be destroyed" (8). If the possibility of creating human beings who do not desire power is at all feasible, then much blood will have to be spilled. Under the cover of Darwinian science, dependent upon the vagaries of genes and environments, Conner espouses a Promethean and even transhumanist liberation, looking forward to "the crystalline erections"— a revealing *double entendre* that suggests a mineral rather than an animal sexuality—"that in his heart he felt certain would arise, once his old people were gone" (64).

Yet one of the more intriguing aspects of *The Poorhouse Fair* is that Conner and Hook are equally frustrated by the contemporary world because of its lack of opportunities for heroism, a lack associated with the ascendancy of feminine values. Readers may be appalled by intimations of bloodshed in Conner's worldview, but Hook too admires martial values, and even though he speaks of "a war we can wage without blood" (160), he also thinks of virtue—which he at one point defines as "obedience to the commands of God" (111)—as "[a]n austerity of the hunt, a manliness from which comes all life, so that it can be written that the woman takes her life from the man" (160). It follows that because such manly austerity is almost gone—Hook opines oracularly that "[t]his last decade . . . has witnessed the end of the world, if the people would but wake to it" (152)—the United States has become feminized and pathetic: "Women are the heroes of dead lands" (160). Conner's preferred metaphors are vegetative rather than feminine, but his own sense of the contemporary scene is much the same: "He wanted things *clean*; the world needed renewal, and this was a time of history when there were no cleansing wars or no sweeping purges, when reform was slow, and decayed things were allowed to stand and rot themselves away" (64). It seems to him unaccountable that the heroic humanist forebears should have produced a modern world with "few opportunities for zeal anywhere" (64), and he "envie[s] the first rationalists their martyrdoms and the first reformers their dragons of reaction and selfishness" (65). He has little of the delight in creation that even O'Connor's

Rayber perceives, and when he finds himself "content to gaze at nothing, or what amounted to nothing," he can think only that he has been "infected with the repose that was only suitable to inmates waiting out their days" (66). Against the humanist vision of perfected humanity and the Christian eschatological hope looms the decadent present of political consensus ("[t]he opposition of Republican and Democrat had been unreal since the Republican administrations of a generation ago" [93]) that embraces instead "the tendency of the universe toward eventual homogeneity, each fleck of energy settled in seventy cubic miles of otherwise vacant space" (65) and crafts policies toward this end under the rubric of "Settling."

Updike has called *The Poorhouse Fair* "a deliberate anti-*Nineteen Eighty-Four*," explaining that his vision of the near future (the book is set in 1977) does not portray "the death of everything"—the most terrifying implication of Orwell's vision—but rather a milder dystopia in which "it is others that die, while an attenuated silly sort of life bubbles decadently on" (Foreword x). The poorhouse is relatively cut off from this "silly sort of life," because both its elderly inhabitants, remembering an older world, and Conner, anticipating a brave new one, would prefer not to dwell on the realities outside—the decline of traditional values, the shoddiness of contemporary manufactured goods, the soulless "administrators [and] report-readers" who are Conner's superiors (14). Yet the poorhouse fair, at which the townspeople of Andrews come to buy handicrafts made by the residents, is an intrusion of the outside, made more symbolically pointed when a delivery truck, driven by a sullen teenager, breaches the stone wall that surrounds the property. The final third of the novel, consisting largely of glimpses of random townsfolk at the fair, their thoughts, and their interactions with the residents, has an elegiac tone, heightened by the narrator's intermittent declarations that Americans have become a sad lot, aware of their own material and spiritual decline and quicker than ever to seek solace in nostalgia. Demand for the old people's wares bespeaks "a keen subversive need, at least in the cities, for objects that showed the trace of a hand" (145). In the longest of these declarations, the narrator identifies boredom, prosperity, and meaninglessness as the causes of their "silly" life:

> Heart had gone out of these people; health was the principal thing about the faces of the Americans that came crowding through the broken wall to the poorhouse fair. They were just people, members of the race of white animals that had cast its herds over the land of six continents. Highly neural, brachycephalic, uniquely able to oppose their thumbs to the four other digits, they bred within elegant settlements, and both burned and interred their dead. History had passed on beyond them. They remembered its

moment and came to the fair to be freshened in the recollection of an older America, the America of Dan Patch and of Senator Beveridge exhorting the Anglo-Saxons to march across the Pacific and save the beautiful weak-minded islands there, an America of stained-glass lampshades, hardshell evangelists, Flag Days, ice men, plug tobacco, China trade, oval windows marking on the exterior of the house a stair landing within, pungent nostrums for catarrhal complaints, opportunism, churchgoing, and well-worded orations in the glare of a cemetery on summer days. . . . There was to be no war; we were to be allowed to decay of ourselves. And the population soared like diffident India's, and the economy swelled, and iron became increasingly dilute, and houses more niggardly built, and everywhere was sufferance, good sense, wealth, irreligion, and peace. The nation became one of pleasure-seekers; the people continued to live as cells of a body do in the coffin, for the conception "America" had died in their skulls. (158–59)

The shift here toward a discourse of American exceptionalism and decline parallels Conner and Hook's longing for struggle, though with a complex irony that doubles back upon itself and appeals to readerly complicity. The narrator waxes ironic about the racialist overtones of (white) American identity, its bygone belief in Manifest Destiny, its susceptibility to crass commercial appeals ("nostrums for catarrhal complaints"), and even about the belief in human distinctiveness ("highly neural, brachycephalic"). Yet this irony registers both an appropriate liberal discomfort with such notions *and* a conviction that they are nevertheless valuable (even, perhaps, the quack medicines), that irony provides cold comfort when genuine vitality is lost. Moreover, the continued population growth (Updike did not foresee the drop in the birth rate in the United States after the postwar "baby boom"), traditionally associated with ethnic conquest, becomes itself an index of decline, associated not with American destiny but with Third World fatalism. (Here, perhaps, is an early hint of Updike's discomfort with procreation itself.)

If the double irony of this passage seems unpalatable to many readers, it is because Updike has taken too much for granted an audience that believes in the fearful possibility of national decadence, an audience that might be persuaded that shared religious belief constitutes the best defense against it—in short, an audience shaped by the historically specific fears of the early Cold War, when the phrase "under God" entered the Pledge of Allegiance and the struggle against Soviet Communism was widely perceived as a struggle against godlessness.[8] Updike's scriptural epigraph for the

---

8. Although D. Quentin Miller is correct to see expressions of Cold War anxiety in *The Poorhouse Fair*—references to atomic bombs, as well as Updike's prediction that the Cold War

novel—"If they do this when the wood is green, what will happen when the wood is dry?" (Luke 23:31)—evokes both what Updike would consider the thinness of half-secularized mainline Protestantism and the complacency of newly prosperous postwar America, but for a contemporary audience accustomed to think of the Cold War largely in terms of oppression and what Alan Nadel calls "containment culture," it may also appear shocking that anyone might consider a pre–women's movement, pre–civil rights America a land of "green wood."[9] Here the divide between nonacademic and academic readers of Updike might loom especially large: for all the prominence of pop-cultural critiques of the 1950s, nostalgia for that era of putative American strength has not disappeared. From the standpoint of such nostalgia, Updike's worry about the long-term viability of American strength might today appear prophetic.

What finally distinguishes *The Poorhouse Fair* from Updike's later work, however, is its hint that fears of national decline or of creeping meaninglessness must be combated not only with vaunting egoism and with obeisance before God but also with the moral actions that such an attitude demands. Hook's insistence that belief itself, though a necessary prerequisite for a worthwhile life, requires "obedience to the commands of God" (111) is a far cry from the tortured rationalizations for adultery that later Updike protagonists will offer up, all the while proclaiming their belief in the God who forbids it. Indeed, despite the novel's effort to present the debate between Conner and Hook fairly, it is on the question of how their beliefs affect their actions that the tables finally swing against Conner. The key moment occurs when Conner, trying to organize the poorhouse men to help cart away the stones that have fallen when the wall was breached, sud-

---

would still be going strong, reveal as much—his emphasis on a paralyzing fear of nuclear apocalypse is misplaced. The more potent fear is not that the world will be destroyed— "There was to be no war" (159), after all—but that life will become meaningless, that even the antagonism of the Cold War has been safely contained and rendered merely formal. Here, Updike anticipates Walker Percy's more sustained reflections on human beings' attraction to apocalyptic thinking in a time of comfort and boredom.

9. *The Poorhouse Fair* did not anticipate the women's movement, but it did project the successful passage of civil rights laws: "Dark-skinned people dominated the arts and popular culture; intermarriage was fashionable, psychologists encouraged it; the color bar had quite melted in all states save Virginia. The Enforced Reforms, so stirring to Conner's youth, might never have occurred, to hear Hook talk" (93). Here Conner's identification with the post–civil rights order serves to bring the movement itself into question. The coming of racial equality is linked with the disappearance of meaningful distinctions, so that intermarriage becomes both a fashion statement and a kind of therapy, while the older, more vital America is explicitly racialized as white (158). The only redeeming feature of Ted, the teenaged driver of the truck that breaks the wall, is his disdain for "all this Latin stuff. Every other movie star was a Cuban or mestizo or something, as if you had to be brown to look like anything. Some guys he knew wore 'torero' pigtails standing up from the back of their heads and sprayed their hair with perfumed shellac. Ted'd be damned if he'd do this. They could call him a Puritan all they wanted" (55).

denly finds himself being stoned by some of the men who have resented his treatment of them. The assault is over quickly—a show of "disdain" (133) is enough for Conner to quell it—but it brings Conner closer to his desired martyrdom than anything else in the novel, and even Hook, who did not take part in the stoning but witnessed it, "had the thought that here was something glorious. Battles of old had swayed beneath such a canopy of missiles" (132). And indeed, Conner rises to the occasion magnanimously, continuing to gather the stones after the men disperse and telling his enraged friend Buddy that he intends to "forgive them" (134).

Conner's *caritas*, however, is short-lived: he soon feels that "it was not quite enough, merely to forgive them" (135), and he confronts Hook, whom he falsely believes to have been the instigator of the attack. Hook, not understanding Conner's suspicion, attributes the attack to boredom and idleness, which provokes an angry reply: "My patience is not limitless. Any repetition of mass defiance, and there will be measures taken" (136). He then orders Hook to stop smoking cigars, lest he endanger himself and the wooden buildings on the grounds, and permits Buddy to wrench the cigar away and to stamp it into the ground. Even the impulse to forgive cannot long triumph over petty vindictiveness, and Conner's last appearance in the novel—in which he reads, for the tenth time, an angry anonymous letter accusing him of not respecting the inmates' rights—suggests that he will cling to his injuries petulantly.

Hook, on the other hand, receives the final word in the novel, and his actions convey a more genuine desire for reconciliation with Conner. He wakes in the middle of the night because

> [h]is encounter with Conner had commenced to trouble him. The young man had been grievously stricken. The weakness on his face after his henchman had stolen the cigar was troubling to recall; an intimacy had been there Hook must reward with help. A small word would perhaps set things right. As a teacher, Hook's flaw had been over-conscientiousness; there was nowhere he would not meddle. He stood motionless, half in moonlight, groping after the fitful shadow of the advice he must impart to Conner, as a bond between them and a testament to endure his dying in the world. What was it? (185)

Even as the narrator hints at the futility of Hook's desire to give advice— his schoolteacher's "meddling" is, indeed, a humorous counterpart to Conner's "busy-ness"—its poignancy is undeniable. The denotative ambiguity of the final sentence—is it the "testament" or Hook himself that must "endure" (survive? tolerate?) his dying?—also suggests a sympathetic vulnerability, a desire to put accounts in order before death and a fear that he might be unable to do so. Whether readers interpret this passage primarily as the upsurge of a usually suppressed (and quintessentially Updikean) fear of nothingness or as a wholly selfless desire to comfort, what seems crucial here is its direction outward, toward relieving Conner's anguish. Even if I place the most narcissistic construction on Hook's motive here, I must acknowledge that it pushes him toward what is not merely the "right" thing to do but an act of gratuitous kindness. Its placement at the end of the novel, after the less conclusive arguments about the existence of God and the more potentially unsavory arguments about national decline, suggests that Updike intends for this appeal to Christian *caritas* to be decisive. Never again would Updike be so explicit in aligning belief in God with goodness. In the name of the new possibilities for self-affirmation afforded by the sexual revolution, Updike would increasingly come to sunder Christian belief from ethical action. Continuing to reject versions of Christianity that minimize unfashionable dogma and emphasize good works and social justice, Updike would eventually come to suggest that even belief itself is a matter of indifference, given humans' inability to approach God at all—that what truly matters is not being taken in by ethics.

III. The Feminization of American Religion and the Refusal of Argument:
Couples and *Roger's Version*

One year before Updike published *The Poorhouse Fair*, the now mostly forgotten Nebraskan novelist Wright Morris brought out *The Territory Ahead*, a study of the persistence of nostalgia as a major theme in American fiction. For Morris, one of the most revealing traits of American writers—exemplified by Faulkner's famously overblown praise of Thomas Wolfe—is their glorification of failure:

> Failure, not achievement, is the hallmark of success. The romantic origins of this statement are less pertinent to this discussion than the prevailing tendency to find in such a statement a profound truth. The great writer *must* fail. In this way we shall know that he is great. In such a writer's failure the public sees a moral victory: what does his failure prove but how sublime and grand the country is? This point of view has so much to recommend it that to call it into question smacks of un-Americanism. It calls, that is, for a shrinking of the national consciousness. (xiv)

According to this logic, all American writers will fall short of the sheer, raw sublimity of America itself, but in their ambition to do so, they return obsessively to the places and the moments when they first confronted this sublimity in all its transformative power. For earlier generations of writers, this meant, quite literally, taking to the woods and recording the immensity of the American landscape; in the twentieth century, now that the frontier is no more, the same move focuses on the epiphanies of child-hood and youth, which are figured, in Wordsworthian fashion, as intima-tions of privileged glory. There is, to be sure, a good deal of egoism in such strategies, and indeed, the effect among readers is frequently the reverse, so that Whitman or Thoreau, for instance, seems to invest the scenes he describes with meaning rather than being their passive recorder. Yet in both cases, the writer's greatness is achieved by his very woundedness, which he probes by returning to the scene of former glory and contrasting it with the present.

Updike's novels participate in this dynamic, though in a curiously attenuated fashion. Few of his protagonists can be called successful in any conventional sense; many are detached and lacking in worldly ambition, and their obsessive yet complacent attention to the world—what James Wood calls their "quality of fattened paganism" (227)—is matched by a querulous suspicion that things were once better still. Rabbit Angstrom may be prototypical in that he often looks back on the glory days of his youth (in the first paragraph of *Rabbit, Run* [1960], the note is already pres-ent, as the twenty-six-year-old watches a group of youths playing bas-ketball and thinks, "the kids keep coming, they keep crowding you up" [1]), but one of the most striking features of Updike's work as a whole is its wistful dwelling on the *recent* past. The moment so prized shifts from novel to novel—typically, there is a gap of five to twenty years between the relatively disillusioned present of either the novel or the moment of the novel's publication and the splendors of the past remembered or immedi-ately depicted in the novel. This gap, moreover, persists whether the novel is narrated in the first or the third person. *The Poorhouse Fair*, set in 1977, looks back to the moment of the novel's actual publication as a time when "the wood was green"; the notorious *Couples* shortens the interval to a mere five years, valorizing 1963 as the charmed moment after postwar prosperity and the sexual revolution had contrived to create an affluent sexual utopia, but before feminism and the antiwar movements had brought civil divi-sion and rancor between the sexes. In *Marry Me: A Romance* (1976), the same early 1960s moment is the site of a narrative of adultery and remarriage whose cruelty is matched only by its lyricism. And in *Memories of the Ford Administration*, Alfred Clayton, though he acknowledges them to have been a time of "post-apocalyptic let-down, of terrifying permissiveness" (248), nonetheless delights in "those far-off Ford days [when] it was assumed that any man and woman alone in a room with a lock on the door were duty-bound to fuck" (16)—in contrast to the 1980s and 1990s, when AIDS and the recognition of sexual harassment as a crime have imbued relations between men and women with caution and bitterness.

Such depictions of nostalgia are familiar enough when the focus of the nostalgia happens to be (as the previous examples have suggested) youth, sexual delight, or belief in American exceptionalism. The fact that all of these are entangled with Updike's version of Christianity, however, complicates matters, for it raises the question of just when the "fall" away from orthodox Christianity occurred and why. In Updike's fictional world, this fall is rarely personal—which is to say that Updike's protagonists seldom lose their faith, though they do often wonder why they continue to believe and even, like Roger Lambert, glory in the distance between themselves and God. Some are even inclined to consider their faith a moral weakness, an exaggerated respect for conventionality. Piet Hanema, for instance, wonders in *Couples* "what barred him from the ranks of those many blessed who believed nothing. Courage, he supposed. His nerve had cracked when his parents died. To break with a faith requires a moment of courage, and courage is a kind of margin within us, and after his parents' swift death Piet had no margin." As an apparent afterthought, the narrator adds, "Also, his European sense of order insisted that he place his children in Christendom" (20). Such passages, however, seem intended ironically: David Lodge is much closer to the truth when he speaks of Updike's attempt to depict Piet as "a kind of primitive, a rough diamond" (36) who might plunge just as readily into adultery as his fellow Tarboxers but who nevertheless stands apart from them, lacking the secular alienation that makes their own attempts to "break back into" hedonism so unsatisfying for them (48). Piet's faith remains secure, but it depends for its resonance on a sense that everyone else's is irretrievably lost, and that believers and unbelievers languish—though with considerable compensations—"in one of those dark ages that visit mankind between millennia, between the death and rebirth of the gods, when there is nothing to steer by but sex and stoicism and the stars" (31). Has so much changed in the four years between the publication of *The Poorhouse Fair*, when it is still possible to imagine that in 1977 a few elderly folk might still abide by Christian morality, and the events depicted in *Couples*?

Updike's work as a whole suggests that the collective American fall from Christian orthodoxy took place long ago, but that Americans have only begun to perceive this fall and its effects in the recent past. It may be, in fact, that his characters' personal nostalgia for lost youth or American self-confidence is misplaced, that it serves to conceal an authentic desire for God that can no longer declare itself without irony in a world of waning belief. Perhaps the clearest sign of this argument can be found in Updike's sustained engagement with the work of Nathaniel Hawthorne, who even appears as a minor character in *Memories of the Ford Administration*.[10] David Lodge has argued that *Couples* is, in part, a rewriting of *The Blithedale Romance* ("Post-Pill" 33), and it has become common to speak of the later novels *A Month of Sundays, Roger's Version,* and *S.* (1988) as a *Scarlet Letter* Trilogy, whose three protagonists are modeled upon Arthur Dimmesdale, Roger Chillingworth, and Hester Prynne. Updike's own claim that "[a] very vivid ghost of Christianity stares out at us from [Hawthorne's] prose, alarming and odd in not being evenly dead, but alive in some limbs and amputate in others" ("Hawthorne's Creed" 76) seems, particularly in the novels written after *Couples,* to be a description of his own stance. Moreover, both Updike and Hawthorne associate their sense of the decline of American religious orthodoxy with the ascendancy of not only women in general but also with a cloying and sentimental ideology of femininity. Hook's claim in *The Poorhouse Fair* that "women are the heroes of dead lands" takes on additional resonance in light of this comparison and suggests that Updike's often-remarked antifeminism, though certainly no less narcissistic for being so, is not merely a matter of misogyny.

In *The Feminization of American Culture,* Ann Douglas famously argues that a sea change in American Protestantism took place between roughly 1820 and 1875. The Calvinist orthodoxy of Presbyterian and Congregational denominations that had dominated the American colonies until soon after the Revolutionary War was, after a protracted struggle, disestablished in the states where it had been an official creed, and in the free marketplace of religion that ensued, it quickly lost ground to upstart denominations (Baptists, Methodists, and in New England, Unitarians) that competed for souls by stressing an emotional rather than an intellectual relationship with God, holding out the possibility (if not always the likelihood) of universal salvation, and promoting a saccharine and overtly feminized cult of domestic and necrophilic piety. Douglas discerns in this development the beginnings of American mass culture and describes its ascendancy as a remarkably successful push for power on the part of

---

10. Perhaps it is more accurate to speak of Updike's Hawthorne as a character conceived by a character. Alfred Clayton, the novel's narrator, is writing a fictionalized biography of James Buchanan, and Hawthorne appears in this section of the novel as the focalizer of a scene in which he and Buchanan converse, during the days of the Pierce administration, in Liverpool, where Hawthorne was serving as the American consul.

two allied but culturally marginalized groups—American clergymen and white, middle-class women. Douglas's account sheds considerable light on Hawthorne's ambivalent relation to the Calvinist culture that these women and nineteenth-century clergy routed. Wendy Piper notes that Hawthorne "believed the Puritan doctrine of natural depravity, despite its severity, to be a more accurate understanding of human nature than that suggested by the optimism and ideals of the Transcendentalists" (40–41). Accordingly, he admired the Puritans' unsentimental sounding of human depravity and rigorous habits of thought—both virtues traditionally coded as "masculine"—while deploring their scorn for fleshly life, including sexuality, which bespeaks a false belief that spirit and matter are opposed to each other and leads to what Aquinas called *libido dominandi*. The tension in such an attitude is evident in Hawthorne's depiction of Hester: she is celebrated for her own emotional strength, resilience, maternal ardor, and sexual warmth—qualities that Hawthorne attributes in lesser degree to her contemporaries, with "broad shoulders and well-developed busts, and . . . round and ruddy cheeks, that had ripened in . . . far-off [England], and had hardly yet grown paler or thinner in the atmosphere of New England" (161). Yet she is also implicitly condemned for her own antinomianism, which is well-nigh Transcendentalist—when she tells Dimmesdale, "What we did has a consecration of its own!" (286), she replaces a Puritan conviction of evil with an even less tenable sense of natural goodness. Both she and the Puritans who condemn her, however, appear in a more favorable light than many of Hawthorne's contemporaries, who have abandoned both a rigorous, unsentimental religion and a robust emotional life for a cloying sentimentality.

Updike's own beliefs about the relationship between orthodox religion, femininity, and national decline follow Hawthorne's in broad outline, although where Hawthorne suggested both irreconcilable difference and comfortable proximity—preventing Hester from ever achieving a full reconciliation with her community yet maintaining her in a relationship with it nonetheless—Updike exaggerates the impossibility of reconciliation, even hinting that orthodox religion gives a more delectable savor to one's adulteries than atheism, agnosticism, or Transcendentalism would. As many commentators have observed, when lightning destroys the Congregationalist church at the end of *Couples*, this is presented not as God's wrath against an epidemic of adultery, but rather as further evidence of God's self-withdrawal, his taking leave of a house that has become an empty shell. Being abandoned by God in this way might be painful, but it is nothing new—it is only to be expected from the Calvinist God who selects a few as his elect and predestines everyone else to eternal damnation. The distance and otherness of God becomes, paradoxically enough, the surest license for one's own narcissistic pleasures.

Once one has gone so far, the distance between a Calvinist God who may be *absconditus* but remains no less real and the human God whose death is plangently announced by Nietzsche becomes very small indeed, even if Updike cannot join Nietzsche in his brand of tragic affirmation after such an announcement, tending instead toward what I called before an attenuated celebration of failure. *Roger's Version* suggests how small the difference between these two conceptions might be by making its central religious debate occur not between an atheist and a believer but between two believers. The first, Roger Lambert, is a middle-aged professor of theology and former minister, an avid Barthean, misanthrope, and connoisseur of pornography; while the second, Dale Kohler, is a young "Jesus freak" and computer scientist who wishes to prove the existence of God mathematically. Whereas in *The Poorhouse Fair* Updike attempted to present both sides of a debate on religion fairly, in *Roger's Version*—as the novel's very title suggests—Roger's victory is a foregone conclusion, and Dale's eventual loss of faith is presented with malevolent glee. Roger considers Dale's desire to prove God's existence "blasphemy" and "loath[es] the icy-eyed fervent way" Dale declares Christ to be his Savior (22); he even goes so far as to name the Devil "the absence of doubt . . . [that] pushes people into suicide bombing, into setting up extermination camps" (81), thus suggesting that atheism may be preferable to much of what passes for Christianity. He also prefers to keep his own faith as secret as possible, hating the fact that his "hot Barthian nugget insulated within layers of worldly cynicism and situation ethics" are "dragged toward the light by this boy's earnest agony" (180). Dale, for his part, is genuinely needy in his own faith— when he loses it, "he can't sleep . . . because he always used to pray and that would put him to sleep" (315–16). While Roger does believe Dale's approach to be wrong and blasphemous, it is clear that he is repulsed even more by how obvious Dale's neediness is: the pathos of Dale's loss of faith only strengthens Roger's contempt for him.

Readers of *Roger's Version* have judged Roger and Dale in diametrically opposed ways, despite general agreement that the game is rigged against Dale. James Wood, for instance, maintains that "Dale is, throughout, a repulsive character; Roger Lambert, a genial, mild professor" (229), while Frank G. Novak, Jr., making much of the parallel between Lambert and Hawthorne's Chillingworth, considers Roger a "satanic personality" who deceives many readers into believing that Updike endorses his Barthean theology (3). Such divergent responses are themselves enabled by Updike's severing of ethics and morality from Christian orthodox belief. It is tempting to conclude that those who rate orthodoxy higher than morality, perceiving them as separable, will prefer Roger, while those who maintain that orthodoxy must be demonstrated by a moral life will prefer Dale. Even this judgment, however, is too simple. Viewed from the standpoint of orthodoxy, Roger is correct that only revelation guarantees the truth of Christianity, and any response to that revelation is always "subjective," in that it engages us not merely intellectually, but (as the She'ma puts it, "with all your heart, and with all your soul, and with all your strength" [Deuteronomy 6:5]). Yet it does not follow that reason is worthless and has no place in theological reflection. It is significant, moreover, that despite his professed allegiance to Barth, Roger is an academic specialist in Christian heresy and a former teacher of a course on blasphemy.[11] In the central section of the novel, when he imagines (or, implausibly but not impossibly, has revealed to him in a vision) his wife's possible adultery with Dale, his pornographic description of the scene is juxtaposed against passages from Tertullian, the orthodox champion who became a heretic (though Roger proposes that the work from which he quotes is not heretical at all). Indeed, Roger accuses himself of heresy after his affair with his niece, Verna—"that of committing deliberate abominations so as to widen and deepen the field in which God's forgiveness can magnificently play" (289). On the other hand, although Dale professes belief in Jesus as his Savior, he admits that his efforts to prove God's existence, if successful, will only prove deism: "we're not trying to prove anything about the Incarnation, or the Trinity—a Hindu could be just as happy with this news as a Christian" (25). In this way, for all

---

11. It is also, of course, possible to compare Roger's quotations from and commentaries about the texts by Barth and Tertullian in the novel, taking into account such factors as when these texts appeared in their author's careers. Such an effort requires a familiarity with theology beyond what most educated general readers will possess. Frank G. Novak, Jr., for instance, has argued that Updike sides decisively against Roger in part because his favorite passages from Barth come from earlier works whose ideas Barth himself later corrected by placing less emphasis on the total otherness of God and more on the Incarnation. Although my own theological commitments lead me to agree with Novak more than I disagree with him in my own judgment of Roger as a character, his reading implies a degree of gamesmanship in Updike's novel that complicates the rhetorical situation that is my primary interest here—the communication from an avowedly Christian author to a (probably) secular audience. Unlike Walker Percy, for instance, whose own engagements with philosophy and theology in his novels are presented accessibly and in a way that leads little doubt as to how the author intends for readers to interpret his work, Updike makes the relationship between these passages and his own purposes more obscure—even going so far as to leave several of the quoted passages from Tertullian untranslated into English. I am not sure that Updike intends for readers to come to particular conclusions about *how* Roger's use of Barth and Tertullian reflects upon his theological or moral beliefs; rather, I take this use primarily in a broad, sociological sense: Roger is the kind of man who reads theologians to justify his actions, and other men aren't. Even if he misreads them, the only readers who might be able to identify this misreading are those who are *already* interested in theology.

the fervency of his belief, Dale's actual project seems congruent with the long nineteenth-century effort to "rescue" Christianity with science, and in the process of doing so discarded much of its dogma as mere myth. At the same time, however, if Roger's allegiance to Barth is more consistent with Updike's own professions of faith, Dale's terror of nonbeing suggests something of Updike's own similarly professed fear.

Nor does judgment become clearer if one shifts its criteria from orthodoxy to morality. Both Roger and Dale are adulterers, and Roger's adultery is also incestuous. Though it is eventually confirmed that Dale did have an affair with a woman who could have been Roger's wife Esther (318–19), it is not fully established that it was Esther, or that Roger's pornographic visions were true, though there is some circumstantial evidence to suggest as much. Esther herself, however, is not very compelling as a Hester Prynne: readers are led (though by Roger) to believe that her affair with Dale is the result of suburban housewifely boredom and resentment against her husband's relative freedom, and though Roger's callousness toward her is evident throughout the novel, it is balanced against her desire to remain with him because she enjoys "the solid and lively social matrix" that her position as his wife gives her (293). Dale's own relative sexual inexperience and immense gratitude toward Esther might make his participation in the adultery less culpable, but the novel prevents us from making an informed judgment on this point: readers are never shown how he reconciles the fact of the adultery with his professed Christianity. The novel ends with Roger triumphant and Dale crushed, but with a wide variety of specific judgments of both characters left open. Indeed, the final sentences of the novel open yet a new possibility: Esther, an avowed atheist throughout the book, decides one Sunday to attend church. If one takes her at her word when she tells Roger that she does so to annoy him (329), one might be led to the conclusion that nothing has changed, that her attendance merely begins a new cycle of boredom, resentment, and possible adultery; if, however, one assumes that behind this stated motive there is a genuine interest and even an incipient faith that might have been stimulated by her interactions with Dale, one might reach an altogether different conclusion about the mysteries of divine grace.

Ultimately, I would argue that Updike creates such ambiguous ending in order to suggest that none of these judgments, however one might personally resolve them, necessarily follow. The primary fact is that God, after having intervened through the Incarnation, crucifixion, and resurrection of Jesus, has withdrawn, and in the long interval until Jesus returns, there is no practical difference between believers and unbelievers. Roger is closer to the atheist Myron Kriegman (and indeed, to the atheist critic James Wood) than to Dale precisely because he believes that God cannot be proven, and while he may derive a certain comfort from his faith, the nature of this comfort seems no different from Dale's—it is, inevitably, a response to the fear of death. Moreover, if belief or unbelief has no bearing on one's moral life—so that Updike reflects what Ralph Wood calls "an ethical quietism" (*Comedy* 190)—then why not indulge in all that the modern world has to offer? Wood is correct to note that "[u]nlike Nietzsche, Updike does not envision humanity as the inventor of life's meaning and value" and that he "is not finally a tragedian but an ironist" (204). A "tragic" view of the death of God, like Nietzsche's, offers something to reckon with. A merely ironic view might serve, as Booth claims that irony inevitably does, to build a community—in this case, Updike implies, the entire human race, which needs God and yet cannot approach him. But this very need becomes a focus for complacency, both in those who acknowledge it (and in doing so, forgive themselves for almost anything) and in those who profess to have overcome it. God becomes an object among others that might help one get one through the night, chosen for reasons that are therapeutic at best and irreducibly selfish at worst. Those who choose objects other than God for this purpose have no reason to gloat, and if they fancy that they have freed themselves from the irrationality of "needing" God, they condemn themselves to false consciousness. Though Updike theoretically acknowledges the existence of people who do not share his terror of death and whose belief or unbelief might therefore be grounded on something else, the major work of his last two decades, *In the Beauty of the Lilies,* suggests that he finds it increasingly hard to credit such positions. Roger may share Dale's fear of death, but he takes a stubborn pride in not admitting as much. There is no such pride in the later novel—everyone needs God, and those who profess not to are whistling in the dark, proving themselves pathetic.

IV. The American Sadness:
In the Beauty of the Lilies

In the Beauty of the Lilies follows four generations of an American family from the period 1912 to 1990. The novel reaffirms Updike's implicit claim that Christian belief has been waning for decades yet remains as necessary as ever to the psychic health of Americans. George Steiner's judgment that "[o]ne puts down this novel with the intimation that America is, very near its center, the saddest country on earth" (106), rings true, for here Updike suggests, more clearly than in any novel since *The Poorhouse Fair,* that without the conflation of American identity with doctrinally Protestant commitments and a capitalist work ethic, Americans are condemned to a profound sense of emptiness. The novel begins with the loss of faith of Clarence Wilmot, a Presbyterian clergyman in Paterson, New Jersey, and ends when Clarence's great-grandson Clark, having joined a religious cult that is almost too heavy-handedly called the "Temple of True and Actual Faith" (360), loses his life in a conflagration modeled on the 1993 Branch Davidian disaster in Waco, Texas. Paralleling the vicissitudes of the Wilmot family's faith is a transformation in American life, in which traditional virtues of industry and Protestant self-reliance (presented, as in *The Poorhouse Fair*, with an irony that doubles back upon itself in an effort to redeem its ethnocentrism) yield to the solipsistic pleasures of motion pictures and pornography and the hollowing out of American identity itself. Clarence loses "the last particles of his faith" (5) at the very moment that Mary Pickford, who is being filmed by D. W. Griffith in Paterson, faints—as if to suggest that faith in God and faith in the illusions of film serve the same purpose and are similarly vulnerable.

One significant historical context for the novel is provided by the industrialization of Paterson and the waves of immigrants that it attracts. As Clarence adjusts to life without his faith, Paterson becomes the scene for a confrontation between the Industrial Workers of the World (the "Wobblies") and the owners of textile mills, between a largely Catholic and Jewish population of workers and the "born Protestants" (26) who own the mills. Though the strike is broken, in the long run the immigrants win precisely by embracing a superficial Americanness without also adhering to the religious (and capitalist) values that sustained such Americanness in the past. "The climate of the times," opines the narrator, only half ironically, "was against [Clarence]. The immigrant hordes had brought to America German radicalism and Italian anarchism and Semitic materialism; this was no time for native-born Protestants to grow lax and abandon the sublime values and articles of faith that had induced God to shower down upon them the blessings due a chosen people" (89–90). It is fitting that when Clarence gives up his pastoral duties, he finds work selling *The Popular Encyclopedia* door to door—an inferior product whose chief appeals are that it "is edited entirely by Americans, and is much superior on American subjects" (91) and that its articles on religion are "uniformly respectful and studiously neutral" enough for "[n]o child's faith, of whatever denomination," to be disturbed" (94). Even more fittingly, in this capacity he is patronized by his former housekeeper, an Irish immigrant now pregnant out of wedlock, who takes pity on him. The loss of national faith entails that "real" Americans of Protestant background are becoming aliens in their own country. Seventy-six years later, Clarence's son Teddy will write to his own grandson about the eventual fate of Paterson: "Pretty near everybody is black. Those that aren't are spic. Market Street looked like something out of Haiti, it felt to me like carnival time, all these boom boxes and the girls in bright rags and not much of them, the men standing around laughing as though every day was a legal holiday" (417–18). Though Teddy professes not to be "put off" by the scene and to prefer "people jigging down the middle of Market Street than huddled in those slave shacks over on Beaver Road [as in Paterson's industrial heyday]" (418), the irony is palpable.

More significantly for Updike's theological purposes, Clarence's loss of faith conforms to Douglas's account of the feminization of American culture and religion. As a Calvinist minister, Clarence must be committed both to the dogma of double predestination and to *sola fide*. Yet even though he reads atheist writers such as Robert Ingersoll, Herbert Spencer, and Nietzsche and eventually comes to agree with them, the initial cause of his loss of faith is his reading in the Higher Criticism: "They called themselves theologians, these Teutonic ravagers of the text that Luther had unchained from the altar and translated out of Latin, and accepted their bread from the devout sponsors of theological chairs, yet were the opposite of theologians, as in the dank basement of Greek and Aramaic researches they undermined Christianity's ancient supporting walls and beams" (15). Clarence concludes: "For all its muscular missions to the heathen and fallen women and lost souls of city slums, the nineteenth century had been a long erosion, and the books of this century that a conscientious clergyman collected . . . Clarence now saw as so much flotsam and rubble, perishing and adrift, pathetic testimony to belief's flailing attempt not to drown" (16). The older, orthodox books of Bunyan, Kempis, and Calvin, by contrast, were "ignorant but not pathetic" (16). Because faith is a "force of will," Clarence accuses himself of listening to the feminizing blandishments of liberalizing Christianity: "the failure was his own, an effeminate yielding where virile strength was required" (18).

A turning point occurs when Clarence is called to comfort Mr. Orr, a dying, elderly member of his congregation. Much to his surprise, even though Mr. Orr is concerned about his salvation, he chides his pastor for not emphasizing damnation enough in his sermons, for shrinking from what he perceives to be a logical consequence of Christian teaching: "Take away damnation, in my opinion, a man might as well be an atheist. A God that can't damn a body to an eternal Hell can't lift a body up out of the grave either" (47). Just as the Barthean Roger Lambert has more in common with his atheist colleagues than with Dale Kohler, Clarence Wilmot finds himself agreeing with his congregant despite his loss of faith, and when, the following Sunday, he preaches a sermon that culminates in the claim that "election . . . is *choice*" (54), he loses his voice immediately afterward. As if to consummate the feminization of religion, his wife Stella finishes the service for him and continues to do so on future occasions, enjoying her new power immensely. The implication that it is better to be an atheist than to subscribe to such an effete version of Christianity, with its "sickly" talk of compassion (41), is unmistakable. Even Stella's faith, however, proves not to be solid: when Clarence finally confesses to her his loss of faith, she becomes angry, advises him to "stop this tedious mooning about faith" (65), and complains bitterly about the loss of income and social standing that will follow should he give up his position. Indeed, after Clarence's death, once the family has relocated to the small town of Basingstoke, Delaware, she lies to her son Teddy about the end of her husband's career as a minister: "He didn't lose his faith, he lost his voice" (140). Teddy discerns in such lies further evidence that Christianity is false, and resolves to remain loyal to his father's unbelief: "He used to wonder how the stories of Jesus' miracles and Resurrection could have been spread across the world if they were not true, but his mother had showed him how" (140).

Yet though Stella is lying here, she may be speaking more truly than she knows. Clarence loses his faith, yet the passivity into which he sinks, which he at first attributes to relief at no longer having to maintain "an immense strain of justification" (7), becomes more serene even as his health and his family's economic position deteriorate, as if he comes eventually to abandon himself to God's mercy. The brief, despairing prayer that he speaks, "smiling at the futile sound of it," in the immediate aftermath of his loss of faith—"Have mercy" (24)—is repeated at the end of his chapter by the omniscient narrator (108), hinting that it has become more genuine. Even Teddy comes to suspect as much: "Looking back I wonder if Dad didn't believe more than he knew, and that's what made him so serene at the end" (417). Because Teddy considers faith a security blanket, he does not begrudge other people's faith and does not object when his grandson joins the cult. Indeed, his own attitude is less active disbelief than anger at God: "[I]t seemed to me God could have given Dad a sign. To help him out. Just a little sign would have done it, and cost God nothing much. Damned if I'd go to church to sing His praises after that" (410). Teddy himself inherits much of his father's passivity and spends years after his father's disgrace "waiting for some second, even bigger blow to fall" (114), but ultimately his life is more successful than his extreme caution would suggest: he marries the woman he loves, lives into old age, and attributes his own serenity to the fact that he "never expected too much out of life" and thus escaped disappointment (418). His melancholy does not cross into genuine despair, and he retains both a sense of basic decency and a genuine curiosity about the world. Though I agree with Ralph Wood's judgment that the novel "tells us, with great power and poignancy, what is happening to us and why," I do not share his sense that Teddy becomes "something of [Updike's] self-portrait," nor the implication that Teddy, because he does not blame others, fails to regard others as fully human ("Updike's Sloth" 457). Both Clarence and Teddy believe more than they know, if only because they know what they have lost. A truly committed atheist would neither pray even so vague a prayer as "Have mercy" nor feel any anger toward God. Their very existence confirms Updike's inability to believe, as it were, in disbelief—they belong to the ranks of those who claim to have overcome a need for belief yet merely channel their need into substitutes.

Of the four Wilmot protagonists whom *In the Beauty of the Lilies* follows, it is Teddy's daughter Essie, eventually the movie star Alma DeMott, whose obsessions and self-image correspond most closely to those of Updike himself. Whether his decision to filter his own convictions so largely through a female character springs from an ironic response to hostile feminist critics, or an ironic rethinking of what the feminization of American culture might portend in the age of film, Updike chooses to combine his own reverent yet contemptuous attitude toward sexuality in the person of Alma, for whom sex is both bliss—"an entertaining smooth chute into the dark red bliss of things" (313), a phrase worthy of Piet Hanema—and an unsentimental, devious livelihood: "sex was at the heart of show business, but was not worn, actually, on its sleeve" (305). She stands in contrast both to her father and grandfather, who for Updikean protagonists are mostly diffident about sex and completely uninterested in adultery. Alma's breathtaking narcissism, which her career permits her never to outgrow, also raises the question of whether feminine narcissism is qualitatively different—and thus either more or less culpable—than the masculine narcissism that is Updike's usual trademark. Her girlish sense that God's love "pressed down from Heaven and fit her whole body like bathwater in the tub" (233) never leaves her: as a teenager, she reasons that "God understood" her sexual desires because "He made us, after all" (267), and even as an experienced, middle-aged star, she regards moments of unusually felicitous acting as instances when "something from God would flow into her face from behind" (336). As a child, she associates her feelings with God with the stories she hears about her grandfather Clarence; when she is old enough to learn the particulars of his story, she pities him for having "fallen into a shining white hole of damnation forever" (334), but remains secure that her own faith will compensate for her own ethical failures—above all, her promiscuity and her benign neglect of her son Clark, who grows up appropriately jaded.[12]

What ostensibly distinguishes Essie's faith from that of Updike's previous protagonists is her sense that God remains continually close to her. Unlike Roger Lambert, she does not envision God as remote, awful, and self-concealing—on the contrary, she marvels at one point at the fact that "God always answered [her] prayers" (277). This difference, however, may be less significant than it seems, for unlike Dale Kohler, Essie does not ground her sense of God's involvement in her life in scientific or philosophical arguments; she simply takes it for granted and lives as she pleases. Both she and the male protagonists struck by God's absence invoke God in the course of licensing their pleasures. On the other hand, Essie's beliefs can be seen, perhaps, in Douglas's terms as signs of the transformation of nineteenth-century post-Calvinist Protestantism into the twentieth-century mass culture of stardom. There may well be more gravity in choosing damnation, as Clarence and Teddy do, than in nodding piously toward God while selling sexual fantasies—yet her character also raises the possibility that Updike himself may not be doing anything so different.

Clark is the most elusive of the four Wilmots. He becomes acquainted with the Temple when he picks up a young woman, Hannah, at a ski resort, who takes him back as a potential convert and sleeps with him. Yet though he does so willingly enough, he has none of the single-minded focus on sexual desire that is typical in Updike, and the experience itself is anticlimactic—"sleepy and dutiful, a poke and a submission" (390). Moreover, the events of his life before the Temple tend to confirm a sense that sex as he has learned about it, in the context of the impossibly beautiful people of Hollywood and the falsity of film, is always distasteful: in one memorable scene, he masturbates to a pornographic film, concludes immediately afterward that "people are disgusting," and resolves "to get out of Los Angeles, out of reach of the fucking movies" (434). Hannah's offer of herself may have been a necessary lure, but what seems to confirm Clark in his decision is not the promise of sex, but the cult leader's declaration that he is "the only person you will meet . . . who is not interested in your

---

12. Interestingly, the consciousness of parental neglect appears to be the one thing that reliably makes Updike's male protagonists feel pangs of remorse for their adulteries and desertions of their spouses—the short story "Separating" and the novels *Marry Me* and *Memories of the Ford Administration* provide especially wrenching examples. Essie, however, has no such regrets. When Clark asks her why she had (briefly) married his stepfather Rex, she replies, "Rex was all cock." Reasonably enough, Clark translates this response as *"Get off my case, kid"* (363, italics in text). Indeed, she is relieved when Clark elects to join the Temple, seeing it as just the latest instance of how God continually provides for her: "Off her hands, and into God's. So be it. Good riddance" (360).

mother. I am interested in *you*" (383). Jessie is also uncannily correct when he opines, "Your mother perhaps was *jealous* of her God and did not wish to share Him with the world, even with her son" (383). Jessie's is a Toc-quevillian appeal to an ordinary young man in a democratic culture preoccupied with the petty object of himself and whose frustrated egoism burns bright. It is also, as Peter Augustine Lawler has noted, the essential (albeit distorted) appeal of Christianity for many Americans: God loves you too, even if you find that hard to believe, and no one has the right to keep you from him. In this, Clark is his mother's son, though either he or the narrator (Updike's use of free indirect discourse makes this distinction ambiguous at this point) seems more clear-eyed about the denial involved: "A company of believers is like a prisonful of criminals: their intimacy and solidarity are based on what about themselves they can least justify" (416)—in theological terms, their fallenness and their need for God's mercy, which they do not deserve.

Though Clark is attracted to the Temple in part because it offers an escape from a world of meaningless sexualization, Jessie's vision of the corrupt American culture and of the impending apocalypse that he believes he will usher in is no less distorted in its understanding of sex. Officially suggesting that women and men in the Temple can sleep freely with each other, in practice Jessie tries to keeps the women for himself, believing that it is his duty to father as many children as possible. His condemnation of the "whoremongering" outside the Temple is directed less against the sin of fornication than against the separation of sexual intercourse from procreation. From the point of view of orthodox Christianity, his preaching on the subject is a mixture of the true and the false:

> "Scientific studies show, brother, that alcohol and tobacco impair sexual potency, and this impairs a man's bounden duty to disseminate his seed, as enjoined in Genesis, Leviticus, and the Song of Songs. In the Song of Solomon, six eight, we read, 'There are threescore queens, and fourscore concubines, and virgins without number' . . . Keep that temple pure," Jesse told him, "and it will *func*tion." (382)

Accordingly, Jessie hates contraception, and one of the few ways in which Clark proves unfaithful to his teaching is by using condoms on the rare occasions when Hannah sleeps with him. As I have suggested above, procreation is a vexing subject in Updike's fiction: men tend to associate it with female wiles, for children, once they are brought into the world, bind men to their wives, and the genuine love that men feel for their children makes this fetter all the more painful. Updike's preoccupation with nonprocreative sex seems in part a defiant effort to bypass this hazard of lovemaking, and Jessie's desire to bring as many children as possible into the world would probably be anomalous enough, even without his bizarre religious framework, to mark him as suspect in Updike's world. When the Temple's compound is eventually attacked by law enforcement and Jessie begins to kill the women and children in the belief that he is sending them to heaven, the implication seems to be that his desire to procreate and his murderousness are complementary: he who makes life has the right to destroy it as well. As insane as Jessie's position is, it sheds additional light on the usual distaste of Updike's heroes for procreation: to bear and raise children is to be responsible for them unto death, and this is a responsibility not gladly embraced, except, it seems, by madmen.

Clark is given the name "Esau" in the Temple, though he is also called "Slick" in mocking tribute to his wealthy and socially adept background, and his sense of having found a home is tempered by a nagging sense of hostility toward him. His mixed motivations ensure that judging him for his violent role in Jessie's endgame will be difficult. As policemen begin to descend on the Temple, Clark kills one—in part, it seems, to overcome "his unease, his virginity in regard to guns" (399) and to gain respect from the hardier men in the compound. Still later, as he finds himself in the same room with a group of women and children and anticipating that he and everyone else will be in heaven shortly, he asks with exasperation, "How had he acquired this clattering scorpion's tail of women and children?" (481). Yet when he is ordered by Jessie to kill Hannah, the woman who brought him to the Temple, and her two children, the narrator abruptly speaks of Clark's "non-coöperative streak," repeating a phrase that had earlier been associated with Essie's judgment of her son (484, 360), and immediately afterward, Clark kills Jessie and another of his henchmen before he is himself shot. His motivations are unclear: is it because he pities Hannah and her children, or because Jessie calls him "Slick" at this crucial moment? Moreover, how does he evaluate his own action in the moments before his death? In this crucial paragraph, Updike's use of free indirect discourse becomes maddeningly ambiguous:

> There was nothing for him on the outside now, just hassle, and embarrassment for Mother. Whoremongers, sorcerers, the whole pack of supercilious shits. He wasn't worried; the living God had laid hold of him, the present-tense God beyond betting on. . . . Even through the chemical filter, the smoke was palpable, like a fine rich coke being stuffed very fast up his nostrils, down his throat, into his eyes. His head was losing its ability to make pictures. *The second death*, when had the first been? *The Lamb*

shall overcome, how could a Lamb overcome, by letting Its throat be slit? That vast indignant beast with seven heads was *whuffing* and beating on the panelled white door as if entitled to admission. Esau was a cunning hunter. He had a twin, somewhere in the smoke. He heard a noise, soft but pointed, over where the cups and plates used to be: a cup settling on a saucer or a twig snapping in the fire or the bolt of a rifle being stealthily slipped back. *Go ahead and shoot. You'll be doing me a favor.* (486)

Is this heroism, stoic resignation before death, panic, or despair? The characterization of the outside world as "whoremongers, sorcerers, and supercilious shits" connotes both theological condemnation and the pain of social rejection. The death-bringing smoke may be a harbinger of his salvation, or a perverse thrill like the rush of cocaine. The distinction between the "living God"—into whose hands it is a fearful thing to fall— and the God on whose existence people merely place bets suggests a sudden fullness of faith (hence the accompanying lack of worry), but Clark's subsequent remembrance of Biblical references bespeak incredulity and irony—doubt at the efficacy of Christ's sacrifice, confusion about whether hell ("the second death") awaits him, whether the seven-headed beast of Revelation is "entitled" to him. There is also, in the reference to Esau's twin Jacob, a question as to whether he sees his role to destroy not just the false prophet but the true patriarch who will become Israel as well. Is it therefore just that the imagined Jacob destroys him? That Updike attributes his confusion to the loss of his ability to "make pictures" is characteristic, for it resonates with Updike's continual gesture of simply pointing to the visible world and celebrating it in all its detail. Perhaps the suggestion is that someone who is no longer able to see properly is beyond any intimation of salvation, and that Clark's apparent welcoming of death should be attributed to despair at losing his vision.[13]

Although the question of Clark's motivation and ultimate salvation is unclear, as news of what happened at the Temple reaches the outside world, he is acclaimed as a hero who has saved the lives of women and children. Essie, in fact, thanks God for letting him achieve this heroism,

---

13. In *The Humiliation of the Word,* the French theologian Jacques Ellul mounts a sustained critique of vision as that which deceives by falsely establishing human perceptions at the center, so to speak, of the universe. Writing itself is problematic insofar as one reads instead of hears it, for faith comes by hearing. What Clark sees in these final moments is fragmentary and ambiguous; what he hears is the harbinger of his death. To the extent that Updike's fictional project privileges sight over sound and associates nonbeing with the absence of visual sensation, it is possible to locate his theological problems precisely in this lack of concern with what one hears—a call not only to believe the Gospel but also to transform one's life in accord with that belief.

once more reinforcing her own egoistic conception of her relationship with God (488). The proverbial last word in the novel is given to Teddy, who, watching the news reports and reflecting on how much more depraved the world has become since his childhood, watches women from the Temple emerging "as if just waking up, carrying or holding on to the hands of their children, too many to count. The children" (491). Ralph Wood calls this final sentence "a blank cry for pity," and though he is correct, such pity is uncharacteristic for Updike, who rarely shows such concern for the welfare of children ("Updike's Sloth" 455). I would argue that this pity is directed less at the children than at the United States, for whose future the children serve as a familiar metaphor. These children have, after all, survived the carnage along with their mothers; if they are to be pitied for what they have lost, the implication is that they may have been better off in the Temple. Leaving it, they enter a world that has its own "whoremongers and sorcerers," but which, lacking the drama of apocalypse, might prove more emotionally barren. Jessie's faith may have been neither "true" nor "actual," but clearly his power drew upon hungers for genuine religious conviction. The novel's title, which quotes the line "In the beauty of the lilies Christ was born across the sea" in Julia Ward Howe's "Battle Hymn of the Republic," seems relevant here. In Ralph Wood's words, "American exceptionalism does not mean, for Updike, that this nation is God's 'last, best hope of earth,' as Lincoln declared. It means that our Union is uniquely blessed and cursed by God's absence. . . . The Christ of Updike's fiction strikes me as stratospherically remote, dwelling in the distant loveliness of lilies that fester far more than they transfigure" ("Updike's Sloth" 455–56). Updike is unable to take disbelief seriously, but he is also unable to take belief in Christ's presence seriously—his attempt to do so in this novel, through the character of Essie, is sincere, but it appears as yet another version of the feminization of religion that he decries. The children are bereft—not, strictly speaking, by their loss of faith, but by their inevitable going out into a disenchanted world, where even Updike's egoistic and cheap version of sacramentalism cannot long prevail.

V. Coda:
Christianity versus Islam in *Terrorist*

Updike's rhetoric of narcissism, as a strategy intended to make Christian belief credible and compelling, is a calculated and audacious risk. The degree to which Updike connects both narcissism and Christian belief to a discourse of American exceptionalism bespeaks a certain shrewdness, for in contemporary democratic culture, egoism is simultaneously reviled (since radical equality regards airs of superiority as intolerable) and celebrated (since equality guarantees the supreme worth of each individual). Readers who are unsympathetic to Updike's Christian project are quite able to see in it nothing but a terrified flailing against death, an interpretation that Updike anticipates and even, at times, appears to endorse: "Of my own case, looked at coldly, it might be said that, having been given a Protestant, Lutheran, rather antinomian Christianity as part of my sociological make-up, I was too timid to discard it. My era was too ideologically feeble to wrest it from me, and Christianity gave me something to write about, and a semblance of a backbone, and a place to go on Sunday mornings, when the post offices were closed" (*Self-Consciousness* 234). Some might add: and it also gave you a point from which you could contemptuously disregard all the accusations of sexism, racism, and sheer personal arrogance that you deserve.

Yet if this were the whole story, Updike would simply not have the following that he has attracted. What might be most compelling in his religious vision, finally, is the way he simultaneously presents Christianity as embattled—a "ghost" in American life since the nineteenth century, despite many Americans' belated realization of this fact—and yet as so necessary that alternatives to it are almost unthinkable. Acknowledging the theoretical possibility of people for whom nonbeing holds no terrors, Updike finds their actual existence incredible, and the effects of this disbelief become more pronounced as his career progresses. The respect accorded both to believers and unbelievers in *The Poorhouse Fair* dissolves into an indifferent embrace, as both come to be seen as advancing their own narcissistic dramas, their own secret forms of belief—dramas that the reader is cordially invited to identify with his or her own. Atheists and lukewarm believers are, in the end, the same, whether they admit it or not—so why not, Updike implies, go all out and wager on eternal life?

And yet, even with his increasing equivocation between belief and unbelief, Updike insists that if one sides with belief, it must be Christianity, and not any other religious alternative—both for the historical reason that the United States was founded and sustained by Christians and for the self-serving reason that no possible competitor affords the same degree of narcissistic delight. This, I would argue, is the main interest of *Terrorist* (2006), Updike's penultimate novel, which was widely criticized for its implausible portrayal of Ahmad Ashmawy, a high school student in north New Jersey who comes to espouse Islam and becomes involved in a plot to blow up the Lincoln Tunnel. Ahmad resembles Clark Wilmot in his disgust for the lax religiosity and triumphant license of contemporary American society—yet, in characteristic Updike fashion, he does not let this disgust prevent him from accepting a sexual favor from a fellow student. The degree to which Ahmad resembles many previous Updike forebears is indeed implausible, as is the epiphany he experiences at the last moment that compels him not to trigger the explosion: "[God] does not want us to desecrate His creation by willing death. He wills life" (306). The novel's final paragraph, however, suggests that Ahmad recoils immediately from his epiphany once he emerges from the tunnel into Manhattan:

> All around them, up Eighth Avenue to Broadway, the great city crawls with people, some smartly dressed, many of them shabby, a few beautiful but most not, all reduced by the towering structures around them to the size of insects, but scuttling, hurrying, intent in the milky morning sun upon some plan or scheme or hope they are hugging to themselves, their reason for living another day, each one of them impaled upon the pin of consciousness, fixed upon self-advancement and self-preservation. That, and only that. *These devils*, Ahmad thinks, *have taken away my God*. (310)

Ahmad may voice something of Updike's praise of creation and refrain from murder, but he does not accept what appears in Updike's work as its necessary corollary—the love of self as the perceiving consciousness that confirms creation's value. It would seem that for Updike, Islam is not a viable alternative to Christianity precisely because it lacks such a conception of the centrality of the self: Ahmad perceives his Updikean epiphany as a fall into the kind of self-consciousness that disgusts him, a desire for self-preservation that he rationalized into a belief that he was doing God's will in not causing the explosion. Ahmad has, it would seem, lost his faith precisely because he has discovered his capacity for narcissism even in the midst of what would seem an act of total submission to God. Yet he does not embrace this capacity, and the chilling quality of the final sentence suggests that for Updike, not to do so compromises one's humanity. Whether Ahmad presents a convincing portrayal of Muslim belief in America in the early twenty-first century or not, Updike wagers that readers will recoil not from his sense of shame but from his refusal to celebrate himself, his dogged insistence that if one believes, one ought to live as if one does. For all of Updike's professions of orthodoxy, in this respect, at least, he drearily conforms to Amy Hungerford's thesis of postmodern belief: orthodoxy is a private matter, and one must accept the trivialization of public and communal life that accompanies such a stance.

4

Walker Percy's
Rhetoric of Time, Apocalypse,
and the Modern Predicament

I. Narrative in the Diagnosis and Treatment of Boredom

Among avowedly Christian writers of merit in the late twentieth century, Walker Percy is distinguished not only by his novelistic achievement but also by the range and sophistication of his intellectual interests. Valued by some readers primarily as a novelist and by others as a philosopher or even a guru, Percy has engaged in his fiction and essays with French existentialism, the civil rights movement in the South, the mid-twentieth-century revival of scholasticism, the theories and fortunes of psychoanalysis, the historical burdens of being a white southern male, the relationship between anthropology and the philosophy of language, the sexual revolution, the critique of scientism and technological hubris, the fascination of apocalyptic fantasy, the possibility that a distinctly southern culture and literature is dying, and the cultural and religious consequences of the Second Vatican Council.[1] There is no doubt, however, that Percy subordinated all of these

---

1. Kieran Quinlan rightly notes that "Walker Percy is one of the few contemporary novelists who has made a difference in the lives of many of his readers" (13). James Atlas confirmed this statement when he interviewed Percy in 1980: "Percy has acquired a devoted, even fanatical following that responds to his work in a very personal way; readers are forever writing and calling him up to discuss their problems" (186).

engagements to his Catholic faith, or that his most devoted admirers turn toward this faith as the key that unlocks all the nuances of his thought. Like Muriel Spark, Percy was a convert who seems to have regarded his conversion as the precondition for his achieving an original writing voice. But he was far more forthright than Spark about his proselytizing impulses and his Catholic critique of culture, once describing his *modus operandi* in fiction as "ass-kicking for Jesus' sake."[2] Yet Percy has also provoked more perplexity and more wide-ranging assessments than this straightforward commitment to "ass-kicking" would suggest—both among secular readers who admire his work and among Catholics who find the positive commitments of his faith blunted by the ironies and even the sheer range of his writing. If Percy's emphasis on evangelization resembles Flannery O'Connor's, how is it that he has largely avoided the polarizing response that surrounds O'Connor's work—so that few readers would either make a case for Percy's sainthood or simply revile him as a benighted reactionary?

The answer to this question, I believe, lies above all in the different stances that Percy and O'Connor take toward their audiences. Like O'Connor, Percy writes for an audience who believes that God is dead—but unlike O'Connor, he neither assumes the hostility of this audience nor believes that shock and violence are the most effective rhetorical strategies to appeal to it. Even when his characters' "moments of grace" are accompanied by literal or metaphorical violence, the shock is muffled by the sheer geniality of Percy's prose and its insistent posture that characters are real people to whom real things happen, not grotesques confronting divine violence. While O'Connor's works do seem, in some readers, to sharpen the pleasures of self-righteousness, Percy's suggest that his readers share the same essential "predicament" (to use one of his favorite words) as his characters—and indeed, as himself—and in doing so projects a reassuring sense of equality. Moreover, unlike Updike's appeal to an American narcissism, which presupposes a theoretical human equality but frequently entails an icy misanthropy in practice, Percy's evocation of a common predicament works, ironically, to strip his characters of their privileges, to render them Everymen despite their marked departures from a generic, late twentieth-century American norm. All of Percy's protagonists, like Percy himself, are white, upper-class males conscious of their familial legacies and increasingly unsure of how they should behave in a South that is losing its faith in blood and breeding, ideologies of white supremacy, and traditional codes of honor. Their efforts to read correctly the markers that determine other

---

2. From a letter of 6 April 1962 to his mentor, Caroline Gordon, quoted in Jay Tolson's biography, *Pilgrim in the Ruins: A Life of Walker Percy* (301).

characters' places in the social hierarchy probably strike contemporary readers as rarefied, comic, or sinister, but above all as anachronistic. Yet one of Percy's most remarkable achievements is to make such characters sympathetic, so that readers discern in their befuddlement not an unpleasant mixture of elitism and self-pity but rather finely observed variations on the Percyan predicament—the mutually reinforcing problems of boredom and sinfulness, as well their somatic expression, clinical depression. Indeed, as befits a physician-turned-Christian writer, Percy conceives of conversion not only as a matter of salvation but also, secondarily, as a therapeutic breakthrough.

It is difficult to overstate the centrality of boredom—often described as a living death—to Percy's work. "For some time now the impression has been growing upon me that everyone is dead" (99), says Binx Bolling in *The Moviegoer* (1961), and the theme continues through Father Smith's conviction in *The Thanatos Syndrome* (1987) that only dying people tell the truth, even though "Everyone else is dying too and spending their entire lives dying to themselves" (244). As Percy put it in "Questions They Never Asked Me" (1977), a "self-interview": "[O]rdinary life in an ordinary place on an ordinary day in the modern world is a dreary business. I mean *dreary*. People will do anything to escape this dreariness: booze up, hit the road, gaze at fatal car wrecks, shoot up heroin, spend money on gurus, watch pornographic movies, kill themselves, even watch TV" (407). Boredom may lie at the intersection of "ordinary life" and "the modern world," but Percy's diagnostic emphasizes the second of these two terms. In *Lost in the Cosmos: The Last Self-Help Book* (1983), Percy maintains that the word "boredom" did not enter the English language until the eighteenth century, and, asking why this should be the case, proposes as one possibility the fact that "for the past two or three hundred years the self has perceived itself as a leftover which cannot be accounted for by its own objective view of the world" (70). According to this account, the "modern world" fully emerged in the eighteenth century, as Enlightenment and historical consciousness drove out myth and religion, forcing ethics to become secularized and the self to lose its formerly privileged yet also dependent position as a fallen creature of God. What began as the promise of liberation—that one can use one's reason, know oneself, and transform the world—soon turned destructive: "If one had to set a date of the beginning of the end of the modern world, 1914 would be as good as any, because it was then that Western man, the beneficiary of precisely this scientific revolution and Christian ethic, began with great skill and energy to destroy himself" (*Signposts* 208).

In Percy's view, Enlightenment promises of liberation cannot succeed, because consciousness and language, the very things that most distinguish human beings as a species, remain inexplicable if viewed through the frames of positivist science and utilitarian philosophy. Consciousness and facility with linguistic signs are the only things that allow humans to place themselves in the world, yet their very existence is absurd, an unaccountable "leftover."[3] Scientists can explain distant phenomena in the universe more fully than they can explain the most mundane daily experiences (*Lost* 1), and their failure to legitimate experience as such leads both to a preoccupation with the self and to an impoverishment of daily life. Paraphrasing Kierkegaard, Percy critiques Hegel as the great exemplar of such an attitude: "Hegel knew everything and said everything, except what it was to be born and to live and to die" (*Conversations* 109). In the wake of Hegel and all his successors who claim to have either transcended or explained away mere experience, boredom flourishes. It is simultaneously a heightened self-consciousness, "the self being stuffed with itself," and a "loss of sovereignty in which the self yields up plenary claims to every sector of the world to the respective experts and claimants of those sectors" (*Lost* 71). Percy's first rhetorical principle, then, is to assume that his readers will find their own experiences "certified" in such a description, no matter who or where in modernity they may be.[4] It is as if all of his works ask readers the questions that, he maintains, would be the most appropriate questions to ask of extraterrestrial intelligences, should any ever turn up on Earth—"Did it also happen to you? Do you have a self? If so, how do you handle it? Did you suffer a catastrophe?" (109). Clearly, Percy expects most readers to nod in recognition.

If such recognition is the necessary precondition for taking Percy's efforts to persuade seriously, then much of his work appears a repetitive examination of different strategies to escape from boredom, to "redeem the time." The most obvious of these seek to abolish consciousness of time, either by grasping a scheme of meaning that transcends time (such as sci-

---

3. Geoffrey Galt Harpham has argued that inquiry into "language alone" has been the dominant intellectual project of the twentieth century precisely because the term "stands as a luminous and highly concentrated token of the multiple mysteries of human life" (236). Percy anticipates this claim when he maintains, "What is involved in a theory of language is a theory of man" ("Questions" 420).

4. "Certification" is defined by Binx Bolling in this way: "Nowadays when a person lives somewhere, in a neighborhood, the place is not certified for him. More than likely he will live there sadly and the emptiness which is inside him will expand until it evacuates the entire neighborhood. But if he sees a movie which shows his very neighborhood, it becomes possible for him to live, for a time at least, as a person who is Somewhere and not Anywhere" (*Moviegoer* 63). Though Binx refers here to the medium of film and to place in a strictly geographical sense, I believe that the same logic describes Percy's choice of fiction as a medium and his notion that selves must "place" themselves temporally as well as spatially.

entific laws and mathematics, or a totalizing philosophy such as Hegel's) or by plunging as often as possible into pure immanent sensation (drugs, alcohol, promiscuity, or mindless consumption). Scientists and artists, according to Percy, can achieve a kind of temporary transcendence through their discoveries and creations, which seem to affirm some kind of truth beyond the flux of temporality, and though scientists suffer less from the inevitably transient nature of this exaltation than artists, this is a difference in degree, not in kind.[5] Those who are neither artists nor scientists either suffer in silence or, embracing the palliatives of a consumer society, live in bad faith.

Yet though Percy focuses on the particular afflictions of modernity, he also holds that all was not well with the self in the serenely religious ages that preceded the Enlightenment. Even before there was what Weber calls "the disenchantment of the world," there was original sin—that primordial rupture between human beings and God that forced humans into time (and death), predisposing them to selfishness and to the boredom and violence that are its inevitable consequences. This "disaster," in which human consciousness "falls into the pit of itself" (*Lost* 212), loomed less large in premodern times not because human beings were qualitatively better (they weren't), but because, at least in the Christian world, the knowledge that Jesus Christ had died to redeem all those who believe in him sufficed to make life meaningful and endurable, even in the midst of boredom. The Incarnation, in which God situates himself in human time and subjects himself to death, provides reassurance that even God has experienced something of the human predicament and loves us enough to deliver us from it. The waning of Christian faith, then, leaves humankind more vulnerable than ever. Condemned to be neither angels nor beasts, but "wayfarers" (a term Percy borrows from Gabriel Marcel), only the conviction of ultimate redemption can deliver humankind from the torments of boredom or from the unprecedented violence (for Percy, the two world wars of the twentieth

---

5. For Percy, the scientist suffers less because "[he] is the prince and sovereign of the age. His transcendence of the world is genuine. That is to say, he stands in a posture of objectivity over against the world, a world which he sees as a series of specimens or exemplars, and interactions, energy exchanges, secondary causes" (*Lost* 115). The artist, lacking both a comparable esteem from society at large and the posture of objectivity that scientists enjoy, is often incapacitated by everyday dreariness: "It is one thing to write *The Sound and the Fury*, to achieve the artistic transcendence of discerning meaning in the madness of the twentieth century, then to finish it, then to find oneself at Reed's drugstore the next morning. A major problem of reentry, not solved but anaesthetized by alcohol" (123). Only in a few, rare instances—Percy mentions Simone Weil, Martin Buber, and Dietrich Bonhoeffer—do writers manage both to "become themselves transparently before God" and "to live intact through difficult lives" (157), and it seems significant that these exceptions are not writers of fiction. For an extended account of how Percy's conception of transcendence and immanence informs his theories of fiction and of life, see especially Farrell O'Gorman (135–36, 141–49).

century and the threat of nuclear holocaust) toward which they tend in a technological age.

If Percy is largely successful in persuading readers that they share a general predicament of boredom and meaninglessness in the twentieth century (and this particular claim has been seconded by many non-Christian writers), he is, perhaps, less successful in persuading readers that conversion is the only effective remedy. In this Percy seems like a twentieth-century successor to Pascal, whose reflections on the misery and greatness of human beings continue to prove more resonant to more people than does his wager that hope for happiness must lie in faith. Pascal was, to be sure, aware of the gap between convincing people that faith might be reasonable and leading them to believe in its truth, and Percy confronts the same gap in his writings. His preferred strategy in negotiating it is indirection. Because the experience of boredom is inextricable from the experience of a time that cannot be redeemed, Percy guides the reader toward his Christian doctrines not by beginning with calls to repent and believe—indeed, the characters in his fiction who do so, such as Father Smith in *Love in the Ruins* and *The Thanatos Syndrome*, are often presented with a certain destabilizing irony—but by suggesting that one's first step should be to reconcile oneself to time.

Edward J. Dupuy, one of Percy's best critics, has suggested that this step is also the fundamental project of autobiography, and in this sense, Percy's novels and essays can be considered as reflections on the autobiographical dimension of all narrative. Drawing upon the work of James Olney, Georges Gusdorf, and Janet Varner Gunn, Dupuy holds that "[t]he autobiographer redeems his time through the interplay of past and present, which takes place in memory" (22), setting into motion a self-conscious repetition of events that reveals their significance. For both Percy and Dupuy, this redemption must involve an acceptance of temporality and one's enmeshment in it, so that the self's here and now becomes not just a limiting condition, but also a source of possibility. Such a project contrasts with certain prominent features of modernism—the spatializing of narrative form and the preoccupation with recurring, mythic structures that always already account for everything. For this reason, argues Dupuy, Percy's work can be considered postmodern in some respects:

> Autobiography and Percy as autobiographer . . . seem postmodern because they are not primarily concerned with the past but with the now. The autobiographer retrieves the past, and is thus preoccupied with it, but always from the perspective of the present. Percy's characters, for their part, want nothing to do with the great southern archetypes of dignity and honor and

duty. Instead, they come to a realization of the possibility of acting now. Allie says in *The Second Coming*: "What was my (your, our) discovery? That I could *act*. I was *free* to act. . . . How does one ever make the discovery that one can actually be free to act for oneself? I don't know. I don't know how many people, if any, do it" (40). For both Percy and autobiography the past serves primarily as a repository of foreclosed potentialities. The possibility for action in time depends on these potentialities becoming actual. (20–21)

Here Dupuy's argument aligns with Peter Augustine Lawler's judgment that postmodernism should be seen as "human reflection on the failure of the modern project to eradicate human mystery and to bring history to an end" (1), and with Lawler's assessment that Percy's work exemplifies such reflection, because it affirms that "[h]uman beings have religious longings that cannot be satisfied by social or political reform" (109). The possibility for free action that Percy illuminates has little to do with politics, let alone with mastery of the world, but rather with the sudden discovery that one is free to love and be loved, wherever and whenever one finds oneself.

If Percy's project is seen as postmodern in this way, one of the features of his writing that has exasperated many readers—his characteristic lack of novelistic closure—becomes more explicable.[6] With the exception of *The Second Coming* (1980), Percy's novels tend to end with their plots resolved but with their characters left nonetheless in a state of ambiguity—in some cases, possibly having converted or on the cusp of a conversion to Christianity (as in *The Moviegoer* and *Lancelot*), but without decisive clues that would confirm such a judgment, and with an overarching sense of irony that even had such an event taken place, life goes on. It is understandable that such ambiguity would frustrate both Christian readers who want a clearer affirmation of Christian dogmas and all ordinary readers who seek the pleasures of closure. Yet Percy's endings in fact represent both the predicament that he diagnoses and the necessity of accepting temporal change. The only genuine closure in human life is death, and novels traditionally impart their sense of the meaning of a human life through their selection of an end that retrospectively determines this meaning—either death or something that functions as its structural equivalent, such as marriage. Peter Brooks's insight that "plot is the internal logic of the discourse of mortality" (22), derived from his reading of Freud's *Beyond the Pleasure Principle*, states the problem well: readers who demand closure from Percy's novels, seeking to read backward from their ends a definitive meaning (and thus

---

6. I have criticized Percy on these grounds myself, but that was in another country. See my *Fears and Fascinations: Representing Catholicism in the American South* (154–55, 166–68).

to redeem the time of reading), are also seeking the "death" of the narrative and enacting through their demand for it the belief that only death can confer meaning on life.[7] Yet the corollary of such a view is that death (as well as the end of a narrative) is desired—the desire of narrative is not to elude its end but to arrive at it in its own individual fashion. Redemption thus becomes identical with individualized, meaningful death. On the other hand, in Christianity the world is already redeemed by Jesus' sacrifice (even as human beings still live after the event), and Christians' greatest difficulty consists of keeping faith with that redemption, perceiving its ultimate closure and promise of more abundant life not only in the hereafter but also in the very flux of banal dailiness. Until the moment of death, the story remains open: even those who have become Christian may fall away, and even the most confirmed atheist may come to believe. The greatest difficulty for Percy's wayfarers is not merely to accept Christianity—or at least the necessity of something like it, since Percy is more explicit about this in some novels than in others—but to continue to live in the ordinary, dreary world after having arrived at this knowledge.

Percy's novels suggest two broad strategies for characters who arrive at this point. Although rhetorically they are opposed to each other, they are shown to be complementary in practice, so that over the course of a novel, the same protagonist often oscillates between the two. The first involves embracing a sacramental understanding of the world, in which what had seemed irredeemably dreary appears in its true light as a splendid, gratuitous gift, charged, in Hopkinsesque fashion, with the glory of God. (Here, Percy follows the example of his mentor, Caroline Gordon, who explicitly conceived of fiction as a sacramental undertaking and declared, "I am

---

7. Although Percy was critical of Freud (in "Questions They Never Asked Me," for instance, he expresses exasperation at Freud's "rather stupid hydraulic model of art as the sublimation of libidinal energies" [405]), both he and his characters—above all, Dr. Thomas More—respect Freud's preference for the long, hard work of analysis. More seems to be speaking for Percy when he says in *The Thanatos Syndrome* (whose very title expresses its debt to *Beyond the Pleasure Principle*), "Though I admired and respected Dr. Freud more than Dr. Jung, I thought Dr. Jung was right in encouraging his patients to believe that their anxiety and depression might be trying to tell them something of value. They are not just symptoms. It helps enormously when a patient can make friends with her terror, plumb the depths of her depression. . . . True, in the end Dr. Jung turned out to be something of a nut, the source of all manner of occult nonsense. Dr. Freud was not. He was a scientist, wrong at times, but a scientist nonetheless" (67). Part of More's professional difficulties spring from the fact that "[o]ld-fashioned shrinks are out of style and generally out of work," having been "mostly superseded by brain engineers, neuropharmacologists, chemists of the synapses" who reject "such a quixotic quest as pursuing the secret of one's very self" (13). More's most authentic mentor is identified in this novel as Harry Stack Sullivan, for his view that "[p]eople can get better, can come to themselves, without chemicals and with a little help from you" (17).

a Catholic, I suspect, because I was first a fiction writer."[8]) Percy's Chestertonian claim that "The only cure for depression is suicide" (*Lost* 75) is informed by the possibility of such sudden illuminations—only the "exsuicide," who knows that his depression is justified by the real conditions of the world and has seriously entertained the possibility of nonbeing, can also know that "he has nothing to lose by being alive. It is good to be alive" (*Lost* 79). More fortunate still are those characters in Percy who already possess such an attitude. Some are committed but unselfconscious Catholics (often lax in practice) who take life easily, enjoy ordinary domestic pleasures, and do not concern themselves much with what Binx Bolling calls "the old longings" (*Moviegoer* 9). Binx's Uncle Jules, for instance, is "the only man I know whose victory in the world is total and unqualified." He is "an exemplary Catholic, but it is hard to know why he takes the trouble. For the world he lives in, the City of Man, is so pleasant that the City of God must hold little in store for him" (*Moviegoer* 31). Binx's mother also falls into this category: her Catholic faith appears to her son as "a bargain struck at the very beginning in which she settled for a general belittlement of everything, the good and the bad" (*Moviegoer* 142)—but a bargain that has worked well for her. Such minor characters do present a potential problem that is related to the novels' lack of closure: if Percy's recommended alternative, Catholicism, is not explicitly shown carrying the day against both modern anomie and rival belief systems—for instance, the cheerful evangelical Christianity in the background of *The Second Coming* and *The Thanatos Syndrome*—then the indirection that Percy employs can lead all too plausibly to conclusions that he would not have endorsed, that turning to Catholicism is merely a matter of therapeutic and aesthetic self-fashioning.

However, such portraits of Catholics ensconced in serene domesticity and aware, whether they verbalize it or not, of the sacramental in daily life, are juxtaposed in Percy's fiction with a preoccupation with apocalypse. The modern world may be coming to an end, but for many of Percy's characters, who believe that meaning can be recovered only in the aftermath of a general destruction, this end cannot arrive soon enough. Percy seems to give a qualified endorsement to his characters' desires by selecting a passage from Romano Guardini's *The End of the Modern World* as the epigraph to *The Last Gentleman*: "The world to come will be filled with animosity and danger, but it will be a world open and clean" (105). Yet it is important not to overstate the violence implied by Percy's apocalpytic intimations, or

---

8. Letter to Brainard Cheney, quoted in Ann Waldron, *Close Connections: Caroline Gordon and the Southern Renaissance* (259).

to equate it simply with the annihilation of humanity. As Gary M. Ciuba puts it, "Composed of all the unquestioned assumptions about reality, the world is the accustomed manner of looking or, for the unseeing seers at the beginning of Percy's novels, the way of not looking. The end of the world is really the end of a worldview" (5). The expiring worldview is that of secular modernity, and Guardini suggests that as it goes, "the unbeliever will emerge from the fogs of secularism. He will cease to reap benefit from the values and forces developed by the very Revelation he denies" (124). Meanwhile, Christianity will not itself become new—that is, it will not respond to contemporary exigencies by replacing its scandalous dogmas with something more appealing—but it will stand out more sharply against a non-Christian, secular world. The "animosity and danger" that Guardini forecasts are a consequence of this contrast, but so is the possibility for a more undiluted witness to the truth—and perhaps also a greater opportunity for unbelievers to be persuaded of it.

Although Percy's protagonists yearn for the possibility of "seeing" in a new way, and thus are accurately described as "apocalyptists" in Ciuba's sense of the word (5), their quests for a redeemed world—what Binx simply calls "the idea of the search" (*Moviegoer* 13)—are marred by confusion and even, on occasion, bloodlust. Actual moments of transfiguration, in which the sacramental erupts into consciousness, are often literally as well as metaphorically violent—such as when Binx counts among his "best times" (10) the moments after being shot in the shoulder during the Korean war and being injured in a car accident; or when Will Barrett, in *The Last Gentleman*, recovers his sexual desire (and saves a child to boot) in the middle of a hurricane (23–24), or discovers a Velázquez painting "glowing like a jewel" (27) only after a skylight in the Modern Museum of Art collapses, injuring a worker. These merely personal instances of the therapeutic effects of violence become more generalized in Percy's later works: a character such as Lancelot Lamar looks forward to what he calls "the Third Revolution," and Percy himself, clearly influenced by Walter M. Miller Jr.'s novel *A Canticle for Leibowitz*, imagines as a thought experiment in *Lost in the Cosmos* the possible lives of survivors of a nuclear war in the deserts of Utah.

The complementarity of these two strategies for overcoming boredom—celebrating the sacramental nature of creation and looking forward to apocalypse—is to be found, as I have suggested, in the fact that the salvation of the world is both an accomplished fact ever since Christ's resurrection, immediately accessible to all who believe in it, and something whose consummation is yet to come. Dupuy's reflections on the autobiographical nature of narrative again seem relevant here—the organizing faculty of memory, which imposes meaning on the past in a way that illuminates the present, is analogous to the understanding of the Christian revelation implied here, and one way to grasp this might be to refer to Augustine's meditations on time and the redemptive nature of both its passing and its perception as a continuous, threefold present in the *Confessions*.[9] The committed Christian, in Percy's view, can "repeat" his experiences in such a way that their wonder and newness remain ever present to him; his being-in-the-world provides a certain inoculation against the despairs of boredom, even though he remains subject, until his own death, to possible fluctuations in his faith, and even though the very nature of the process opens a gap between the narrating and the narrated self that his language both testifies to and struggles to close. The unbeliever or lukewarm believer, on the other hand, might require violence, just as O'Connor predicted—but even these violences will be familiar to us, not necessarily fatal or humiliating, and presented in a spirit of fellow suffering, rather than in the garish, otherworldly light that characterizes O'Connor's violence. Percy's own freely acknowledged reworking of his own experiences in fiction, as well as biographical evidence of his own fluctuations in faith, demonstrates that he does not exempt himself from the struggles of his characters.

If, then, readers find themselves identifying the predicaments of Percy's characters with their own, it would seem that there are two characteristic ways in which Percy's strategies might misfire. First, readers might reduce the sacramental in Percy to the aesthetic, so that its efficacy becomes primarily a function of their form instead of their content. Sacramental intimations could then appear as examples of Hungerford's "postmodern belief." Conversely, readers might take the intimations of apocalyptic violence too literally, concluding that one need not just endure the "end of the modern world" but work to bring it about. Though Percy clearly attempts to balance the two impulses against each other and to forestall the effects that either one might bring about if left unchallenged, in his later work there is a definite shift in emphasis away from the sacramental pleasures of dailiness and toward the urgencies of apocalyptic violence embraced selfishly—as Ciuba puts it, toward the danger that characters will not read their lives in

---

9. Book 11 of the *Confessions* explains the threefold present by noting that whether one reflects on the past, the present, or the future, one does so only in the present: "[W]hatever they [future and past things] are, and wherever there, they must be there in the present" (270). Paul Ricoeur's masterly commentary on Book 11 in *Time and Narrative*, Volume 1, suggests what is at stake for theories of autobiography more generally: "Augustine's inestimable discovery is, by reducing the extension of time to the distention of the soul, to have tied this distention to the slippage that never ceases to find its way into the heart of the threefold present—between the present of the future, the present of the past, and the present of the present. In this way he sees discordance emerge again and again out of the very concordance of the intentions of expectation, attention, and memory" (21).

light of the Book of Revelation, but rather that they will rewrite "Revelation so that it becomes the way the world looks after all but the ego has disappeared" (171).

In an earlier book, *Fears and Fascinations: Representing Catholicism in the American South*, I argued that in *The Moviegoer, The Last Gentleman*, and to a certain degree *Love in the Ruins*, Percy's portraits of domesticity prove so attractive that some readers (and, indeed, some writers who followed Percy) might be tempted to reduce Catholicism to a Lyotardian micronarrative, a set of strategies for living pleasantly in a world perceived to be evacuated of metanarrative gravity (147–68). Beginning with *Love in the Ruins*, however, Percy's work begins perceptibly to shift toward an emphasis on the apocalyptic, rendered in increasingly violent terms. Whereas Binx Bolling and Will Barrett were focused primarily on their own personal struggles with despair, Dr. Thomas More, though struggling with alcoholism himself, is concerned primarily with the civil strife that has engulfed the United States, and though he believes (wrongly, as it turns out) that his therapeutic invention, the lapsometer, has the potential to "save" America, he also simultaneously fears and hopes that the events its distribution has set in motion will create a literal explosion—"the end of the world" (3). In this chapter I will argue that particularly in *Lancelot, The Second Coming*, the "Space Odyssey" section of *Lost in the Cosmos*, and *The Thanatos Syndrome*, Percy runs the risk not of making Catholicism seem too cozy and domestic, but rather either of celebrating violence or of making readers turn away in the belief that his work celebrates violence.

II. Yearning for the End in *Lancelot*

The new departure in Percy's work marked by *Lancelot* (1977) can be seen in the way its protagonist describes his project: "a quest for evil" (138). Whereas Percy's earlier protagonists, either drifting aimlessly in their "sickness unto death" or, like Dr. More, consumed with visions of total transformation, still hope that redemption will be on the side of the good, Lancelot Andrewes Lamar, whose own despair has been interrupted by the accidental discovery of his wife's infidelity, is galvanized into his mock-Arthurian quest because he wonders whether the recovery of evil must precede the recovery of God. In the long monologue that he narrates to his old friend Percival from the "Center for Aberrant Behavior" (3), Lance locates the origins of his quest in his intimation that his wife's infidelity is uniquely intolerable: "Is the sexual offense a special category and therefore unlike other offenses, theft, assault, even murder?" (15). He seems, in fact, surprised by the vehemence of his response to the discovery:

But let me ask you seriously: Why is it such an unspeakable thing for one creature to obtrude a small portion of its body into the body of another creature? Is it not in fact a trivial matter when one puts it that way? I don't think women attach too much importance to it.

But suppose I put it another way. Isn't it unspeakable to me to imagine Margot lying under another man, her head turning to and fro in a way I knew only too well, her lips stretched, a little mew-cry escaping her lips? Isn't that unspeakable? Yes. But why? When I imagined other things happening to Margot, even the worst things, they were painful but not intolerable: Margot seriously ill, Margot hurt in an accident, Margot stealing money, even Margot dead, murdered. The thought of Margot dead was painful but not intolerable. But Margot under another man. . . . (16)

Lance contrasts his own violent response, rooted in his conviction of sex as a supreme good, with the casual ubiquity and consequent devaluing of sex that he sees in the contemporary world. While he had enjoyed "dirty books" and frequented whores as a young student, it was still possible for him to view these experiences as portentous revelations: "Sometimes I think we were the victims of a gigantic hoax by our elders, that there was an elaborate conspiracy to conceal from us the one simple fact that the only important, certainly the best thing in life, is ordinary sexual love" (12). Yet the younger generation, coming of age in a time of triumphant license, seems to have demystified sex entirely. Even from the window of his cell, Lance can see that "the old Majestic Theater" has become "Adult Cinema 16" and is showing a film called *"The 69ers"* (22)—a publicly advertised consumer diversion, different in kind from the private discoveries of erotic literature. And Lance's son, "who got enough of women before he was twenty" and now "appears to be a mild homosexual," is representative of his generation, for whom "[s]ex doesn't even seem to rate among the Top Ten experiences" (17).

Lance's attitude here reflects Percy's belief that sexual activity remains for many a vehicle for escaping temporal consciousness in a world of "leftover selves." Yet even it is endangered by a mindset that makes it not a sacramental experience, but merely the instrumental act of a mind achieving its own mastery and satisfaction through its own and others' bodies. Lance's intimation that sexual transcendence can be recovered only by associating it with sin harks back to Binx's reflections on his own unsatisfactory fornication with Kate: "Christians talk about the horror of sin, but they have overlooked something . . . [T]he truth is that nowadays one is hardly up to it. There is very little sin in the depths of the malaise. The highest moment of a malaisian's life can be that moment when he manages to sin like a proper human" (*Moviegoer* 200). The distance between 1961 and

1977 can be measured by the fact that Binx's sense of fornication as "sin" still has some cultural resonance, as his genial narration presupposes, while Lance's yearning for sin has become all but incomprehensible in a time when "courses in how to fuck for schoolchildren" (220) have reduced the act to a matter of mental hygiene.

Once Lance associates sexuality with a lost sense of sin, he generalizes this loss to his entire historical moment:

> But suppose you could show me one "sin," one pure act of malevo-lence . . . But we have plenty of evil around you say. What about Hitler, the gas ovens and so forth? What about them? As everyone knows and says, Hitler was a madman. And it seems nobody was responsible. Everyone was following orders. It is even possible that there was no such order, that it was all a bureaucratic mistake.
>
> Show me a single "sin."
>
> One hundred and twenty thousand dead at Hiroshima? Where was the evil of that? Was Harry Truman evil? As for the pilot and bombardier, they were by all accounts wonderful fellows, good fathers and family men.
>
> "Evil" is surely the clue to this age, the only quest appropriate to the age. For everything and everyone's either wonderful or sick and nothing is evil. (138)

Lance's very presence in the Center for Aberrant Behavior seems to con-firm his view, for having premeditatedly murdered Margot's lover and blown up Belle Reve, his plantation home—certainly sinful actions accord-ing to any standard—his efforts to retrieve the murder weapon are inter-preted as evidence of mental illness. He is not even "sick," a condition still redolent of irreducibly human and animal consciousness, but "aberrant," a mechanism with a surely explicable and correctable glitch. Moreover, Lance regards his quest as a failure. The very act of cutting Jacoby's throat results not in a consciousness of evil but rather of a fascinated, amoral materialism that echoes his earlier description of sexual intercourse: "steel molecules entering skin molecules, artery molecules, blood cells" (254). For all the vehemence of his ranting and the optimism that it falsely suggests, Lance's depression has returned, and his emotional range has become still more restricted: "I feel so cold, Percival" (253).

It is to Lance's credit that even having achieved a kind of revelation of nothingness rather than of sin, he continues to declare both the depraved world around him and the nothingness that might protect one against it intolerable: "If God does not exist, then it will be I not God who will not tolerate [the world as it is]" (255). An essentially pagan stoicism, obviously indebted to Percy's Uncle Will and given specificity by the southern ideology of honor and chivalry, becomes Lance's own desired code after the apocalypse that he has experienced.[10] In the Wilderness of Virginia, the deserted place where Robert E. Lee "lost," Lance proposes to begin again with like-minded people, to promulgate "a tight-lipped courtesy between men. And chivalry toward women" (158). Such a social order will be founded upon a conscious rejection of truth, for rather than admitting the "truth" of nothingness, it will violently enforce codes of belief and conduct in a manner that suggests fascism.[11] Here, too, Lance's obsession with sexuality as the index of human meaning recurs, even though he no longer claims to endow it with transcendence. If "love," for example, is nothing more than a euphemism for unredeemed carnality, which in turn is nothing more than a collision of molecules, then chivalry and romantic love must be enforced to deny this "truth," which Lance calls "THE GREAT SECRET OF LIFE": "[M]an's happiness lies for men in men practicing violence upon women and . . . woman's happiness lies in submitting to it. The secret of life is violence and rape, and its gospel is pornography" (224). As Lance explains it elsewhere in the text, "[w]omen must be saved from the whoredom they've chosen" (158), but the very word "chosen" reveals an ambiguity: if this "whoredom" is only the natural pursuit of women's happiness, then the code that opposes it must constitute a fierce revolt against matter itself. Yet Lance also hopes that women, perceiving this truth, will join him in rejecting it: "Someday women will admit the truth, will refuse to accept it, and then they will be my best recruits" (252).

Is such a vision merely insane? Ciuba argues that Lancelot's's "merciless cult of good form lacks the splendor of apocalyptic renewal. Its martial values are paltry, middling, even minimal" (185) when compared with the new heavens and new earth described in the Book of Revelation. Yet while a confirmed Christian would assent to Ciuba's judgment, Percy's rhetorical gamble in *Lancelot* probably succeeds only if readers are initially willing to consider the possibility that for all its violence and possible insanity,

---

10. Percy's extended engagement with William Alexander Percy's code of southern stoicism begins with his first important essay, "Stoicism in the South" (1958), and extends through several novels in which particular characters serve as surrogates for Uncle Will or voice his beliefs—most obviously in the case of Binx's Aunt Emily. O'Gorman is correct to note that "[i]n a very real sense, Walker spent the rest of his life reacting to Uncle Will" (35). On the parallels between the elder Percy and Aunt Emily, see Tolson (277, 287).

11. Percy confirms such hints in an interview with Elzbieta Olesky: "So, his solution for his alienation is a kind of fascism, or nazism [sic]. In a way, he admires the nazi ; only he says: 'The nazis were stupid'" (qtd. in Olesky 79). (The exact quotation from *Lancelot* is "Don't confuse it with the Nazis. They were stupid. If in fact there was a need to clean up the Weimar Republic and if in fact they did that in part, they screwed everything up by getting off on the Jews. What stupidity! The Jews were not to blame" [156]).

Lance's vision stands as a compelling alternative to the disenchanted United States of the late 1970s, in which Lance appears merely "aberrant," since a genuinely transcendent alternative is not perceived to be widely available. Jerome C. Christensen describes such readers' dilemma well:

> I can, if I choose . . . reasonably explain away Lancelot's rant by psycho-analyzing him, reducing his unsettling vision of America, of man and woman, to the wholly understandable consequence of childhood trauma. From that perspective all that stuff about the end of the world is merely more of the same. Repetition is the limit of action and knowledge. But the monstrous excellence of this book is that though Percy generously supplies the material and tools for such a reduction, he cannily prohibits any comfort in its execution. If I, rationalist, substitute a bright, tidy psychoanalytic explanation for Lancelot's eccentric narrative, I merely repeat his obsessive quest for the determinate and thereby commit myself to a monologue mad like his but chilling and sterile. Every man has a Ma, but only Lancelot tells his disturbing story.
>
> Repetition is the possibility of action and knowledge. That possibility is realized in the book through the development of the figure who listens to Lancelot's story. (117)

The distinction between repetition as "limit of action and knowledge" and repetition as "possibility of action and knowledge" that Christensen identifies here is key. To read the Lance's monologue as the unfruitful repetition of his murderous rage, and his planned "Third Revolution" as a repetition of violent reactionaries from the Ku Klux Klan to the Nazis, is also to commit oneself to unfruitful repetition: everything can be reduced to the eternal Oedipal triangle, and one can become less "sick" by becoming conscious of it, but there will be no breakthrough, no repetition with a difference that will lead to free action. The ultimate horizon, just as Brooks suggests, is death, but the knowledge said to come with the consummation of death can have nothing in it of love, nothing of the reciprocity and commitment that would render sexuality anything more than a struggle to use the other for pleasure, or contemporary life more than a series of diversions to keep despair at bay. Lance's characterization of the "whoredom" of women may indeed be antifeminist, but one wonders uncomfortably whether an alternative description of promiscuity, in which men and women freely choose their sexual objects and exert control over their own sexual desires, escapes an instrumentalist and dehumanizing conception of sexuality any more successfully.

Unsurprisingly, Percy's preferred alternative both to 1970s America and to Lance's stoicism-*cum*-fascism is Catholicism, the "action and knowledge" of which are only intimated by Lance's interlocutor, Percival, also known as Father John. Listening to Lance's narrative, Percival rarely speaks, and when he does, the words are either repeated or paraphrased by Lance, so that until the final pages of the novel, Percival lacks a voice. Moreover, Lance infers from Percival's "phony casuals" (instead of "priest clothes") (5) and refusal to say a prayer for the dead that a woman requests from him on All Souls' Day (11) that his friend is suffering a crisis of faith. Lance concludes—and "manage[s] to surprise" Percival by saying so—that Percival is "a screwed-up priest or a half-assed physician. Or both" (10). Percival, then, is no less a victim of the contemporary malaise than Lance, though his malaise partakes more of depression than murderous rage. Evidently intending both to minister to Lance and to oppose his arguments, Percival can do so for much of the novel only by repeating the word "love," a possibility that Lance refuses to entertain: "That sort of love is impossible now if it ever was. The only way it will ever be possible again is if the world should end" (56). For Lance, Percival joins the ridiculous nuns "in J.C. Penney pantsuits" (5) as representatives of a post–Vatican II Church that has been infested by "the same fleas as the dogs [it has] lain down with" (157). Even so, Lance opines, Catholicism remains the only other option thinkable: "I could live your way if it were true" (155). At the end of the novel, Lance states, "There is no other way than yours or mine, true?" and Percival responds with a simple "*Yes*" (257).

Given the disadvantages under which Percival labors, any reading of the novel that discovers in it a clear affirmation of Christian belief must place enormous weight on the final exchange: Lancelot asks, "Is there anything you wish to tell me before I leave?" and Percival answers, "*Yes*" (257). The implication is that now Percival will do the talking, Lance will listen, and the fullness of Catholic faith—which Lance has already recognized as the only worthy alternative—will be affirmed in an unwritten sequel. This is, perhaps, Percy's boldest rhetorical gamble yet, for as Reynolds Price asks, "[H]ow many contemporary readers of fiction are equipped or even prone to provide a sufficient counter statement?" (qtd. in Tolson 412). In order for the strategy to work, readers must come to identify not only with Lance but also—and in the end, even more—with Percival, who finally recovers his faith, appears before Lance in priestly garb, and announces that he is off to take charge of a suburban parish in Alabama. If Percy's persuasion depends in part on convincing readers that Lance's Third Revolution is indeed preferable to the social decay and anomie that hold sway, the final step consists of making Percival's Catholic alternative—dismissed by Lance as "more of the same" because it consists of "forgiv[ing] the sins of Buick dealers [and] administer[ing] communion to suburban housewives" (257, 256)—more attractive still.

Percy prepares the way for this possibility in part by exploiting the difference between what James Phelan calls in *Living to Tell About It*, his close study of character narration, "narrator functions" and "disclosure functions" (12). According to Phelan, narrator functions comprise the straightforward telling of material from a narrator to a narratee; disclosure functions, by contrast, are signaled by the redundant telling of material that the narratee already knows but the authorial audience does not. Because Percival is a childhood friend whom Lance addresses as "you" throughout the novel, Percy must construct a plausible rationale for Lance's own redundant telling of material that Percival knows—for instance, that Lance and Percival were classmates at Tulane, or that Percival was a solitary, skinny drinker who converted to Catholicism before becoming a priest. Percy initially suggests a plausible rationale by having Lance plead amnesia, a condition not surprising in an inmate in a psychiatric hospital: "Don't I know you? . . . I've been feeling rather depressed and I don't remember things well" (3). Since the pronoun *you* implicitly places both Percival and the reader in the same position, the awkwardness of having Lance narrate information that Percival knows, readers are led to believe, will be mitigated. Interestingly enough, however, Lance quickly confesses this to have been a ruse *before* the disclosure function begins: "I was not quite honest yesterday when I pretended not to know you. I knew you perfectly well . . . [i]t's just that it was quite a shock seeing you after all these years. No; not even that is true. I noticed you in the cemetery the day before yesterday. Still I hardly knew what to say to you. What do you say to someone after twenty years when you have already said everything?" (9). If the initial explanation of amnesia provided a reason why Lance would have to reconstruct so much of the past not to a therapist but to an old friend, Lance's changed rationale actually builds upon the former one to establish a greater sense of intimacy. Not only does Lance now convince Percival that he is now telling the truth (that is, he does remember him), he also suggests that the very intimacy of their friendship can serve as a pretext for going over mutually known events. "Everything" may have been said, but for precisely that reason, a certain repetition is necessary to discover whatever insights might be new and valuable. The disclosure functions which then follow not only contribute necessary information to the reader's interpretation of Lance and Percival; they also pave the way for the narrator function that predominates afterward, in which the particulars of Lance's story are new both to Percival and to the reader. Ironically, an initial lie framed by the context of mental illness helps to cement a more secure trust, to suggest that whatever Lance's problems may be, insanity, properly speaking, is not one of them. To hold that he belongs in the Center for Aberrant Behavior, instead of in prison, is the real lie.

Yet for all the care with which Percy develops such narrative strategies, readers must still draw their own conclusions at the end—will they concur with Percival's repeated "yeses," acknowledging his truer, more viable Christian alternative to Lance's violent stoicism? Readers might detect an echo of Molly Bloom's "yes yes yes yes yes" in Percival's words and perceive through the allusion Percy's affirmative intent, though the fact that these words are interspersed with Lance's own jaded dialogue limits the likelihood of such an identification. As I argued above, the novel's lack of definite closure here does affirm both Lance's freedom and the fact that until his own death, all he can do is remain faithful to his choice, whatever it may be. The same is true for readers of the novel. Ultimately, Percy makes a wager similar to O'Connor's in "A Good Man Is Hard to Find." O'Connor opined, "I prefer to think that, however unlikely this may seem, the old lady's gesture, like the mustard-seed, will grow to be a great crow-filled tree in the [sic] Misfit's heart, and will be enough of a pain to him there to turn him into the prophet he was meant to become. But that's another story" ("On Her Own Work" 112–13). The very implausibility of such a choice, the very fact that it is not determined by what has come before, might serve to show that it is the freest choice of all. If Lance, no matter how his life with Anna in the Shenandoah Valley may unfold, will have been affected enough by Percival's proclamation of love to live henceforth as a believer, then perhaps this is his truest achievement. But that, too, is another story, and by no means a certain one.

III. Believing the Apostle:
The Second Coming

Biographical evidence suggests that at least some of the uncharacteristic ferocity of *Lancelot* can be attributed to a crisis of faith that Percy experienced during the novel's composition. That this crisis was resolved successfully seems to be confirmed by *The Second Coming*, the most overtly didactic of all of Percy's novels and the one that departs the most from his usual practices of indirection and suspended closure.[12] Picking up the story of

---

12. On this crisis of faith, see Tolson (380–82, 387–88). On its recovery, see especially

Will Barrett many years after the events described in *The Last Gentleman*, *The Second Coming* reveals that he has married a Yankee Episcopalian woman, grown middle-aged and affluent, and survived his wife's death. He finds himself once again experiencing fugues, intense memories of his father, bemusement at the craziness of the contemporary South, and what his psychiatrist calls *"wahnsinnige Sehnsucht,"* or inappropriate longing (303). Alternatives familiar from Percy's previous novels are predictably presented to him: the stoic code of honor that secretly loves death and moves through an inexorable logic to suicide; the transient pleasures of sensory delight; and the inadequacy of most of what passes for religious belief in 1980, whether the vague Episcopalianism the novel satirizes, the practice of astrology or pantheism (lumped together under the rubric "Californian"), or the aggressively cheerful (and powerful) fundamentalist Christianity that flourishes in the South. Desiring apocalypse on his own terms, Will tries to escape his predicament by concealing himself in a cave until God either declares His existence or refuses to appear. (The gesture repeats Lance's resolution in *Lancelot*—instead of implementing his "Third Revolution" at once, he declares, "I'll wait and give your God time" [256]). Such bravado, however, fails: driven by toothache and malnutrition out of the cave, he falls into the arms of Allie, the daughter of his old girlfriend Kitty, who has escaped from a psychiatric hospital and is hiding out in the greenhouse she owns. The two fall in love, resolve to marry, and presumably live happily ever after.

Still more happily, Will ends the novel on the brink of a definite conversion experience—the book's most significant departure from *The Last Gentleman*, and indeed from all of Percy's previous novels. Tolson's appraisal of the novel as a "philosophical fairy tale" in which Percy could indulge his impossible desire for perfection (432) is convincing: the resolution of the contradictions that had plagued Will in the earlier novel is so sudden and unexpected as to suggest an O'Connoresque descent of grace. At one point in the novel, Will begins a long litany that begins "Here are the names of death, which shall not prevail over me because I know the names" (272), then enumerates these "names" over the space of two and a half pages, whooping with joy throughout. His final words in the novel, as he ponders the prospect of married life, are "Am I crazy to want both, her and Him? No, not want, must have. And will have" (360). These moments flaunt their narrative implausibility, but—as is not the case in O'Connor's work or in *Lancelot*—there is no mystery as to how readers should interpret their effect

---

Quinlan (162), who speculates that Karol Wojytla's accession to the papacy in 1978 may have particularly cheered Percy.

on the character, no implicit invitation to make a similar leap. This is the kind of closure that comes only with death, and if readers, like Will, "prevail" over "the names of death," they do so simply by finishing the book.

Two features of the novel, however, pull against this overwhelming sense of closure. The first is that Will converts not to Catholicism but to Episcopalianism. Even in 1980, the Anglican Church was hardly known for its doctrinal uniformity, and in subsequent decades, disputes between traditionalists and progressives have grown bitterer—a situation hardly calculated to win Percy's approval. In Percy's other novels, Episcopalianism figures largely as the preferred religion of backward-looking, stoic southern gentlefolk precisely because of its rich aesthetic tradition, doctrinal fuzziness, and snobbery—Tom More's wife, Ellen, for instance, has become in *The Thanatos Syndrome* "one of those Southern Anglicans who dislike Catholics—Romans, she calls them—and love all things English" (46). For men, Episcopalianism is also bound up with romantic, martial fantasies. Lance Lamar, for instance, is nominally Episcopalian and named for the Anglican divine Lancelot Andrewes (who would have a considerable influence on T. S. Eliot), but he explains that "the Andrewes was tacked on by him to give it Episcopal sanction"—his father really cared more for "Romantic English poetry, Southern history, Robert E. Lee biographies" and other books in which one "could detect no common denominator except a taste for the extraordinary and marvelous, the sentimental, the extraordinary experience . . . the extraordinary glory of a lost cause which becomes more extraordinary as it recedes in time and in fact Robert E. Lee and the Army of Northern Virginia had long since become for him as legendary and mythical as King Arthur and the Round Table. Do you think I was named Lancelot for nothing?" (116). Such an attitude stands in contrast to the sacramental embrace of the mundane here and now that Percy celebrates.

Yet there are two Episcopal characters in the novel who complicate this picture. The first, Jack Curl, is an Anglican priest who pursues Will throughout the novel for donations to a planned retirement community. He is made "uneasy" by talk about religion (138) and can speak of it only if he casts himself as a manual laborer, a "sweaty Episcopal handyman" and "godly greasy super" (125) who wears hideous jumpsuits. In one sense, his approach seems no different from that of such Catholic characters as Binx's mother and Uncle Jules; his is a pragmatic, world-invested Christianity. Unlike these characters, however, Jack Curl is tainted by his blatant pursuit of Will's money and fondness for soothing the troubles of the rich and powerful. For these reasons, as much as for the priest's lack of earnestness about God, Will dismisses him: "Seldom can an Episcopalian (or an Anglican) be taken for a Christian" (189). Yet Will also retains enough respect for

Curl's office to ask himself, when he hears that Curl has been picked to lead an ecumenical meeting, "Could Jack Curl reunite Christendom? . . . Why not? Isn't it just the sort of damn fool thing God might favor?" (309).

The elderly Episcopal priest to whom Will addresses himself at the end, Father Weatherbee, is more admirable. Demanding that Father Weatherbee marry him and Allie despite the fact that neither is yet a Christian believer, Will states, in an interestingly hedged declaration, that he and Allie are "willing to take instructions, as long as you recognize that I cannot and will not accept all of your dogmas. Unless of course you have the authority to tell me something I don't know. Do you?" (358). Will's words here hark back to the 1975 essay "The Message in the Bottle," in which Percy develops Kierkegaard's distinction between a "genius" and an "apostle" and offers these criteria for determining whether an apostle's authority is genuine:

> Faith comes from God, but it also comes by hearing. It is a piece of news and there is a newsbearer. But why should we believe the newsbearer, the apostle? Must the apostle first prove his case to the scientist in the seminar room? No, because this would mean that God and the apostle must wait in the porter's lodge while the learned upstairs settle the matter. . . .
>
> How then may we recognize the divine authority of the apostle? What, in other words, are the credentials of the newsbearer? The credential of the apostle is simply the gravity of his message: "I am called by God; do with me what you will, scourge me, persecute me, but my last words are first; I am called by God and I make you eternally responsible for what you do against me." . . . [W]hat if a man receives the commission to bring news across the seas to the castaway and does so in perfect sobriety and with good faith and perseverance to the point of martyrdom? And what if the news the newsbearer bears is the very news the castaway has been waiting for, news of where he came from and who he is and what he must do, and what if the newsbearer brought with him the means by which the castaway may do what he must do? Well then, the castaway will, by the grace of God, believe him. (146, 147, 149)

Percy makes the intended parallel between this passage and his preferred Episcopal priest Father Weatherbee all too clear, for not only does Father Weatherbee have a professed interest in the Apostolic Succession—a doctrine which aligns him with the Anglo-Catholic wing of Anglicanism (and which Curl rejects as something that "sounds more like the ancestor worship of his Mindanao tribesmen" [311])—but he also has spent fifty years as a missionary in the Philippines, where he found a happy simplicity of faith among his congregation that Americans lack: "They believed the Gospel whole and entire, and the teachings of the church. They said that if I told them, then it must be true or I would not have gone to so much trouble" (359). These words confirm what Will had already suspected, that Father Weatherbee "seem[s] to know something—and that by the same token Jack Curl does not" (358). Father Weatherbee's apostolic authority is genuine, and, it would seem, sufficient to convert Will, despite Father Weatherbee's own bewilderment and his belief that Will is a "madman" (357). Clearly Jack Curl's ambition of "reuniting Christendom," however worthy a goal, takes a back seat to the more fundamental effort of bringing the good news to people, one by one.

The question remains: even granting the very Catholic kind of Anglicanism that Father Weatherbee professes, why Anglicanism at all? Kieran Quinlan, professing uncertainty here, suggests several possibilities: perhaps "it was just too cumbersome for Percy to have Will jump through all the hoops in one novel"; perhaps "Percy deemed that the most theologically obtuse of all his protagonists was unworthy to become a member of the church of the great St. Thomas Aquinas"; or perhaps in the novel, as in *Lancelot*, "the Catholic faith is most present by its relative absence: the radical inadequacies of *all* alternatives reinforce its supreme necessity" (173). I am inclined to agree most with the third possibility, not only because such a stance is consistent with Percy's statements elsewhere but also because it provides an obstacle to complete closure in the novel.[13] Will may be about to convert, but he will not have arrived at what Percy perceives of as the fullness of Christian truth, which can be found only in the Catholic Church. Moreover, readers unaware of Percy's Catholicism may well perceive a different message altogether—as did Richard Gilman, who, reviewing the novel in the *New Republic,* identified its "religious sense" but considered it to be "without creed or dogma" (31). Indeed, as Quinlan observes, *The Second Coming* "seems to have had an especial appeal for those sympathetic with a New Age style of Christian gnosticism [*sic*], an outcome that hardly would have pleased its by now ultraorthodox author" (172). *The Second Coming* may well be Percy's most orthodox novel, if its sense of urgency and its presentation of a genuine conversion are the measures of orthodoxy, and I share the sense of many readers that it is also

---

13. In *Lost in the Cosmos,* Percy asserts that "Catholic Christianity" is the "most preposterous" religion in the triad of Judaism, Protestantism, and Catholicism because of the counterintuitive nature of its claims, but he also holds that "in the end it is precisely this preposterous remedy, it and no other, which is specified by the preposterous predicament of the human self as its sole remedy" (253, 254). As preposterous as Will's conversion is, it may not be preposterous enough.

his most tendentious. Even here, however, there is just enough of a gap to make its intended good news genuinely contestable, to emphasize the genuine freedom of its readers and the genuine leap that belief requires.

IV. Living after the End:
"A Space Odyssey"

With *Lost in the Cosmos*—a parody of the self-help book genre, an introduction to semiotic theory, and a compendium of "thought experiments," several of which are recycled from his previous works, Percy provides the most concise and in many respects most entertaining summation of his thought. From the standpoint of an inquiry into the use of narrative as rhetoric, its most interesting feature is "A Space Odyssey," two variations on a short fictional narrative that play out the logic of apocalypse that characterized earlier works by Percy to its limit. Whereas Percy's protagonists often longed for an apocalypse that either did not come or arrived with a whimper, here the theoretician proposes the real thing—a nuclear holocaust that leaves only a few survivors and their descendants on the earth—as a test of whether Percy's theories of the self, language, and redemption would still operate in the most extreme conditions imaginable. Predictably, the theories are verified—not even a literal end of the world, as opposed to a metaphorical one, can transfigure recalcitrant human nature.

In the first part of "A Space Odyssey," a group of astronauts on a mission to discover intelligent extraterrestrial life in the universe mysteriously loses contact with Earth and begins to fear that a nuclear war has destroyed human civilization. Discovering evidence of extraterrestrial intelligence on a planet orbiting Proxima Centauri, the astronauts attempt to land but are prohibited from doing so, because the planet's inhabitants determine, after a lengthy conversation with the astronauts' captain, that human beings are afflicted with self-consciousness and will probably bring nothing but violence and sexual disorder to their planet.

In the second variation on the narrative—which borrows its setting, premises, and even the name of its central character from Walter J. Miller, Jr.'s science fiction novel *A Canticle for Leibowitz*—a similar group of astronauts who lose contact with Earth return to discover that nuclear holocaust has occurred in their absence. Landing in the desert of Utah, they discover an unlikely group of survivors: Abbot Liebowitz [*sic*], a Brooklyn Jew who has converted to Catholicism, presides over a Benedictine abbey, and suspects himself, in the absence of contradictory evidence, to be the Pope; the two African American monks who with him comprise the abbey; a young

Californian astronomer named Aristarchus Jones who wears special clothing to protect him from ultraviolet light; and a group of children suffering from deformities and disabilities as the result of radiation.

Percy's habitual presentation of privileged southern males who can skillfully read the social distinctions implied by clothing and mannerisms becomes amusingly obsolete in this narrative, for race, disability, Judaism, and southernness have ceased to mean much at all: a Jew might be the Pope, and the resemblance of Jones's protective garb to the robe of a Ku Klux Klansman (243) reveals not the persistence of racism but the fact that even the most entrenched images associated with racism now signify differently. The only stereotype that seems to survive concerns the extraordinary intelligence of Jews: Abbot Liebowitz hopes to "revive the University of Notre Dame around a nucleus of Jewish scientists whom [he] shall lure from Israel" (249). Indeed, the disappearance of all other social distinctions seems dependent upon the survival of Jews and Catholics, the particular people called by God and the universal church that descends from them. As Liebowitz puts is, "the two, Jew and Catholic, are inextricably attached to each other like Siamese twins at the umbilicus, whether they like it or not, and they both detest it, until the end of earth time" (249). In the irradiated deserts of the West, what matters is that the apostolic succession goes on, that the Church keeps its promise to endure, while the fact that a Jew leads it also points to God's continued covenant with his chosen people.

Percy offers two "options" for readers to choose regarding the future of this fledgling society. The first option, proposed by the astronomer, involves the survivors removing to the Jovian satellite Europa, breaking completely with the past, and initiating a kind of behaviorist utopia to be named New Ionia and grounded in a combination of Skinner-style conditioning and Jungian theory. He invites the monks, though he also envisions "a sexually free and peace-loving society where the sciences and arts can flourish freed from the superstitions and repressions of religion" (246), and he refuses to invite the malformed children, because "[i]t would make no sense to perpetuate genetic defects" (247). Such a plan is not so different from the arrangements that prevailed among the astronauts on their spaceship, in which an equal number of men and women were enjoined to practice free love and bear children outside the context of a nuclear family. The first variation on "A Space Odyssey," however, suggests that such an arrangement cannot last: three of the original men were killed in "quarrels over the women" (214), and one of the women, though she was deemed "culturally liberated" by "the screening procedure," now wants to revert "to the old monogamy" and marry (216). Clearly, the implication is that marriage is preferable to sexual anarchy—and, as if realizing that in its absence other measures must be taken to prevent such disorder, Aristarchus resolves to codify his teachings in a "Little Green Book" and to demand group exercises of "self-criticism and honest appraisal of others. . . . No more lies, no more self-deception, no more secrecy, no more guilt, no more shame" (257). Needless to say, such a regime must prescribe "punishment, even exile, for aggressive, jealous, hostile, solitary, mystical, or other antisocial behavior" (256)—with the result that those who are dissatisfied learn to keep their unhappiness to themselves.

In the second "option," the survivors eventually move to Lost Cove, Tennessee, begin to multiply and to attract immigrants, and soon reestablish some markers of southern identity. Denominational divisions reappear among the Christian members of the group, as do racism, anti-Semitism, anti-Catholicism, agrarian ideals, and homemade whiskey. The five Jews in the colony—"one orthodox, one reformed, one conservative, one humanist, and one Yemenite Israeli" (259)—are too fractious to establish a temple. Even one of the two African American monks has "discovered his roots in nearby Alabama, resigned his priesthood, and joined the Shiloh Baptist Church" (259). When contact is made with a "Celtic enclave across the old Carolina line, a growing community with a reputation for violence and snake-handling" (260), the old, long-suppressed social hostilities erupt into plain view, as the Celts propose an alliance of white Americans and Christians against the African Americans, Catholics, and Jews. In the words of the Marcus Aurelius Schuyler, captain of the spaceship and Percy's inevitable spokesperson for old-fashioned southern stoicism, "Jesus Christ, here we go again" (261).

The juxtaposition of these two options reprises the alternative that Percy presents at the end of *Lancelot:* only Catholicism and some form of fascism (an unusually "light" version in this case, with its emphasis on behaviorism and self-interrogation) are viable solutions to the predicament of the self in modernity, and of the two, only Catholicism has the benefit of being true as well as more tolerant—a colony that was created under Catholic auspices welcomes Jews and unbelievers, and exiles nobody. Neither option, however, obviates the need for the self to go on living, to confront everyday problems even as it embraces everyday grace. Human beings may be already redeemed, but not even a nuclear holocaust can obliterate their tendency toward sin and disorder. Even committed Catholics, such as Percy's African American monk, sometimes fall away; even committed agnostics might, even if they do not come to accept Christian belief itself, might come to admit how necessary it is. Percy's choice of Marcus Schuyler—a man "like a Christian who had lost his faith in everything but the Fall of man" (229)—as his central focalizer both in the New Ionian and the Tennessean options, in fact, suggests that an unbeliever might be more cognizant of the radical nature of Christian teaching than many professed Christians.

Marcus's habitual boredom in New Ionia, where nothing except sex, Shakespeare's *Henry IV* plays, and Mozart's string quartets move him, is contrasted with his genial, if no less ironic, disposition in Lost Cove. As Peter Augustine Lawler puts it, "He knows why he has affection for the priests and their Church. He knows, as he did not before, the limits of his independence. His freedom depends on the cave; his skepticism depends upon belief, and his pleasurable experiences of the goodness of life depend upon his love for others. He knows he is more alike than different from other human beings. He lives well with all sorts of misbegotten selves, because he knows that he himself is far from free from trouble or disorder" (103–4). In this conviction of the basic shared experience of flawed human beings, there is even a basis for democracy, in contrast to the false egalitarianism that fascism violently creates—and a basis for love and desire, which in turn nourish science and art. In New Ionia, there is nothing to strive for and nothing to love. In Lost Cove, love exists—and one must accept the existence of hatred, too, as its corollary—"Wherever there is love of particular troubled selves for others, there is hatred too"—but this makes for a view of the human condition as "more comic and genuinely mysterious" (103), not for despair. Percy's two post-apocalyptic visions of the future in *Lost in the Cosmos* manage to escape, more clearly the texts that precede them, the temptations of losing the self in violence and building a new, but inhuman and loveless, order.

V. Fascinations with a Culture of Death:
The Thanatos Syndrome

After the unprecedented novelistic closure of *The Second Coming* and the attempt to follow apocalyptic thinking to its limit in "A Space Odyssey," Percy's final novel, *The Thanatos Syndrome,* has struck some readers as a belaboring of material that Percy had brought to more successful fruition elsewhere. Kieran Quinlan, for instance, calls it "repetitious of his earlier themes" and full of "careless errors," and speculates that "as he moved toward the conclusion of his life, Percy might have wanted simply to reinforce his ideas without worrying too much about 'art'"—he had, in fact, praised *A Canticle for Leibowitz* "for precisely this achievement" (198). A reader familiar with Percy will certainly find little in the novel that surprises, but what is new about *The Thanatos Syndrome* is not its ideas but its form: unlike the earlier novels, it is a concerted attempt at genre fiction, with the rapid, suspenseful plotting that characterizes thrillers. If Quinlan is correct that Percy attempted a more lowbrow style out of a sense that "literary" fiction may have become an obstacle to his theological arguments, then perhaps his repetition is deliberate as well—an effort, so to speak, to get new readers up to speed while relying on the plot to maintain their interest.

This plot concerns a secret experiment in social engineering performed by Bob Comeaux and John Van Dorn. Drawing on the work of Dr. Tom More, Percy's protagonist from *Love in the Ruins*, the two men have released heavy sodium into the water supply of the region of Feliciana, Louisiana and the city of Baton Rouge. People who consume the water experience "an average twenty percent increase in I.Q.—plus an almost total memory recall" (192), as well as the disappearance of anger and anxiety. There are also profound changes in sexual behavior and its consequences. Because women now experience estrus instead of a menstrual cycle, unintended pregnancy disappears. Homosexuality also disappears—the Gay and Lesbian Club at Louisiana State University, for instance, voluntarily disbands. On the other hand, people feel less sexually inhibited, and their characteristic sexual overtures resemble those of chimpanzees—"presenting rearward" (20) instead of facing each other. Facility with language, that distinct attribute of human beings, also deteriorates, so that people communicate in factual, "two-word sentences," which Comeaux, speaking for an unimaginative scientism, touts as "a lot more accurate than once upon a time there lived a wicked queen" (197).

This is a familiar scenario, whose literary ancestors include Aldous Huxley's *Brave New World* and whose philosophical touchstones include such thinkers as Alexandre Kojève, Richard Rorty, and Francis Fukuyama.[14] Human self-consciousness, described by Comeaux as "not only an aberration of evolution but . . . also the scourge and curse of life on this earth, the source of wars, insanities, perversions" (195), is eradicated, leaving relatively happy, extremely intelligent animals able to live productive lives and to lose themselves in sexual happiness. Van Dorn, believing sexual energy to be the source of human beings' greatest accomplishments, wishes to "combine the high sexuality of [Don Giovanni] and Einstein without the frivolity of the Don or the repressed Jewish sexuality of Einstein" (220), and though he considers the heavy sodium to be a crude means to this end, he is willing to experiment with it until a more total sexual liberation can be

---

14. On the continuity between these philosophers' views, see especially Lawler (15–76).

achieved, because he believes, like Lance Lamar, that the social decay of the late twentieth century is intolerable. Comeaux, committed to respecting "the rights of the unwanted child not to have to suffer a life of suffering and abuse, the right of the unwanted aged to a life with dignity and a death with dignity," is an advocate of euthanasia, responsible for disposing of "neonates" and "euthanates" at facilities called "Qualitarian Centers" (199), and his enthusiasm for heavy sodium springs from the same desire to maximize a so-called "quality of life," even at the price of killing or rendering subhuman those who cannot attain it. Indeed, Percy has described the "only message" of *The Thanatos Syndrome* as the claim that it is "[b]etter to be a dislocated human than a happy chimp" (*More Conversations* 202).

As could have been predicted, the secret of such a vision of perfected humanity is that is based upon domination. Neither Comeaux nor Van Horn undergoes the experiment, understandably preferring not to be guinea pigs and to be able to control their subjects. Moreover, it is clear that both enjoy dominating people in other ways: Comeaux entertains the fantasy that the experiment will "restore the best of the Southern Way of Life" (197), complete with "darkies singing" (331) as they work happily in the fields; while Van Horn is a predator who molests children at his "traditional Southern academy founded on Greek ideals of virtue and to avoid the integration of the public schools" (214). The euthanasia that Comeaux advocates is merely the logical consequence of such an attitude: human beings must conform to the pattern established by the experts who know best, or they prove themselves unworthy of life. Helpless infants and suffering elderly people may be unable (and sometimes unwilling) to resist their extermination, but the heavy sodium experiment, performed without the consent of its subjects, precludes resistance altogether. Lawler has cannily connected the heavy sodium experiment in *The Thanatos Syndrome* to some of the more chilling implications of Richard Rorty's pragmatism. If, as Rorty maintains, one should cease to concern oneself with death, because "[f]ear is of something concrete, and so one cannot fear nothing or one's obliteration" (Lawler 43), then not only is there no reason not to practice euthanasia in certain circumstances, there is also every reason to stigmatize dissenters who ground their arguments in a metaphysics of the human as dangerous: "We should say we have no transcendent or transhistorical truth . . . That way, anyone who has such metaphysical or theological opinions about the truth can be excluded from discussion in a liberal democracy. They can rightly be labeled mad" (Lawler 63). In *The Thanatos Syndrome*, the character of Father Rinaldo Smith, who has sequestered himself atop a firetower (in imitation of St. Simeon Stylites) and refuses to speak to most people because he is disgusted by the fact that his hospice is being shut down in order to build a Qualitarian Center, is in danger of institutionalization. Tom More, who knows Father Smith, sympathizes with his anti-euthanasia stance, and suffers from guilt for having indirectly enabled the heavy sodium experiment through his own scientific research, is the novel's narrator and hero: he must race to stop the experiment, save Father Smith and his hospice, and, after he learns of his crimes, bring Van Dorn to justice.

Although these tasks are accomplished, in its lack of theological and even moral closure, *The Thanatos Syndrome* resembles Percy's earlier novels more than *The Second Coming.* A certain comic ambiguity, for instance, undercuts the novel's outrage against sexual predation, suggesting either that even the most heinous of crimes can be forgiven, or that a nation so addled as to look to Phil Donahue for moral guidance has no right to condemn Van Dorn.[15] More significantly, Dr. More, who has lost his faith before the novel begins, shows no sign of regaining it. He assists Father Smith at a Mass when called upon on the spur of the moment, but emphasizes that he will not do so again, because "since I no longer was sure what I believe, didn't think much about religion, participation in Mass would seem to be deceitful" (363). Such an ending is consistent with Percy's familiar strategies of indirection and his conviction that even for those who, unlike More, have made the leap of faith, life's intractable problems do not disappear; they are merely rendered comic and bearable. Yet if More resembles a typical Percy protagonist in this respect, it is striking that Father Smith, whose convictions are demonstrably Percy's own for long stretches, is made such an unappealing figure. Like Lance Lamar, he can be read as simply mad, and even Dr. More, his ally and friend, never denies this possibility. Moreover, though his position as a believing priest would render him Lance's opponent if the two were to engage in debate, the terms of the debate seem much the same as the agreement that Lance and Percival reach at the end of *Lancelot:* there is Catholic Christianity as a solution to the problems of modernity, and there is fascism, but nothing else.

15. In *Lost in the Cosmos,* Percy had mocked primatologists who, denying the uniqueness of human language, were devoting considerable effort to teaching chimpanzees and gorillas sign language. In *The Thanatos Syndrome,* Van Dorn regresses to a prelinguistic consciousness after being forced to take his heavy sodium overdose as a punishment for his crimes, and as a result, is unable to stand trial. More eventually suggests that Eve, a gorilla who knows some sign language, teach Van Dorn. He moves in with her under the watch of a primatologist and soon fully recovers, though only after he has established a sexual relationship with her. Once he is able to stand trial, he is convicted—but because he writes a popular book called *My Life with Eve,* he is eventually pardoned and makes frequent appearances "on the *Donahue* show, often with Dr. Ruth" (344). Neither his imprisonment nor his unwilling participation in an experiment seems to faze him—what seems to be poetic justice at first loses its irony and suggests that even the crime of sexual abuse can be erased through shrewd self-marketing.

Indeed, Father Smith is far more explicit than Lance in identifying fascism as the unwittingly chosen remedy of a secular world to modern anomie. Having spent some time visiting family in Germany in the 1930s, Father Smith was impressed enough by his cousin Helmut, a member of the SS—"I had never met anyone ready to die for a belief" (247)—to have been willing to join him, had he remained in Germany. The parallel between the culture of the Nazis and the traditional southern love of military glory is clear enough: both are rooted in a sentimental (and, in Percy's view, therefore cruel) romanticism, which stoically prefers noble death to muddled life. Father Smith goes on to argue, however, that the true implications of such a worldview are to be found in the Nazis' programs of abortion, eugenic euthanasia, and eventually, the attempt to exterminate the Jews. Helmut's father, a doctor who was contemptuous of Hitler, nevertheless became the murderer of children in Hitler's eugenics program, and fled at the end of the war, apparently to Paraguay. Father Smith's point is that noble love of country and the humanitarian zeal to end suffering, both forms of sentimentality, lead to atrocities. As he puts it in a ceremony to celebrate the reopening of his hospice, "More people have been killed in this century by tenderhearted souls than by cruel barbarians in all other centuries put together" (361). He paraphrases Flannery O'Connor's words—"Tenderness leads to the gas chamber" (360)—and builds up to the following peroration:[16]

> "Listen to me, dear physicians, dear brothers, dear Qualitarians, abortionists, euthanasists! Do you know why you are going to listen to me? Because every last one of you is a better man than I and you know it! And yet you like me. Every last one of you knows me and what I am, a failed priest, and old drunk, who is only fit to do one thing and to tell you one thing. You are good, kind, hardworking doctors, but you like me nevertheless and I know that you will allow me to tell you one thing . . . no, beg one thing of you. Please do this one favor for me, dear doctors. If you have a patient, young or old, suffering, dying, afflicted, useless, born or unborn,

---

16. O'Connor's well-known reflections on this theme are from her introduction to *A Memoir of Mary Ann*: "One of the tendencies of our age is to use the suffering of children to discredit the goodness of God, and once you have discredited His goodness, you are done with Him. . . . In this popular pity, we mark our gain in sensibility and our loss in vision. If other ages felt less, they saw more, even though they saw with the blind, prophetical, unsentimental eye of acceptance, which is to say, of faith. In the absence of this faith now, we govern by tenderness. It is a tenderness which, long since cut off from the person of Christ, is wrapped in theory. When tenderness is detached from the source of tenderness, its logical outcome is terror. It ends in forced labor camps and in the fumes of the gas chamber" (*Mystery* 226–27).

whom you for the best of reasons wish to put out of his misery—I beg
only one thing of you, dear doctors! Please send him to us. Don't kill them!
We'll take them—all of them! Please send them to us! I swear to you you
won't be sorry. We will all be happy about it! I promise you, and I know
that you believe me, that we will take care of him, her—we will even call
on you to help us take care of them!—and you will not have to make such
a decision. God will bless you for it and you will offend no one except the
Great Prince Satan, who rules the world. That is all." (361)

Father Smith's conviction that the doctors "like him" and will permit him
to speak a necessary truth echoes the claim in *The Second Coming* that the
apostles and their designated successors have the authority to proclaim the
truth, that all one needs to do is listen. Moreover, he suggests that one's
motivations do not necessarily matter—he will care for the sick and the
unwanted, not out of love for them or even love for God, as a truly saintly
Christian would, but simply because, as he tells Tom earlier, "dying people were the only people I could stand . . . Dying people, suffering people,
don't lie. They tell the truth . . . Everyone else lies" (244). The truly kind-
hearted are the ones most likely to usher in what Pope John Paul II called
a "culture of death," and the political progressives who endorse abortion
and euthanasia are already fascists in practice, though they would deny the
claim vociferously, and though their historical moment resembles the Weimar Republic more than Hitler's Reich.[17]

Because Father Smith emphasizes right conduct itself over the authenticity of the motives behind it, his stance does locate itself at some distance

17. Percy would amplify his argument about the links between humanitarian sentiment
and Weimar-era euthanasia in "An Unpublished Letter to the *Times*," written on 22 January
1988 and later published in *Signposts in a Strange Land*. In this letter, Percy cites the influential
book *Die Freigabe der Vernichtung lebensunwerten Lebens* [*The Justification of the Destruction of
Life Devoid of Value*], published in 1920 by Karl Binding, a jurist, and Alfred Hoche, a professor
of medicine and medical ethics and points out that the Nazi genocide took emerged from a
democratic and humanitarian climate, that the justification for Hitler's eugenics program did
not originate with the Nazis themselves. Though Percy professes not to imply that "*The New
York Times*, the United States Supreme Court, the American Civil Liberties Union, the National
Organization for Women, and suchlike" are "similar to corresponding pre-Nazi institutions,"
he maintains that "once the line is crossed, once the principle gains acceptance—juridically,
medically, socially—innocent human life can be destroyed for whatever reason, for the most
admirable socioeconomic, medical, or social reasons—then it does not take a prophet to
predict what will happen next, or if not next, then sooner or later" (350–51). Quinlan suggests that the editors of the *Times* might have found Percy's view "rather oddball" (206), but
it is interesting that many of the same questions Percy raises here reappear—albeit with a
different emphasis—in Giorgio Agamben's *Homo Sacer: Sovereign Power and Bare Life*, which
includes an extended discussion of how Binding and Hoche's book provided considerable
justification for "the integration of medicine and politics, which is one of the essential char-
acteristics of modern biopolitics" (143).

from the emphasis in much of Percy's earlier work. Percy's preoccupation with the particularity of the self, the uniqueness of its predicament,
and the existential search for authentic being that consciousness of such a
predicament provokes becomes less important than the demand that the
self should do what is right. To be sure, in preaching against abortion and
euthanasia, Father Smith is repeating the teaching of the Catholic Church,
and in this sense one can also say that orthodoxy and right conduct are
shown to go together, even in the absence of authentic motive. Such a move
is implicitly Pascalian—even those who do the right thing for the wrong
reason, such as Tom, who does not believe but agrees with Father Smith on
abortion and euthanasia, might come to believe if they practice the actions
of belief long enough. Yet it also suggests a sense of exhaustion and a belief
in the futility of argument that is surprising to see in a novelist so theologically committed.

Percy prepares the way for this devaluation of argument with Tom
More's admission that unlike Comeaux, he doesn't like to argue (34).
Comeaux, who knows of Tom's opposition to euthanasia, tries to engage
him in argument but is repeatedly frustrated by Tom's refusal to do so,
which usually takes the form of agreeing with particular statements that
Comeaux makes without accepting the conclusions that Comeaux draws
from them. Comeaux reminds More of his fellow white-collar prisoners
at Fort Pelham, Alabama (More has spent two years in prison for deal-
ing drugs to truckers), "ideologues . . . [who] could argue plausibly for
and against religion, God, Israel, blacks, affirmative action, Nicaragua"
(34). More found the arguments themselves "boring," because they never
changed anyone's mind, but he was nonetheless "interested in the rage":
"[W]hat is it the passionate arguer is afraid of[?] Is he afraid that he might
be wrong? that he might be right? Is he afraid that if one does not argue
there is nothing left? An abyss opens" (34, 35). Later, Father Smith suggests
that argument cannot convince because in these dark times, words no longer signify: "It is not a question of belief or unbelief. Even if such things
were all proved, if the existence of God, heaven, hell, sin were all proved
as certainly as the distance to the sun is proved, it would make no difference . . . Because the words have been deprived of their meaning" (118).
More concludes from Father Smith's words that the man "has gone batty"
(120), but the priest's claims are already implicit in More's earlier speculation that argument serves to conceal an abyss. They also explain why he
is so nonchalant about More's continued refusal to profess belief: "You
have been deprived of the faith. All of us have. It is part of the times. . . . So
don't worry about it. . . . Do what you are doing. You are on the right track"
(364, 366). It is perhaps this apparent indifference toward the question of

belief that leads Ralph Wood to ask whether Smith and More "are drawn to Christianity mainly as a transcendent means for making their own cultural critique," which, in his judgment, renders the novel "disappointingly abstract" ("Thanatos" 858).

If Father Smith's argument about the priority of right action over belief clashes with Updike's proclamation of the very opposite, his suggestion that in the late twentieth century there may be little to distinguish believers from unbelievers (though much to distinguish moral from immoral action) is very Updikean. Indeed, it may be tempting to read into his remarks a falling away from Percy's orthodoxy. That this would be a misreading, however, is confirmed by Father Smith's conviction that only one word has maintained its proper signification: *Jews.* Jews are "unsubsumable" (352) under any other signifier, precisely because they are "the actual people originally chosen by God" (124). Whether they continue to believe in God does not matter: God may have withdrawn, but Jews still exist and through their particularity testify to the truth. This unsubsumability is a scandal to all those who would erect their own universal orders to challenge God, and this, Father Smith argues, is the original reason both for anti-Semitism generally and for the Nazi attempt to exterminate the Jews in particular: "an anti-Semite who despises Jews actually believes them deep down—that's why he hates them!" (125). The implication seems to be that anyone who can recover the Word and its glad tidings must do so through the portal of the word "Jews"—as Father Smith maintains, quoting Jesus, "Salvation comes from the Jews" (124; John 4:22).[18]

How is one to evaluate Percy's heterogenous rhetorical maneuvers in *The Thanatos Syndrome*? Apocalyptic motifs, perhaps cheapened but also made more accessible to a wider audience by being packaged in a thriller, are combined with a declaration of the futility of argument on the one hand (with the corresponding suggestion that what one does is more important than what one believes) and a strident fidelity to orthodoxy nonetheless, starting with its beginnings in God's original revelation to and choosing

---

18. Here, Percy is in considerable agreement with Philip Rieff. Rieff sees what he calls "remission" as central to the maintenance of culture, but credible only when it claims a divine mandate. He attributes the Shoah to the destruction of belief in such a mandate: "Revelation . . . refers to the unalterable directive word of God. . . . Displacing and humiliating the absolute word and its open tradition of meanings, there has happened in history an absolutely human and faithless series of events commonly and mistakenly called 'the Holocaust.'" In these acts, as in the crucifixion, the carrier elites of world-immanent 'values' have affirmed themselves and so reduced the theological differences between the Jewish and Christian motifs of commanding transcendent truths to tired old theological quibbles between retreating and dwindling carrier elites of the second culture, still blind to that freedom of decision exploited and perverted by swarming new elites going about their business of creative destruction" (*My Life* 57).

of the Jewish people. The critique of technology as a means to dominate despite its promise of liberation has a long history, but Percy's working of new variations on it seems fresh, especially in light of the way such attitudes both spring from and reinforce a dominant therapeutic ethos in the culture of the contemporary West. On the other hand, by insisting on the absolute particularity of the Jews and their narrative, Percy risks—and even admits, through More's incredulity—the danger that such a position will seem monomaniacal. As in *Lancelot*, Percy's fundamental wager is to be prepared to listen to what the purportedly mad have to say, for it just might be the truth.

The unacceptability of that option to many readers is reflected in Kieran Quinlan's rather gleeful prediction that Percy might come to be seen, at least "among some of his less discriminating readers," as "appealing in the way that the New Age religions he has so forcefully dismissed do: for their 'mythical liveliness.' Thus would this champion of Roman Catholic orthodoxy join that 'amorphous group ranging from California loonies like Shirley MacLaine to the classier Joseph Campbell'" (227; internal quotation is from Percy's *Signposts*, 308). And indeed, the ambiguity that attends the commitments of Percy's protagonists—reflecting a comfy, domesticated belief in some instances and in visions of egoistic apocalypse in others— can easily be misread. People seeking God must, of course, begin where they find themselves, but Percy leaves considerable room for his readers to conclude that such a belief, confessed in fullness and in truth, is less important than the therapeutic practices that it legitimates. Readers might agree with Percy's diagnosis, yet conclude that Catholic Christianity can be only a palliative, not a cure—since even Percy admits it will not yield continuous bliss.

Quinlan's judgment reflects, to be sure, his own conviction that Percy's arguments are simply unconvincing, that he is "the *last* Catholic novelist" (218) because the historical moment that shaped his conversion is no more, and because "[a] resigned skepticism about ultimate questions rather than a dogmatic denial characterizes the present intellectual community. But in so far as this is the case, such positive assertions as the Catholic church makes seem at best of dubious validity" (225). The appeal to the authority of "the present intellectual community" is an appeal to a historicist mode of apprehending truth, and I have argued elsewhere about the limits of historicism.[19] The "present intellectual community" is not exactly the same now as it was in 1996 (even if there is much continuity), and to make its convic-

---

19. See Allen Dunn and Thomas F. Haddox, "The Enigma of Critical Distance; or, Why Historicists Need Convictions," in *The Limits of Literary Historicism*.

tions the basis for what one ought to profess—in this instance, "a resigned skepticism"—is to acknowledge that one might believe something completely different hundreds of years from now, without necessarily having better or worse reasons for doing so. Quinlan slides between maintaining that the rhetorical strategies of argument may be more or less persuasive at different historical moments and suggesting that differences in persuasiveness amount to differences in truth. The fact that belief in Christianity has waxed and waned over the last two millennia (and it is by no means certain that secularization is the irreversible process it once seemed) obviously proves that some people have found it more or less persuasive at different times; the question of its truth is separate and primary. Percy affirms its truth, even when he is well aware that doing so makes him (and his surrogate, Father Smith) look ridiculous. If he persuades, it is likely to be because some readers will find its very defiance of conventional intellectual attitudes bracing, its leap out of the prison of historicism compelling. If he fails to do so, it may well be because of the all-too-plausible misreadings that Quinlan identifies and Wood fears—that either therapeutic play or cultural critique take precedence over the truth.

5

The Uses of Orthodoxy

Mary Gordon and Marilynne Robinson

I. Triumph, then Collapse:
Vatican II and American Mainline Protestantism

Nearly fifty years after its commencement, few topics continue to gener-
ate as much debate within Roman Catholicism as "the spirit of Vatican
II." Should the pastoral council of the 1960s be understood as continuous
with earlier magisterial teachings or as a dramatic departure from them
that redefines what it means to be Catholic? Numerous observers have
offered conflicting interpretations of the council and of its effects in the
lives of Catholics.[1] Most agree, however, that whether the changes should
be applauded or deplored, Vatican II coincides with the collapse of a distinctly Catholic subculture in the United States—one founded largely by
immigrants; one considered dogmatic, pious, and self-consciously insular;
and one long regarded with suspicion by mainstream America. Ironically,
this collapse followed swiftly upon what many American Catholics perceived to be their moment of cultural arrival. In the period following the
Second World War, the celebrity of Catholic television personalities such as

---

1. Representative examples include Jacques Maritain's *The Peasant of the Garonne: An
Old Layman Questions Himself about the Present Time* (1968); Garry Wills's *Bare Ruined Choirs:
Doubt, Prophecy, and Radical Religion* (1972); and the second half of Charles R. Morris's *Ameri-
can Catholic: The Saints and Sinners Who Built America's Most Powerful Church* (1997).

Fulton Sheen, the idealized portrayals of priests and nuns in Hollywood films, the association of Catholic politicians such as Joseph McCarthy with an adamant anticommunism, and above all the election of John F. Kennedy as president contributed to a short-lived sense of American Catholic triumphalism. Its sudden disappearance provoked consternation among many mainline Protestants as well as Catholics. As Garry Wills put it, "Catholics were the last believers; dubiety among them is an omen. . . . if this thing falls, then what can hope to stand?" (4).

Wills's tongue-in-cheek description of Catholics as "the last believers" was published in 1972, at a time when the postconciliar tumult was perhaps obscuring a comparable shift in American Protestantism—the rapid decline of mainline Protestantism and the corresponding growth of Protestant churches that, for all their differences (expressed under such labels as "fundamentalist," "evangelical," "charismatic," and "emergent") emphasize a relative indifference to extrascriptural traditions, liturgies, and ecclesiology. The denominations that constitute the mainline have long histories that extend back into the colonial era, rich theological traditions, and a history of frequent dispute with each other that did not preclude broad agreement on morals and manners—indeed, arguably, enough of a consensus to determine the distinct character of American society. As Joseph Bottum puts it, "Perhaps precisely because they were aimed inward, the Protestant churches were able to radiate outward, giving a characteristic shape to the nation: the centrality of families, the pattern of marriages and funerals, the vague but widespread patriotism, the strong localism, and the ongoing sense of some providential purpose at work in the existence of the United States" (24). For Bottum, the decline of mainline Protestantism and its cultural effects are unprecedented:

> The death of the Mainline is the central historical fact of our time: the event that distinguishes the past several decades from every other period in American history. Almost every one of our current political and cultural oddities, our contradictions and obscurities, derives from this fact: The Mainline used [sic] has lost the capacity to set, or even significantly influence, the national vocabulary or the national self-understanding. . . . [S]ince the 1970s, we have faced a unique kind of political dilemma, in which no agreement can be reached even on the terms by which we will disagree with one another. (24, 25)

Bottum's thesis about the political implications of the decline may be overstated, but the decline in numbers is indisputable, as is the bitterness of struggles within the denominations since the 1970s—struggles typically described, like comparable clashes in Catholicism, as disputes between "traditionalists" and "progressives."

To date, Vatican II has generated more interest among fiction writers and literary critics than the decline of mainline Protestantism, though this interest has taken largely predictable forms. Catholic writers who depict the effects of the council do tend to portray a general sense of triumph followed by collapse, as well as little consensus about what either the triumph or the collapse portends. In *Testing the Faith: The New Catholic Fiction in America,* Anita J. Gandolfo, borrowing Thomas Kuhn's notion of "paradigm shifts," argues that while the preconciliar church "reflected the classical paradigm of a fixed and static reality . . . the rest of Western civilization responded to a more modern paradigm informed by the Renaissance, the Enlightenment, and the Age of Romanticism" (5). Though Gandolfo's opposition between "classical" and "modern" paradigms is crude and overdrawn, it cannot simply be dismissed, for it does reflect something of the self-understanding of American Catholics and non-Catholics alike, who have tended to view Vatican II as one aspect of the broader rubric "the Sixties." Gandolfo is faithful to this general understanding, which implies belief in a progressive concept of history and conceals unacknowledged affinities to Hegel behind its more up-to-date Kuhnian vocabulary. Because history is progressive, its movements are authoritative and irreversible— so that when the conditions for a "paradigm shift" are present, the old paradigm necessarily crumbles, no matter how strenuously its partisans might protest. For Gandolfo, the predicament of the postconciliar church is that while the old paradigm has been discredited, a new one has not yet been identified to take its place. Catholic fictions reveal this confusion, yet because they deploy "the imagination as a source of knowledge about reality," one might, through a synthesis of such texts, be able to pursue "the present task of Catholicism"—namely, "to discover the new paradigm" (21, 22). The very use of the word "discover" here suggests the systemic, impersonal nature of the shift—it has already happened, and one can understand its nature only after the fact. One cannot consciously forge it, in the sense of arguing on its behalf and hoping that one's efforts will succeed—or, more precisely, one *can,* but it will not avail unless one's position happens to conform to the historical avant garde. And this one can know only by studying and plotting the course of history, whose path is the primary means through which God (or *Geist*) reveals himself.

There is a forced quality in Gandolfo's argument, as in most attempts to discern the teleology of contemporary events. If the old paradigm has been shattered, and evidence of the new can be gleaned from current fiction, why the persistence of "conservative" Catholic novelists, or the emergence of newer novelists such as Andrew Greeley, whose work, though undeniably popular, does not correspond to Gandolfo's sense of what the new paradigm ought to contain?[2] Indeed, how does the synthesizing work proceed—how does one recognize the insignia of the new? That differing, incompatible opinions about Catholic teaching and life exist is undeniable, and at times Gandolfo offers little more than a survey of them. Yet in implying that this confusion has a foreseeable end—that beneath it, a new and better paradigm already exists—she obscures her own argumentative commitments about this emerging paradigm's content. At the very least, it is clear that Gandolfo *is* committed to an unspecified new paradigm and considers challenges to the old to be *prima facie* evidence of the shift underway.[3] In the larger debate as to whether Vatican II signifies continuity or rupture within Catholicism, she stands on the side of rupture, rejecting

---

2. Greeley's work, indeed, provides the biggest problem for Gandolfo's argument, for popularity would intuitively seem a marker of fidelity to the *Zeitgeist*. If one can only "discover" a new paradigm, then Greeley's combination of success and novelty ought to reveal something about what the new paradigm actually is, unless one wishes to deny that his work is "Catholic" in any meaningful sense at all. Gandolfo elides this problem. She views Greeley both as reactionary in his hostility to theological liberalism (a stance associated with the "old paradigm") and as not genuinely Catholic in any sense because of his unacknowledged debts to what Leslie Fiedler called the "Sentimental Love Religion" and which Gandolfo calls the "Sentimental Love Ethic" (Gandolfo 49–50). These are defensible propositions, but precisely because her argument is premised upon the necessity of the paradigm shift underway, she must explain why so popular a novelist (who is also a Catholic priest) has nothing to teach about the new paradigm, why his work can only be a projection of his own obsessions or a relic of an irrelevant past. Gandolfo's answer is that Greeley's readers are stupid: "Unfortunately, the more passive readers to whom these slick narratives appeal are internalizing not only Greeley's unvarnished hostile opinions of the Catholic hierarchy, liberation theologians, nuns, feminists, academic administrators, and other assorted victims of the Greeley mythic system, but they are also absorbing his theology of sex, a view Greeley propagates with the same glibness that characterizes his self-defense" (59–60). Even if this is true, it remains to be shown why stupidity, bad sexual theology, and Sentimental Love Religion cannot possibly be elements of the new paradigm. To do so, however, would be to make Gandolfo's own commitments more explicit, instead of letting them surreptitiously float under the passivity of "paradigms." Richard Rorty, who radicalizes Kuhn's notion of the paradigm shift, is more forthright about the sleight-of-hand involved here: the existence of paradigm shifts suggests that change of some kind will probably happen, but since I cannot honestly regard any change as an inevitable change for the better (that would be buying into the metaphysics of an inevitable historical progress), I am better off appealing to the impersonality and inevitability of changes that I desire instead of arguing about their merits. My rhetorical efforts work thus work to convey that resistance is futile, even though I know there is nothing inevitable about the program I espouse.

3. This is not to say that the content of Gandolfo's desires for a new paradigm are altogether concealed—only that it must be inferred from her positive references to thinkers such as James Fowler, Carol Gilligan, Mary Daly, and Pierre Teilhard de Chardin. The resulting picture is impressionistic but discernible as what I described in the introduction as a "spirituality."

the possibility that recent developments might be either historical dead-ends or recuperable, given enough hindsight, within the framework of the older paradigm. Surely a more prudent investigation would find the jury to be still out on this question, and a more confident advocate of the new would not shrink from arguing boldly on its behalf, instead of gesturing toward its inevitability or reacting irritably to those more skeptical of its superiority.

In *Postmodern Belief*, Amy Hungerford proposes an interpretation of the fate of "belief" in American literature after about 1960 that parallels Gandolfo's account of the "new Catholic novel" but seems especially suggestive (and far more subtle) when applied to mainline Protestantism. Beginning during the Eisenhower administration—and coinciding with the rise of New Criticism, which Hungerford reads as the latest stage in the effort to make literature fulfill the function or religion—the notion of "faith in faith . . . a version of religious thinking that minimizes the specificity of religious doctrine in service to usually nationalistic goals of civil connection" comes to stand "in contrast to the version of religion that stresses doctrinal content, a kind that in 1950s America most prominently includes the multiple version of Christianity, from committed mainline Protestantism and Catholicism to the more evangelical strains" (3). A harbinger of this development in American political life can be found in a widely quoted speech by Eisenhower: "[O]ur form of government makes no sense unless it is founded in a deeply felt religious faith, and I don't care what it is. With us of course it is the Judeo-Christian concept but it must be a religion that all men are created equal" (qtd. in Hungerford 2).

As Hungerford notes, the notion of the "Judeo-Christian tradition," developed by "the star theologians of the day, including Paul Tillich and Reinhold Niebuhr," is "itself a notion that mediates between pluralism and doctrinal specificity" (3), making up in civic idealism for what it lacks in robust particularity. As I have suggested in chapter 3, the career of Updike can be viewed in part as a reaction against this emerging conception of American religion, which looks to the Reformed tradition and especially to Karl Barth in its rejection of Tillich and his half-secularized Protestantism. Updike is, undoubtedly, the most prominent doctrinally Protestant American novelist since the 1960s, and his example might suggest that something as bland as the "Judeo-Christian tradition" proves thin gruel for Christian novelists, for whom the rendition of the particular remains a key criterion of aesthetic success. Despite the narcissism that I have identified as the central preoccupation of his work—and even despite the Emersonian commitments that he evinces in his most autobiographical writing—I maintain that in resisting this "faith in faith," Updike proves not only a better Christian but also a more aesthetically satisfying writer than many of those whom Hungerford considers exemplary.

In this chapter I turn to the work of Mary Gordon, a Catholic, and Marilynne Robinson, a Congregationalist—two writers who, unlike Updike, appropriate Christian orthodoxy in the period after 1960 rather than arguing straightforwardly on its behalf. For Gordon, the turmoil that followed Vatican II provides both opportunities and losses for the Catholic who wishes to identify with the Church's aesthetic heritage yet withholds assent from much in Catholic moral teaching. Robinson, writing in the first decade of the twenty-first century, looks back to the mainline Protestantism of the 1950s, at exactly the moment when large sections of it were beginning to espouse something like Hungerford's "postmodern belief," in order to highlight what she perceives as a suppressed link between political liberalism and Christian faith. The fictive commitments of both writers, I argue, are primarily political and aesthetic rather than religious, for both ultimately affirm tolerance and spirituality more than the content of orthodox Christian doctrine and practice. Gordon's project of affirming aesthetic value and sexual freedom—two values mediated by the concept of "the body" that are not endorsed by Christian orthodoxy in the terms that she prefers—is an intelligent effort that nevertheless proves, in the end, even more narcissistic than Updike's work. Robinson, a greater novelist than Gordon, has nevertheless been misread by many of her recent critics, who do not perceive that the doctrinal content that she so lovingly examines in her novels and essays is not the main point but rather a means to her own political and aesthetic ends.

II. The Church and the Body:
The Aesthetic of Mary Gordon

Gandolfo's half-acknowledged desires for a particular *kind* of new Catholic paradigm find stronger advocacy in the work of Gordon, who is probably the most prominent postconciliar Catholic fiction writer in the United States to enjoy both mass appeal (her first two novels, *Final Payments* [1978] and *The Company of Women* [1980], were bestsellers) and widespread critical acclaim. Like Gandolfo, Gordon regards Vatican II as an event that divides American Catholic experience into a "before" and an "after." "Before" was as much a place as a time, the milieu of Gordon's own childhood—working-class Irish communities in and near northeastern cities, with their traditional religious piety and gender roles, right-wing politics, and suspicion of the larger world. "After" is the world wrought by the 1960s and their aftermath, characterized by sexual and economic freedom for women on the one hand and the rush of American Catholics into the cultural mainstream on the other. If the trajectory of Gordon's own life as recounted in her memoirs and imaginatively transformed in her fiction resembles an immigrant success story—perhaps a kind of Catholic feminist counterpart to Norman Podhoretz's *Making It*—it never turns its back on the world of her childhood, seeking, in a manner that Gandolfo would probably approve, a just yet deeply personal measure of what has been gained and lost since Vatican II.

Gordon portrays sexuality, politics, and aesthetics as the primary lenses through which to scrutinize these gains and losses, and her general assessment is that changes in Catholicism have been good for the first two (indeed, Gordon's central political commitments, being feminist, turn primarily on sexual matters) but bad for the third. Although she dissents from magisterial teaching on a range of matters related to sexuality and gender— the permissibility of pre- and extramarital sex, divorce, birth control, abortion, the ordination of women—Gordon also continues to identify herself as a Catholic. Rhetorically, such a stance both exaggerates and minimizes the status of sex. In a 1986 interview with Lynn Neary, Gordon explained her position:

> I refuse to lose the richness and truth of the Catholic Church for issues which do not make up the whole of a religious life. . . . What in fact the Church hierarchy does is, by placing so much emphasis on a very narrow interpretation of sexuality, they cut many people off from a religious life, because most people who are in the modern world and live as moderns cannot go along with the Church's position on sexuality. Therefore, what the Church does is say: if you don't agree with us on this one small issue, you must leave. Most people do. It seems to me that both the Church and those people lose a lot. I'm not going to let them do that to me. (*Conversations* 40–41)

The church's teachings on sexuality are "one small issue," nothing close to "the whole of a religious life," but they are also, for "most people who are in the modern world," impossible to affirm. It follows that remaining Catholic even when one identifies as "modern" in this way requires a redefinition of Catholic identity, a distinction between the "institutional church" and the church proper that, Gordon suggests, is thinkable only after Vatican II. In a 1987 interview, she clarifies: "I come in and go out of the institutional church as I have more or less patience for it. . . . It's not a great cost to me to be in or out of the church" (*Conversations* 42). Secure in her knowledge of the "richness and truth" of Catholicism—a formulation that suggests the priority of the aesthetic over the ontological—the "institution's" teachings become greater or lesser inconveniences, not provocations that one must address.

On the other hand, if Vatican II has made such flexibility conceivable, it has also trashed the aesthetic heritage of the Catholic Church—what Gordon calls, in the same interview, "a kind of solemnity in the sense of formal beauty—the beauty of the prayers, the beauty of the music." Current Catholic ritual, she maintains, is, "at best . . . nondescript. Sometimes it's actively ugly. . . . It's really a grief to hear ugly music, to be in ugly buildings, to hear ugly or stupid or hackneyed language. It hurts me." Unfortunately, however, Gordon finds many Catholics who appreciate and wish to revive the older rituals to be "politically abhorrent" (*Conversations* 43), and this mismatch among politics, sexuality, and aesthetics was evident to her even as a college student, as she recounts in her memoir *Seeing Through Places:*

> The archdiocese was presided over by Cardinal Spellman, a great supporter of Vietnam. If I went into a church, everyone would know I was having sex, and would order me to stop, and I knew I wouldn't because I liked it too much. I understood that there were priests who opposed the war, but they were saying folk masses, and I couldn't stand singing about transubstantiation to the tune of Peter, Paul and Mary songs, and I suspected they loved themselves too much for consecrating whole wheat bread instead of Hosts, and that, despite the antiwar protest and the whole wheat bread, they would still be telling me to stop having sex. I needed formality, but formality was in the hands of men who were shouting about communism and free love, just as the country was in the hands of men who were lying about burning the flesh of children. (244–45)

Gordon's desire not just for purely subjective aesthetic delights but for "formality" suggests that despite the influence of second-wave feminism on her politics, she does not subscribe to either of the aesthetic stances most often associated with this feminism—the wholesale debunking of the aesthetic as a patriarchal ideology on the one hand or the embrace of a fluid and avowedly "feminine" aesthetic on the other.[4] Her tastes are traditional,

---

4. There is, of course, an enormous range of feminist criticism, but the two poles I identify here are clear enough and have the benefit of having been espoused by certain enormously influential texts from the 1970s—texts roughly contemporary with the beginning of Gordon's career. The debunking of the aesthetic is best represented by Judith Fetterley's *The*

even in the visual arts, where her admiration for painters such as Pierre Bonnard complicates any attempt to align her with feminist critiques of the male gaze.[5] Yet her delight in a formal aesthetic is not presented merely as preference—for Gordon it is *objectively* better, as measured by competent authorities (which is to say, artists themselves) who know whereof they speak. Gordon proposes, in short, the sovereignty of art within its own realm and denies its necessary connection to ethical, religious, or political stances of any kind.[6] The implication is that while feminism may be essential to Gordon's own art, it would be inappropriate to use feminist (or indeed, any other ethically charged) criteria to critique non- or antifeminist art *qua* art. Gordon's own artist-protagonists, such as Monica Szabo from *Spending,* are consistent in separating aesthetic judgments from politics in this way.

In *Cathedrals of Bone: The Role of the Body in Contemporary Catholic Literature,* John Waldmeir has argued that for a number of post–Vatican II Catholic writers, including Gordon, "the body in all its physical specificity—desire and pain, aroma and sweat—becomes . . . a source for mediating God's presence to the world [and] takes shape as a sacramental reality" (7). Such an approach has the merit of proposing a mediating term—"the body"—at the juncture of Gordon's primary interests: religion, aesthetics, and sex. Aesthetics, as Terry Eagleton notes, "is born as a discourse of the body" (*Ideology* 13), and the sensory nature of artistic production and perception is irreducibly corporeal. Liturgy, too, is bodily in nature: the congregating of worshippers at Mass; the physical movements of standing, kneeling, sitting, and approaching the altar; and, above all, the Eucharist, in which bread and wine become the Body and Blood of Christ and are consumed by faithful who themselves constitute the Body of Christ. Vatican II, Waldmeir suggests, placed a corrective emphasis on the reality of the body as a vehicle for sacramental grace, in contradistinction to an earlier

---

Resisting Reader, while the turn toward a "feminine aesthetic" finds its strongest example in the theoretical writings of Hélène Cixous.

5. On Gordon's admiration for Bonnard and his famous portraits of bathing women, see *Circling My Mother* (3–16).

6. To characterize Gordon's position as affirming the sovereignty of art in its own realm is not, necessarily, to make of the aesthetic a religion. As she puts it in "Getting Here from There": "Well, how did I get from there to here? An easy answer would be that I substituted art for faith, so that I found my new priesthood. That would be an easy answer, but it's not true. I don't believe in the religion of art, although I do believe in the vocation of the artist—altogether a more slogging enterprise. I don't believe that the aesthetic and the religious are one. . . . Great art need have nothing in it of the ethical, although the greatness of some great literature is enhanced by ethical components. But some is not" (173). As I hope to show, the aesthetic, the ethical, and the religious may not be "one," but Gordon's work reveals them to be far more mutually implicated than this summary definition would suggest.

"anthropology that privileges the cognitive domain of human experience, specifically, human rationality" (12).

What is the significance of this emphasis on the body for Gordon's work? One can agree with Waldmeir that human life, art, and religion, are necessarily embodied, and yet not be convinced that constant, loving attention to this fact is any more successful at resolving the problem of mind-body dualism, or any less selective in its investments, than an approach that overinvests in the cognitive.[7] Waldmeir's readings of texts draw attention to moments when bodies are foregrounded, as if the very act of dwelling upon the corporeal were *a priori* an outpouring of grace, irrespective of what the body in question does or thinks. His method has affinities with Bakhtin's celebration of the grotesque, in that human equality is affirmed in bodily lowliness. Moreover, it resonates with Gordon's own preoccupation with bodies—her narrators frequently scrutinize bodies, in an effort to grasp not just their aesthetic features but also their phenomenology and agency. Yet what rings false in Waldmeir's frame when applied to Gordon is its blanket dismissal of hierarchy and its concomitant urging not just to *accept* human limitation and failure, but to *celebrate* it—two impulses that I identify in Gordon's nonfiction but not in her fiction. As a committed liberal, Gordon is programmatically hostile to hierarchy in political terms, yet sexually and aesthetically, she affirms it: some bodies, some works of art, and some liturgical practices are more beautiful than others, and to say otherwise is to lie. Insofar as "the body"—itself an abstraction from the multitude of actually existing human bodies—lives and acts in the political, the sexual, and the aesthetic realms, it is no less entangled with hierarchy and with the necessity of hierarchical judgments than "the mind." (Indeed, it may be that it is impossible to escape the problem of dualism, that the overemphasis on one of these terms leads inevitably to an overemphasis on the other, and that one still, perhaps as a result of one's fallenness, lack a vocabulary for speaking of the whole human person in a coherent and meaningful way.)[8]

---

7. Much of Waldmeir's argument is rhetorically deployed against the notion of hierarchy wherever it rears its head, but his own preferences reinscribe hierarchies of their own: the Church Fathers and Renaissance Humanism, not the wasteland between the Council of Trent and Vatican II; in the New Testament, the letters to the Romans and Corinthians but not those to the Ephesians and Colossians; the John Paul II who wrote *Fides et Ratio*, not the one who wrote *Theology of the Body* (5, 11–13). The problem is not that Waldmeir cannot make his argument—of course he can—but that he writes as if making this argument precludes hierarchical judgments or remains faithful to the totality of Christian thinking any more than do the arguments of those whom he opposes.

8. This is why, for instance, Gordon is only half correct when she defines *abstraction* as "the error that results from refusing to admit that one has a body and is an inhabitant of the physical world," and "[d]ualism, its first cousin" as that which "admits that there is

Beginning with the fact of such entanglement and with her own commitments to a particular sexual politics on the one hand and to a formalist aesthetic on the other, Gordon's novels ask the questions that such divergent commitments compel: how does one recognize the legitimacy and interaction of different kinds of moral, religious, and aesthetic authority? How does one weigh their various claims against each other? Of what does readers' authority consist, and what justification beyond desire does it require, if any? Why is hierarchy essential to aesthetic judgments but inadmissible in matters of politics or sex? Catholicism cuts across all of these questions in unpredictable ways. The church claims for itself binding and ultimately infallible authority in the realm of faith and morality, so Gordon's dissent from its teachings becomes rhetorically figured as a blow for freedom.[9] (Hence her assertion that as a student she would not stop having sex because she "liked it too much"—no argument, she implies, could or should hold sway against her own desires here, even if there might be reasonable points to make about the advantages of sexual abstinence.) Yet when one turns to strictly aesthetic matters, the church professes no competence to judge, and there is no necessary relationship between the moral and theological claims that the church propounds and the media through which artists might engage them—certainly no single approved style or set

a physical world but calls it evil and commands that it be shunned" ("Getting There" 160). The mainstream of Catholic theology rejects dualism, as, for instance, it is understood in the work of Descartes or in the Jansenist heresy. Gordon's claim that she "was born into a church shaped and ruled by celibate males who had a history of hatred and fear of the body" ("Getting There" 161) is an overstatement, though one cannot deny the existence of particular priests and even theologians whose own examples do reflect such an attitude. Here Gordon's affiliation with Irish Catholicism may have much to do with her perspective, for Jansenism had a much stronger (and longer-lasting) influence in Ireland than in much of Catholic Europe. If Gordon sees herself as correcting a particular distortion in thinking about the embodied nature of human beings, I would argue that a more urgent distortion today consists of precisely the abstraction involved when one refers to "the body."

9. "Infallible" here does not refer solely to statements of the Pope spoken *ex cathedra*, which carry the explicit mark of infallibility. According to the *Catechism of the Catholic Church*, "Christ endowed the Church's shepherds with the charism of infallibility in matters of faith and morals. . . . The infallibility promised to the Church is also present in the body of bishops when, together with Peter's successor, they exercise the supreme Magisterium, above all in an Ecumenical Council" (256). But even teachings not expressly marked as "infallible" are nevertheless binding: "Divine assistance is also given to the successors of the apostles, teaching in communion with the successor of Peter, and, in a particular way, to the bishop of Rome, pastor of the whole Church, when, without arriving at an infallible definition and without pronouncing in a 'definitive manner,' they propose in the exercise of the ordinary Magisterium a teaching that leads to a better understanding of Revelation in matters of faith and morals. To this ordinary teaching the faithful 'are to adhere to it [sic] with religious assent'" (256–57). The consistent teachings of the Church on sexuality, whether stated in a "definitive manner" or not, fall under this "ordinary Magisterium," so that challenging them is an act of dissent.

of techniques. Catholicism has inspired great art *and* kitsch, and if today the kitsch predominates, this may be because modern artists find intolerable the subordination of their egos to the service of God that earlier religious artists freely acknowledged—which, arguably, leaves a freer field for the always numerous purveyors of kitsch ("Getting Here" 172). Gordon often seems to endorse Milan Kundera's famous claim that "[t]he brotherhood of man on earth will be possible only on a base of kitsch" (251)—and if so, she wants no part of it.

In practice, it is not so easy to distinguish aesthetic from ethical values, and Gordon is honest enough to grant that the poor and the afflicted are frequently ugly, spiteful, unintelligent, and distinctly unlovable. Such admissions, however, pose a problem for avowed leftists, and especially for those influenced by the Christian injunctions to love the poor and to care for the needy, whether this love is appreciated or not. Like Muriel Spark, Gordon gestures toward the superior aesthetic pleasures of Catholicism while casting a jaundiced eye upon the mass of Catholics oblivious to them. Yet there is little of Spark's cold whimsicality or assured snobbery in Gordon's fictive world: aesthetic pleasures are always more sensual than intellectual, and there is a note of defiant indulgence in their depiction, as if Gordon's characters assert that they deserve such pleasure, as if their superior taste ensures greater freedom from conventional moralism. It is difficult not to conclude that the aesthetic is Gordon's supreme value, despite her disavowal of the "religion of art," and that political and religious judgments are, ultimately, aesthetic as well: Catholicism thus deserves credit for enabling Chartres Cathedral or the music of Palestrina but blame for preventing people from pursuing sexual delights outside of a fairly restricted context. It deserves credit for making notions of human equality an ideal toward which to strive but blame for trying to realize these ideals primarily through charity—which necessitates contact with the unappealing, and which can be redeemed only if it takes on an aesthetic of self-renunciation that few can make work convincingly. As Isabel Moore puts it in *Final Payments*, "Charity is tedious, and sacrifice is not, as Christ deceived us into thinking, anything so dramatic as a crucifixion. Most of the time it is profoundly boring" (46).

Indeed, despite Gordon's hostility toward Updike and often her shrewd observations about his unacknowledged assumptions, the narcissism of her characters often resembles the pervading attitude of his work: her protagonists, no less than Updike's, resonate with Tocqueville's observation that democratic people are preoccupied with themselves and bestow value on objects only insofar as the objects flatter their self-images or prove forceful enough to tear people away from themselves. Broadly speaking, aesthetic commitment and sensitivity serve the same role as Christian orthodoxy in much of Updike's work—they make up for a multitude of sins, including selfishness, contempt toward the dull and unsexy, and the tendency to instrumentalize human relationships. Moreover, if Updike associates orthodoxy with good fortune and primordial innocence of being an American, Gordon associates her own aesthetics with the good fortune of being a Catholic woman privileged enough to live after feminism and Vatican II.

In a harsh critique of Gordon's early work, Carol Iannone argues that her novels "are about the monumental self-centeredness released by the collapse of orthodoxy, the agitated emptiness that finds an expression in movements like feminism." They resemble "those books and articles on 'having it all' that are written for women, with their advice on cramming in as much as possible, keeping track of one's needs, making sure they're satisfied, the whole informed by a lurking fear that nothing will really suffice" (66). Such an account is probably overstated, and Ross Labrie is no doubt correct that more nuanced judgments of Gordon's work will come in the future, after its "artistic merits . . . become separated from her role as a feminist ideologue" (265). Yet the linking of Gordon's novels to a posture of self-centeredness is appropriate, even if the connections between this self-centeredness and feminism are contingent rather than necessary. If Updike's work suggests that a commitment to Christian orthodoxy, however strained, may in practice coexist alongside a monstrous selfishness, Gordon's suggests that orthodoxy's value lies precisely in its aesthetic potential, which can also facilitate selfishness. Both writers' work, accordingly, is problematic yet also revealing of the dilemmas that even appeals to or uses of orthodoxy must confront in the contemporary world.

III. The Daughter, the Father, the Body:
Final Payments

Gordon's first novel, *Final Payments*, derives much of its power from the way its working-class American Catholic world is at once familiar and unbelievably distant—a place of constriction and horror from which one escapes, but which, one must admit, continues to mark one's life, in many ways for the better. Isabel Moore, the protagonist, introduces herself in this way:

> I gave up my life for [my father]; only if you understand my father will you understand that I make that statement not with self-pity but with extreme pride. He had a stroke when I was nineteen; I nursed him until

he died eleven years later. This strikes everyone in our decade as unusual, barbarous, cruel. To me, it was not only inevitable but natural. The Church exists and has endured for this, not only to preserve itself but to keep certain scenes intact: My father and me living by ourselves in a one-family house in Queens. My decision at nineteen to care for my father in his illness. We were rare in our situation but not unique. It could happen again. (4)

If "keep[ing] certain scenes intact," rather than saving souls, is the *raison d'être* of the Church, then the Church must be judged on the desirability of these scenes. Are they in fact merely "barbarous" and "cruel"? Isabel's insistence that she feels pride rather than self-pity for her actions suggests that choosing a figurative martyrdom provides aesthetic bliss and confirms one's superiority. The equivocal claim that "it could happen again," no doubt shocking to those who, like Isabel's future lover Hugh Slade, consider her background "as strange . . . as if [she'd] been brought up in the Fiji Islands" (160), emphasizes that such situations do not persist unless people derive some benefit from them, and such conditions could conceivably return. In this way Gordon proves less susceptible to the teleological grandiosity of a critic such as Gandolfo—she does not believe progress to be irreversible, nor does she see the past merely as something to be overcome.

Even though Isabel calls her case "rare but not unique," she locates its rarity less in the actual care for her father than in the extraordinary nature of her relationship with him. A devout Catholic intellectual who "loved the sense of his own orthodoxy, of holding out for the purest and the finest and the most refined sense of truth against the slick hucksters who promised happiness on earth and the supremacy of human reason" (4), David Moore rejects the Enlightenment and all its works, but he nourishes his daughter's aesthetic sense and encourages her intellectual aspirations: "He always said he was raising a Theresa of Avila, not a Thérèse of Lisieux: someone who would found orders and insult recalcitrant bishops, not someone who would submit to having dirty water thrown on her by her sisters in Christ and die a perfect death at twenty-four" (28). Above all, however, he expresses his love for her with shocking, even blasphemous, honesty: "My father looked had once looked at me and said, 'I love you more than I love God. I love you more than God loves you'" (251).

At the heart of Isabel's relationship with her father, then, is the association of Catholic orthodoxy with beauty and intellectual accomplishment—an association unusual in the working-class, largely Irish American world that she inhabits—and a tendency to measure the genuineness of love by

one's capacity for its betrayal. David's love for his daughter is proven precisely because it endangers his soul. The six-year old Isabel who hears his
declaration knows the statement to be sinful on its face, because the claim
that his love exceeds God's cannot be true—yet Isabel suggests that this
sin in no way calls into question his love for God. It seems retrospectively
fitting that Isabel elects to care for her father only after she has betrayed
him, by sleeping with his favorite student and, she believes, thereby causing the stroke that incapacitates him: her betrayal proves the occasion for
demonstrating the depth of her own love. In this relationship, then, Gordon manages to compress many of her characteristic preoccupations—the
capacity of Catholicism to nourish beauty and (within limits) independence
of thought, the privileged status of sexual desire, and the attractions and
possible dangers of martyrdom. If Isabel remains proud of what she has
done, even after she has changed radically, she does so not out of any commitment to the Church or to its way of life, but because her father, bestow-
ing such astonishing love on her, deserves comparable love in return, the
exercise of which allows even greater opportunities for self-satisfaction.

Gordon has acknowledged that Isabel's father is largely modeled upon
her own, David Israel Gordon: a convert from Judaism, a self-taught Catholic intellectual and polemicist, an admirer of both Franco and Joseph
McCarthy, and, the evidence of his published texts suggests, an anti-Semite.[10] Suggesting in her memoir *The Shadow Man* (1996) that she never presented him outright as a fictional character because "the details of his life,
presented as fiction, would be too bizarre to be believed" (xiv), Gordon
presents him as a tissue of contradictions: a brilliant and sincerely religious
man who was also a fraud ("[h]is 'work' was a series of schemes to bankroll
him and his magazines" [xv]), a convinced antifeminist who nonetheless
envisioned his daughter as a great intellectual, an insecure man whose own
writing was hopelessly marred by name-dropping, a liar who concealed
from his family the real place of his birth (Lithuania, not Ohio) and the fact
that before his conversion he had edited a "girlie" magazine called *Hot Dog*.
The Shadow Man is, simultaneously, an indictment of her father and a desire
to understand him and in doing so, perhaps, to exculpate him. Hence its
peculiar tone, which veers sharply from self-aggrandizing righteousness to
an almost abject sense that her beloved has been taken from her. At one
point she sententiously declares, "[m]y silence about his part in the evil [of

---

10. Here is the real-life counterpart of David Moore's declaration of love to his daughter,
as Gordon reports it in *The Shadow Man*: "'I love you more than God,' he once told me. This
was serious; he was a religious man. I didn't know, and still don't, if he meant he loved me
more than he loved God or more than God loved me. It almost doesn't matter. It was a serious thing to say and it scared me. Whichever he meant, he was right" (xviii).

the Holocaust] would be a sin. Against the commandment 'Thou shalt not bear false witness'" (94); at another point, she lines up photographs of Bernard Berenson, H. L. Mencken, Ezra Pound, and Henry Roth, "looking for the face that stalked my father" (182), and accuses them of "murder[ing] the father I could have loved without stain" (185).

The intense particularity of this love, threatened by the "stain" of his political convictions, becomes, in *Final Payments*, the background against which Isabel's confused negotiation of the post–Vatican II world must be evaluated. Isabel insists both on the philosophical rightness of her devotion to her father—the day on which she learns of his stroke is the day "[she] felt most purely alive," because "[c]ertainty was mine, and purity; I was encased in meaning like crystal" (6)—and on justifying this rightness in terms of bodily connection: "[W]e were connected by the flesh, so if anyone should minister to the decay of my father's, it should be I" (7). Waldmeir argues that the novel's central thematic concern is the home, the place where one lives and where one's body has its appropriate work, and that Isabel's loss of her father is simultaneously a loss of home and a loss of identity for her body. Accordingly, this "sense of homelessness leads Isabel to treat her own body as though it were an object, something wandering and foreign to the rest of her" (50). Isabel is free now, as she was not when she cared for her father, to equip herself with an IUD and to pursue affairs with two married men, but it is true that in all of these cases, the text emphasizes her detachment from her body. The first affair, with the husband of a high-school friend, is unsatisfying because it is based only on lust (and because he will not leave her alone after she loses interest in him). The second affair with Hugh Slade, however, is described as falling in love, and the language Isabel uses recalls her relationship with her father: "I was saying over and over, 'I am the beloved; the beloved is mine.' And I thought of the depths of selfishness in those words" (162). Even when she exposes her breasts as a kindness to the elderly Mr. Spenser (one of her cases in her new job as a social worker), because he has not had sexual intercourse in eight years, she distances herself from the act: "I had given him what he wanted and neither of us had suffered loss. . . . I had not believed it possible: giving and getting, as if no one had to suffer, as if it were possible not to feel cheated in the act of giving" (200). Even if no one has been "cheated," the language of economic exchange here testifies to the use of the body, and hence to one's alienation from it.

But if Isabel suffers alienation both from home and body in the wake of her father's death, she also expresses unalloyed revulsion against the body (and person) of Margaret Casey, the woman who had worked as her father's housekeeper and who had loved him:

You can imagine how unbearable the brown patches on her skin—they were not moles but large, irregular in shape, like the beginning of a cancer—were to a child, or even worse, to an adolescent. I wondered how she managed to keep the house so tidy and yet look so inevitably germ-ridden herself. All her clothes seemed damp, as if her body were giving off a tropical discharge. I believed it to be contagious, although I could neither isolate nor identify it. Her feet were flat as fish, except where the bunions developed like small crops of winter onions. The sound of her slopping around the house in her slippers is the sound of my nightmares. (28)

Margaret has always distrusted Isabel, regarding her as a spoiled child and taking every opportunity to chide her for her sinfulness and ingratitude. Isabel remains proud of the fact that at thirteen, she managed to drive Margaret away by provoking her into declaring her love for her father— whereupon he fled in disgust. Since then, Margaret has lived in poverty, working in a box factory in a small town in upstate New York. When Isabel is confronted by Hugh's wife, she feels such an extremity of guilt that she elects to go live with Margaret, explaining to Hugh, "If we can love the people we think are most unlovable, if we can get out of this ring of accident, of attraction, then it's a pure act, love; then we mean something, we stand for something" (243). Here Isabel wishes to surpass the martyrdom of caring for her father, doing so without the self-interest of personal love or the unshakable responsibility implied by bodily connection. As she lives with Margaret, her detachment from her body becomes contempt toward it: not only does she renounce sex, she also allows herself to become overweight, subjects herself to anachronistic hairstyling à la Annette Funicello, and cultivates self-disgust as a mortification that would further validate her disinterested charity. Indeed, Gordon emphasizes the penitential nature of Isabel's stay with Margaret by making it coincide with Lent. Her actual "final payment" to Margaret—a check for twenty thousand dollars—is delivered on Good Friday, and immediately afterward, Isabel is spirited away by her closest friends.

The turning point of the novel occurs when Isabel shouts "The poor you have always with you" in response to Margaret's repeated proclamation of her poverty:

It is one of the marvels of a Catholic education that the impulse of a few words can bring whole narratives to light with an immediacy and a clarity that are utterly absorbing. *"The poor you have always with you."* I knew where Christ had said that: at the house of Martha and Mary. Mary had opened a jar of ointment over Christ's feet. . . . Judas had rebuked her; he had said that the ointment ought to be sold for the poor. But, St. John had noted, Judas had said that only because he kept the purse and the thief. And Christ had said to Judas, Mary at his feet, her hair spread out around him, *"The poor you have always with you: but me you have not always."*

And until that moment . . . it was a passage I had not understood. . . . What Christ was saying, what he meant, was that the pleasures of that hair, that ointment, must be taken. Because the accidents of death would deprive us soon enough. We must not deprive ourselves, our loved ones, of the luxury of our extravagant affections. We must not try to second-guess death by refusing to love the ones we loved in favor of the anonymous poor. (288–89)

Because Isabel cannot love Margaret for who she is, the best that she can do is to provide for her, just as governments, motivated not by charity but by an impersonal mandate, distribute money: "Governments gave money and did not ask for love. Money was beautiful; if you could give money and did not want love in return, you could change lives without giving up your life" (295).

How are readers to understand this ending? Having "given up her life" for Margaret, Isabel wants it back, but because she wants to resume the relationship with Hugh, she must also make herself beautiful again, and doing so involves a further objectification of her body: "The body changed, went on changing, and could be changed. What I had done to myself was not final. It would take time, but I believed, with the unlikely faith of an early Christian, that I could make things happen to my body that would allow [Hugh] to love it again" (291). For Waldmeir, Isabel's relationship with Hugh is problematic not because it is adulterous but because "Isabel's persistent sense of self-detachment contrasts so sharply with Hugh's confidence" (51). Isabel is wounded, for instance, when Hugh confronts Isabel with a moldy coffee mug in her apartment and asks, "How could I even contemplate living with someone who could live in such filth?" (203). Waldmeir implies that the relationship might have a future if Isabel could learn to inhabit her body and home—moldy mugs and all—without being so easily reduced to shame. Yet because Waldmeir follows Gandolfo in regarding novelistic closure as a "vestige of the preconciliar paradigm" (Gandolfo 207), he also rejects the possibility that Isabel might find love with Hugh on programmatic grounds. Indeed, he states simply that "their relationship fails" (51), ignoring Hugh's desire to get Isabel back and her own desire to change for him—and criticizes Gordon for providing "the illusion of closure" (55) in Isabel's escape from Margaret.

If Waldmeir's rejection of closure resembles Walker Percy's own preference for open-ended endings and conviction that even conversion does not eliminate the messiness of life, he is nonetheless vague about what is at stake in this rejection. How does closure, for instance, denigrate "the body"? Isabel does continue to think of her body instrumentally, but she also acknowledges that it changes and might change again; she also states that the only real closure is death, the "accident" that would deprive one of one's extravagant pleasures and commitments. She also affirms the particularity of her body's desires—not the impersonal charity extended to Margaret, but the irreplaceable bonds between her and her father, between her and Hugh. I suspect that Waldmeir finds the end unsatisfying less because of its closure and more because it continues to affirm hierarchy, even—perhaps especially—where bodies are concerned. Isabel and Hugh's bodies *as* bodies, instead of as metaphors deployed against the habit of abstraction, simply matter more than Margaret's, and nothing can change this. In *Final Payments*, an ugly body reliably mirrors a petty, self-righteous, and grasping mind; a beautiful body, whether it embraces its loves or shrinks from its antipathies, can do no wrong.

One must acknowledge Gordon's admirable honesty in *Final Payments*. Margaret is credible as a character, and her presence effectively demonstrates that if one chooses to love selflessly, one must not expect to be loved in return, just as Christ's sacrifice was rewarded not just with his resurrection, but also, as Isabel points out, with "[y]ears of atrocities, monstrous ingratitude: who could make up to God for the stupidity, the selfishness of his people?" (293). Isabel's relationship with Hugh is credible precisely to the extent that it celebrates the egoism of the lovers and argues that such egoism transcends merely moral concerns. Gordon's error, from a Christian standpoint, is that God's love for his people is never a matter of mere calculation, an attempt to secure martyrdom on behalf of "anonymous poor." Nor is love for God properly understood as something equally anonymous and bloodless. Though it can be misdirected and tainted with selfishness, human desire points toward love of God, and God's love is an individual love, demonstrated not by a painless act of divine will but through the incarnation and death of Jesus. Peter Augustine Lawler is closer to the truth when he writes (apropos of Alexandre Kojève and Francis Fukuyama) that Christians "believe in the empirically unverifiable existence of a God who sees clearly into men's hearts and judges them according to their intentions. Each Christian believes that he or she is recognized by God as unique, free, and infinitely valuable" (33).[11] A father's love for his daughter should intimate God's love, but by its very nature, it cannot transcend it. Isabel is correct to perceive in a love that *claims* to transcend it "depths of

---

11. Incidentally, Marilynne Robinson's John Ames, the narrator of *Gilead*, makes a similar point, invoking Augustine's authority for the claim: "[T]he Lord loves each of us as an only child, and that has to be true" (245–46).

selfishness" (162). She is a human being of her time, and of ours. Her representative status is most clearly signaled by her willingness, in a time when spirituality rather than outright atheism is a dominant ethos, to appropriate the Christian gospel for selfish purposes instead of arguing directly against it.

IV. Nuancing Narcissism:
The Company of Women, Spending, Pearl, and "The Deacon"

Final Payments is the keynote of Gordon's career. Her subsequent novels complicate and deepen its commitments to the aesthetic and to the primacy of the self, registering occasional doubts about these commitments but not departing significantly from them. *The Company of Women*, Gordon's best novel, surrounds its protagonist, Felicitas Taylor, with an ensemble cast that consists of Felicitas's mother Charlotte; her circle of friends, all of whom she met while attending religious retreats for working women; Father Cyprian, a "conservative" and contentious priest, usually at odds with his superiors, who led these retreats; and Robert Cavendish, Felicitas's professor at Barnard College, who seduces her and gets her pregnant. As in *Final Payments*, much of the novel's skill comes from the rendering of a detailed world that has, after Vatican II, suddenly vanished. Felicitas herself shares much in common with Isabel Moore: A beloved, intellectually gifted child who is held up by Father Cyprian as "our only hope" (7) in degraded modernity, she has an even keener conviction than Isabel of her self-worth: "'*Domine, non sum dignus.*' She said the prayer but did not mean it. She believed she was worthy. Her soul she saw as glass filled with sky or water, as beautiful, as light, as silvery and as important" (6). Though she suffers from the doubts and confusions of adolescence, she never abandons this posture of certainty—loathing herself when she falls short of her ideals, professing that "she wouldn't lie to make people happy" (72), and acknowledging only as an adult that the main reason she wants to marry her (intellectually inferior) lover Leo is that she "want[s] to be more human" (260).

The superiority of *The Company of Women* lies in its wider canvas, its revelation that all of its characters have crosses to bear and struggle against their private narcissisms. By following two sections set in 1963 and 1969–70 and narrated in third person with a section set in 1977 in which the major characters narrate in first person, Gordon suggests that however much readers may need to understand the historical moment of the novel and see its characters as shaped by larger social forces, their responses to events and the retrospective significance that they attribute to them are always irreducibly personal. Waldmeir's claim that the novel's "'open-ended' narrative structure" (56) marks an advance over *Final Payments* also seems justified: the last word is given to Felicitas's daughter, Linda, and its simple affirmation—"We are not dying" (291)—reminds the reader that, until death, anything remains possible. Father Cyprian and the circle of women have tried to be faithful Catholics, and their struggles against a variety of mundane but very real trials—the insane husband who has been committed but whose insanity does not render his marriage invalid (33), the younger generation of priests who dress inappropriately and "let souls under [their] care risk eternal damnation to swim with Methodists, eat hot dogs with Baptists" (51), even the fact that Shakespeare and Jane Austen can be more enthralling than Dante despite their purported lack of "a deeply spiritual vision" (74)—are genuinely moving, even when Gordon's narrator makes her own ironic stance toward the commitments that fuel these struggles clear.

Ultimately, however, Felicitas remains the moral ideal of the novel, and, like Isabel Moore, her superiority is indicated both by her willingness to draw upon the best of the Catholicism that she has grown up with and her determination to reject it when it inconveniences her or offends against her reason. As a girl, she idolized Father Cyprian; as an adult, she continues to "revere him for his labor, for his passionate, excluding love, for the dignity of his priestly calling . . . the habit of his grand, impossible life" (264). She even values the fact that he "trained me too well, trained me against the sentimental, the susceptibility of the heart," despite its consequences: "I will not accept the blandishments of religious life; I will not look to God for comfort, or for succor, or for sweetness. God will have to meet me on the high ground of reason, and there He's a poor contender" (264). Yet she perceives Father Cyprian to be intellectually deficient: "He has three ideas: the authority of the Church, the corruption induced by Original Sin and the wickedness of large-scale government. All the rest is instinct and effusion" (264). It is arguable, however, that both Felicitas and Father Cyprian have been wrong here. Cyprian's claim that "reason is a whore . . . [who] goes with anyone" (40) echoes Martin Luther rather than Thomas Aquinas and overlooks the real possibility that the modern world may have too little reason in it, not too much. Conversely, Felicitas's belief that there can be nothing reasonable in one's religious life, that it is primarily a matter of "instinct and effusion," partakes of an admirable zeal against sentimentality and kitsch but also defines itself too narrowly, holding that the face of God would be worth something only if it could be perceived, as Kant might put it, "free from all necessity" (265). Even as she affirms Felicitas's stance more reliably than the positions of her other characters, Gordon honestly expresses doubt about whether her vision will prevail by turning at the end toward Linda, the representative of the future. Linda is an appealing blend of the old and the new: on the one hand, she knows, unlike her classmates, "four Greek words, ten Latin words, the names of angels" (290); on the other, she persuades Cyprian to pray for the ordination of women (288). It is tempting, if one subscribes to a teleology of succeeding paradigms, to see in this blending a synthesis that will reveal the new paradigm. But the novel's last words suggest otherwise: as long as Linda isn't "dying," she can come to any possible relation with God and with the Church. Nothing is inevitable.

Indeed, as Vatican II has receded in time, Gordon's novels have acknowledged—albeit with varying degrees of equanimity—that younger Catholics may feel little need to define themselves in relation to the Council, and even that there may be something inaccurate about the sense of world-historical rupture that Catholics of Gordon's generation perceived in it. *Spending: A Utopian Divertimento* (1996) has relatively little to say about Catholicism, and its primary concern—the trials, opportunities, and significance of the woman artist—more explicitly subordinates religion to aesthetics than Gordon's early work does. At one point, Monica Szabo, the painter who narrates the novel, remembers the devotional self-forgetfulness of Sister Imelda, a nun who taught her in the first grade, and emphasizes both the differences and the similarities between her vocation and Sister Imelda's: "The object of my attention isn't what Sister Imelda's was. I tried to make it, for a while, the same as hers: God. It didn't work. The object of my attention is the visible world. Whenever I feel I'm working the right way, I know it has something to do with that self-forgetfulness and attention I saw when I looked at Sister Imelda in the beam of blue light." Her own series of paintings, depictions of the Deposition of Christ meant to suggest postcoital exhaustion, is described as "[t]he coming together of art and faith in the hands of a woman—me—whose life was no longer shaped by belief. The light presence, not oppressive, of a former impression, something traced, but lightly, barely visible" (132). What religion and art have in common is an aesthetic experience of self-forgetfulness, not content or doctrine, and the experience itself is what matters most. Moreover, artists themselves, not spectators, are the only ones who can properly judge the experience and the work that it produces. As Monica puts it, "I really envy brain surgeons. People aren't always coming up to them . . . and saying, 'You know I do a little brain surgery myself. Maybe you could come over . . . and look at a brain I just operated on'" (14).

It follows that whatever restricts this experience or calls into question the authority of artists is to be deplored—financial constraints, prohibitions against certain subject matters, received ideas about the gender of artists. *Spending* is "utopian" because it asks what it might be like for a woman painter in the late twentieth century to enjoy the same advantages as the greatest painters of the past. Unlike feminist critics who would reject their art as tainted by sexism, Monica declares her admiration for their work: "There was nothing I was making fun of, no fault, either in execution or in interpretation, I was trying to show up. There was only the one thing that, as a woman artist, I was occasionally stunned to remember: for most of history, no woman was allowed to do what they did" (88). Monica gets the opportunity to "do what they did" when B., an immensely wealthy futures trader, stands up at a talk that Monica gives in Provincetown and declares his willingness to be her muse. He provides her with money for a new apartment, trips to Italy, luxurious meals, and lots of sex; he even agrees to serve as a nude model for her work. Monica embraces the arrangement despite periodic doubts about its implications, and the novel is indeed thought-provoking about the relationship between money and art and its ethical consequences.

Monica's greatest enemy, however, is a former schoolmate, Alice Marie Cusalito, the representative of "the Catholic Defense League" (186), who leads a protest against the exhibition of Monica's paintings of Jesus, arguing that they are blasphemous and offensive. Monica argues in response that people like Alice are stupid, for they disregard "the history of art and the history of thought," "reinforcing [the world's] prejudices that Catholics are a bunch of ill-educated, bigoted yahoos." They believe that "[t]he truth is simple," whereas "[w]hat I believe in won't fit into a sound bite" (203). Alice herself is, predictably, ugly, with a "puddingy face" and "bad hair" (181)—indeed, when the Catholic Defense League's efforts lead to a debate on the Charlie Rose show, Alice is replaced by "one of those exceptionally well-groomed right-wingers" (196)—and her deepest motive is probably a long-nursed desire for revenge: "[S]he didn't even get nominated for senior class president at St. Augusta's High School and I won the election" (194). When Monica tries to come to "a calm understanding of what they were doing," she imagines that "what was driving [them] crazy was that I was taking images that they thought of as theirs and using them in a way that they didn't like"—a formulation that concedes, at least provisionally, some validity to the criticism of spectators. Even so, "I didn't want to come to a calm understanding of what they were doing. I wanted to pound their heads on the pavement" (188). The only way, Monica tells Theresa, to combat them in the public sphere is "to get across" that "they're against fucking" (199). The autonomy of the artist, it would seem, is also the autonomy of the man or woman pursuing sexual satisfaction, and no one, least of all the Church, has the right to infringe upon it.

What is most interesting about *Spending*, however, is the novel's reluctant suggestion that this argument about art and blasphemy, though it might (in Charlie Rose's words) make for "good television" (204), is essentially a battle within Gordon's generation, able to be plausibly recast as a high-school feud. Monica's daughter Rachel, indeed, seems not only unconcerned with the debate but disapproving of her mother's arrangements with B.—she goes so far as to suggest that her mother is lying to herself, that the arrangement amounts to prostitution, even if the money involved is ostensibly taken for "painting" rather than "fucking" (83). When her other daughter, Sara, decides to marry despite not being pregnant and to "live in the country and teach music to preschool children" while her husband "direct[s] a nature study center in Montana," Monica is appalled because "[i]t's so unadventurous" (261). While neither daughter speaks about Christianity—and while Sara even reassures her mother, "It's not that I'm not a feminist" (264)—the implication is that a whole array of matters related to art, religion, and the politics of gender may no longer carry the heavy symbolic baggage that Gordon has perceived in it.

In *Pearl* (2005), Gordon takes the theme of daughters unwilling to fight their mother's battles even further. Maria Meyers, a feisty, middle-aged woman of devout Catholic background who broke with her father and joined the political underground in the 1960s, has always been vaguely disappointed by her daughter, Pearl, who knows "that some things were hopeless," that "some things no one could do anything about" (82). When Pearl, studying the Irish language in Dublin, becomes emotionally involved with partisans of the Irish Republican Army, she decides to starve herself to death because she believes that she has been responsible for a death and because she believes that her death will bear witness to the rightness of the Good Friday peace agreement of 1998. As in *Final Payments,* belief in one's own responsibility for a loved one's catastrophe leads to an embrace of martyrdom, which is simultaneously self-destructive and full of unsuspected potential for narcissism. Maria, having passed beyond the belief in martyrdom and the ideal of purity that it reflects, was perhaps "too hopeful about the ability of the human species to absorb quick change" (128), finds Pearl's actions incomprehensible; Pearl, in turn, was once "obsessed with hatred for her mother's body," in part because she discovered and read her mother's "adultery diary" (129). The anonymous narrator tacitly grants that there may be nothing unique about the changes that Maria lived through: "I am not a good enough historian to say whether or not there were other periods in history like those ten years, eleven maybe, 1962 to 1973 . . . years in which so easily, so quickly, you became a person you would not have recognized" (53). If such admissions gesture toward the possibility of repeating struggles that were once thought to be finished, of daughters who seem to their mothers like throwbacks to an earlier era, then they also emphasize the lack of finality in any statement made about Vatican II, its legacy, and indeed, about the telos of the contemporary world.

If, despite these admissions, Gordon's later novels still constitute a continuation and a nuancing of narcissism rather than a departure from it, it is because they do not finally question the subordination of orthodoxy to the aesthetic in any meaningful sense. Monica can accept Sara's marriage if it can be reframed as a question of Sara's own satisfaction rather than as a rebellion against Monica's values; Maria and Pearl can exchange mutual forgiveness, and Maria can forgive her father, but the question of an ultimate value that transcends the self must remain in abeyance. When Pearl, having been saved from starvation, asks her mother, "Why is it that it's life we want?" (339), Maria thinks, "It is a ridiculous thing to say, Life is worth living because of ice cream and your dog. But it seems preferable to saying, Life is worth living because you must live for me" (340). Her response to Pearl, "It seems we're meant to" (341), is, as she realizes, inadequate.

From the perspective of orthodox Christian doctrine and practice, Gordon's most successful work might be "The Deacon" (1999), a short story which, like *Final Payments*, associates Jesus' words *"The poor you always have with you"* with an epiphany. Sister Joan Fitzgerald, a shrewd and competent nun, is made to accompany Gerard, an inept and unlovable (though not, like Margaret, hateful) deacon, to a celebratory meal on the twenty-fifth anniversary of his ordination. Though Gerard inspires in her nothing "but a wish to flee from [his] presence" (82), she discovers that Gerard believes her to have cared about him, merely because she relieved him of his teaching duties at the parish school and installed him instead in the computer lab, where his incompetence would do less damage. In fact it had been the parish priest, Steve, who "had prevented her from throwing him out on the street" (82). Like Isabel Moore, Joan longs for—and interprets Jesus as enjoining—"an active love that fills the soul and lightens it, that draws people to each other with the warmth of the spirit, that makes them able to be with each other as a brother is with a sister or a mother with her child" (82). Because she cannot feel such a love for Gerard, she is initially horrified to discover that Gerard believes that she has loved him. Yet the recollection of Jesus' words eventually reconciles her to her role and clarifies the more difficult nature of Christian love: "[S]he knew that she would always have Gerard. He was poorer than Estrelita Dominguez, thirteen years old and three months pregnant, or LaTrobe Sandford, who might be in jail this time next year" (82). Yet while Isabel believes that she can fulfill her duty to the comparably poor Margaret with money instead of love, Joan acknowledges the need to go on doing what she can for Gerard, despite her feelings. When the waiter appears at the end of the story to offer her a drink, she orders only water because he "was an Irishman; he'd be scandalized by a nun's ordering Scotch. She didn't want to disappoint him" (83). It is clear that Joan appreciates the gustatory pleasures that Scotch represents; she apparently realizes that true charity involves not just doing good for others but refusing to let self-serving professions of honesty create scandal. This is a far cry from Maria's claim at the end of *Pearl* that one should live because one is meant to. Perhaps Maria represents the best that a particular kind of contemporary consciousness—lacking any cultural consensus about what constitutes virtue—can muster when it is forced to look beyond itself. Joan's example in "The Deacon," however, provides grounds for hope that something much better remains available.

V. The Liberal Calvinism of Marilynne Robinson

When Marilynne Robinson's *Housekeeping* was published in 1980, it was praised as an extremely impressive debut, yet for nearly two decades afterward, critics of the novel betrayed little suspicion that Christianity might be relevant to its interpretation. And with good reason: not only does *Housekeeping* lack an overtly Christian thematics, its spare but luminous prose, its suspension of traditional closure (its narrator becomes a drifter), and its meditations on desire, dailiness, transience, and the physical world seem to align it with one of the major critical trends of its historical moment: a discourse of second-wave feminist spirituality and poetics that includes writers as different as Hélène Cixous, Mary Daly, and Adrienne Rich. The keywords that regularly appear in published criticism of *Housekeeping* are characteristic: domesticity, feminine subjectivity, spirit, ecocriticism, women's writing, pre-oedipal desire. In the terms that I invoked in the introduction of this book, many of the novel's readers have regarded *Housekeeping* as "spiritual" but certainly not as "religious."

After eighteen years of such a critical response, *The Death of Adam* (1998), a collection of essays, came as a surprise. "I miss civilization, and I want it back," she declared in the opening pages (Introduction 4). Getting it back requires attending to the works of the past "in their own terms" (Introduction 3), rather than cynically assuming their lack of relevance except as a record of oppressions now overcome, ideologies now demystified. It might even require the resuscitation of John Calvin's reputation. As if such statements were not difficult enough to reconcile with prevailing readings of *Housekeeping*, her essay "The Tyranny of Petty Coercion" (2004) forthrightly announced, "I will make a shocking statement: I am a Christian" (16). The publication of *Gilead* (2004) seemed to confirm as much: its narrator, John Ames, is an aging Congregationalist minister in the town of Gilead, Iowa in the year 1956. He is, moreover, a good man and a reliable narrator, sincerely occupied with matters of religious faith and with self-criticism. In short, Ames is so square that Lee Siegel could write that *Gilead* "almost makes you—it's embarrassing to admit this—want to start being ironic and urbane again" (83).

How does one reconcile such apparent traditionalism with the putatively feminist achievement of *Housekeeping*? Readers who prefer not to do so, it would seem, also prefer the earlier novel and are distinctly uncomfortable with the thought that it might be tainted by Christian concerns. Stefan Mattessich, for instance, acknowledges that Robinson's Christianity complicates readings of *Housekeeping*, but rather than inquiring into how Christian doctrine might inform the novel, he assimilates it to metaphysical thought more generally, arguing that the novel "thinks the metaphysics that persist in every denial of metaphysics" (61)—a thesis, derived from Derrida and Jean-Luc Nancy, that violates Robinson's own desire to take writing on its own terms.[12] On the other hand, readers who laud *Gilead* and its sequel, *Home* (2008) (which presents the same story told in *Gilead* from another perspective) seem to value (sometimes with pleasant surprise, sometimes with unpleasantly self-righteous vindication) its demonstration that unfashionably Christian doctrines and virtues can remain, even after so much secular tub-thumping, the raw materials of great art.

In what follows, I will argue that *The Death of Adam, Gilead,* and *Home* reveal Robinson's use of Protestant Christianity to be more slippery—though not necessarily ineffective as a rhetorical tool—than both groups of readers allow. On the one hand, in declaring allegiance not just to mainline Protestantism but to the thought and legacy of John Calvin (whom she prefers to call Jean Cauvin, so as to minimize the prejudices that have accumulated around his more familiar name), Robinson does indeed challenge a pervasive contemporary cynicism, which she defines as "nothing more than an understanding of how arbitrary morality is, how unpredictable and unenforceable, how insecurely grounded in self-interest" ("Puritans"

---

12. Mattessich, to be sure, is quite honest about doing so: "It may be that *Housekeeping*, refractory to the secular presuppositions that critical culture brings to bear on it, rejoins her readers' interest in agency only by driving its stakes more willingly than we might like into the ground of a metaphysical tradition of thought about subjectivity" (61). The implication seems to be that "we," the practitioners of "critical culture," might not find what "we might like" in such an overtly Christian writer, though we might be generous enough to admit that we, too, might be haunted by metaphysics even in our denial.

170). Second-hand judgments of Calvin, deriving from the work of Weber or from blinkered understandings of what the term "Puritan" connotes, have reduced Calvin's career to the doctrine of double predestination and the death of Michael Servetus, his legacy to the triumph of unrestrained, exploitative capitalism. Robinson is correct that such judgments are not just distortions but obstacles to Americans who seek ways to implement a more humane future that are nevertheless rooted in the national past. Merely by presenting the goodness that a Calvinist worldview has nourished, whether in Jonathan Edwards's condemnation of his New England congregation's neglect of the hungry ("Puritans" 151) or in the fictional John Ames's capacity for self-scrutiny, moral action, and joy in creation, Robinson powerfully testifies to the benefits of Christian orthodoxy.

On the other hand, I maintain that this presentation remains, in Robinson's work, a use of orthodoxy more than a commitment to it. This is not to doubt Robinson's explicit statements of Christian belief, but rather to suggest that in her work, the starting points for a consideration of Christianity are always the primacy of religious experience and the benefits—including civil order and prosperity—that Christian belief can afford. In some respects she resembles Percy, whose foregrounding of the modern predicament is, nearly always, the place from which his protagonists struggle toward Christian belief. Yet while Percy used a similar rhetorical strategy both in his fiction and his essays, Robinson uses the two genres for different purposes. In *The Death of Adam,* she emphasizes the deficiencies of contemporary life that might be remedied if Christianity were taken more seriously; in *Gilead* and *Home,* she creates a fictional world in which Christianity is the norm, a quietly sustaining reality against which the central unbelieving character, Jack Boughton, appears to be less an existential hero (as some readers might initially suspect) than one who torments himself needlessly—even, perhaps, one predestined to perdition. Her strategy has been so successful that Siegel has gone so far as to declare (wrongly, I believe) that one "cannot truly understand" *Gilead* unless one is "a believing Christian with strong fundamentalist leanings" (82). If I describe her rhetoric, then, as a "use" of orthodoxy, it is because ultimately she does not press the claims of whether the Calvinist Christianity that she advocates is true—only that it is more humane, and less obviously false, than the theories promulgated by the central theorists of modernity. I identify Robinson's primary value as equality and hold that according to her novels, the value of Calvinism lies primarily in the degree to which it validates it. Here she departs from Percy, for whom the truth of Catholicism was precisely what guaranteed its efficacy against the modern malaise.

Robinson is, to be sure, aware of her somewhat unorthodox relationship to Christianity, and in the autobiographical essay "Psalm Eight," she accounts for it as the continued unfolding of the mystic intimations that she enjoyed as a young girl:

> All the old writers on the subject remark that in every age and nation people have had the idea of a god of some sort. So my archaic self might have been nothing other than a latter-day pagan whose intimations were not altogether at odds with, as it happened, Presbyterianism, and so were simply polished to that shape. Or it might have been that I was a mystic by vocation and, despite Presbyterianism, suffered atrophy of my gift in a life where I found little use for it. For all I know I am a mystic now, and simply too close to the phenomenon to have a clear view of it. In any case I began as a pagan and have ended as one, though only in the sense that I have never felt secure in the possession of the ideas and loyalties that are dearest to me. I am a Saxon in a basilica, refusing to admire so that anyone can see me, thrown back on impassivity as my only notion of decorum. I am surely wrong if I blame history for this sense I have of tenuous claim, wrong to invoke the notion of blame at all. Interloper thought I may be, I enjoy the thief's privilege of pleasure in the simple preciousness of things that are not my own. I enjoy it far too much to attempt to regularize my situation. In my childhood, when the presence of God seemed everywhere and I seemed to myself a mote of exception, improbable as a flaw in the sun, the very sweetness of the experience lay in that stinging thought—not me, not like me, not mine. (229–30)

Robinson's rhetorically subtle self-characterization begins with an appeal to the universality of religious experience ("the idea of a god of some sort") rather than to the doctrines of Christianity. Her own experiences might then be conceivably filed under one of William James's "varieties," so that her religious belief could be assimilated to her psychology. Yet Robinson immediately complicates such a notion by aligning primordial religious consciousness with the word "pagan," applying the term to herself, and then amplifying this term with the word "interloper." To profess Christian belief while using such labels is to suggest that one's claims upon Christian faith, tradition, and forms of life are "tenuous." This is, in one sense, a confession of epistemic humility—an engaging admission that whatever she might say about God or faith will be inadequate to the reality of religious experience, combined with the presumption that others, for whatever reason more secure in their connection to these things, may be more knowledgeable or more devout than she, though not (an interesting exception) more "historically" entitled to their security. A "pagan" sensibility, then, grasps the divinity that imbues creation—what could be characterized as a sense of the sacramental, but which here tends more toward panentheism—but professes not to deserve its relation to this divinity. (In this sense, the term is perhaps analogous to "Gentile," as it is used in Christian discourse to refer to those who lack God's original commitment to the Jews but who have nevertheless been "adopted" by him after Jesus' sacrifice.)

The expression of humility, however, almost at once slides into an expression of privilege, even the defiant privilege of a "thief," who will affirm what she finds experientially valuable in Christianity while reserving the right to judge its people and practices from this very position of the "outsider." Robinson does not so much reject Calvinist doctrinal commitments as hold them at arm's length, always evaluating them on the basis of whether they affirm or occlude this mystical consciousness. Theology must be judged in this light, and can be found lacking precisely to the degree that it can be intellectually understood. The Bible itself, Robinson maintains, is never lacking, because the sheer luminousness of its language cannot be mastered by the human intellect. She especially prizes "the devout old custom . . . of merely repeating verses, one or another luminous fragment, a hymn before and a hymn afterward. By grace of my abiding ignorance, it is always new to me. I am never not instructed" ("Psalm" 230–31). Again, Robinson deploys the double move of humble receptivity and judgment predicated on exclusion: she is instructed only by virtue of her "abiding ignorance," and thus implies that others, less ignorant, are to that degree incapable of "instruction." So far, Robinson seems to position herself in relation to the many people who, in contemporary Western societies, might identify themselves as "spiritual but not religious," but she also seems to suggest that to be spiritual *within* a religious tradition (an "interloper") might be best of all, for religion is at bottom (as she explains elsewhere) a "framing mechanism," a "language of orientation that presents itself as a series of questions" (Interview). Such a position need not reject other traditions within Christianity, although the differences between the traditions in such a view become differences in experience and in aesthetics: "[W]ould we be richer for the loss of Catholicism? Would we be richer for the loss of the Quakers? Isn't it true that every one of these traditions expresses Christianity in a way that the other traditions could not? It's prismatic" (Interview).

Robinson affirms her own doctrinal identity in this way: "I have shifted allegiances the doctrinal and demographic inch that separates Presbyterians from Congregationalists, but for all purposes I am where I ought to be, as sociologists calculate, and I should feel right at home. I will concede only that the sensation of exclusion is more poignant to me in these precincts than in others, being after all these years so very familiar" ("Psalm" 231). A reader of Updike confronted with this passage will be reminded of the difference presented in *Couples* between Piet Hanema's childhood faith and the religion of those Tarboxers who still go to church: "Piet had been raised in a sterner church, the Dutch Reformed, amid varnished oak and dour stained glass where shepherds were paralyzed in webs of lead. He had joined this sister church [Congregationalist], a milder daughter of Calvin, as a compromise with [his wife] Angela, who believed nothing" (20). From Updike's standpoint, the Congregational church in Tarbox is insufficiently orthodox, and its destruction by lightning at the end of the novel confirms, as it were, God's displeasure with it. Robinson, again, cannily positions herself both within and yet outside of an orthodox tradition: she is "sociologically" where she belongs, given (one presumes) her ancestry, politics, and aesthetic allegiances, yet the content of her belief is only imperfectly contained within Congregationalism, and she enjoys the piquancy of being not "at home" despite her long years of membership. She marvels on the occasions in church when "the minister will conclude something brave and absolute," because she is "so far unregenerate that they never cease to impress [her] deeply" ("Psalm" 231). Once again, the implication is that those who take such statements as a matter of course are not "unregenerate" enough—too comfortable in their habitual piety to let the force of the words change them. At the same time, the doctrinal latitude of Congregationalism imbues such statements with a certain irony: how often, indeed, Robinson implies, does one hear something "brave and absolute" preached within such a venue? Only "[f]rom time to time, on the strength of the text" ("Psalm" 231).[13]

Here the question of how Robinson wishes readers to take the doctrines most associated with Calvin becomes relevant, for in the popular conception, few ideas are more "brave and absolute" than double predestination. In the two-part (and misleadingly titled) essay "Marguerite de Navarre," Robinson affirms that for Calvin, the doctrine is a necessary consequence of his belief in the absolute freedom, power, and knowledge of God, and that Calvin's opponents, such as Ignatius of Loyola, also affirmed predestination, though with greater caution and with a degree of "nuance" that one should understand as a rhetorical appeal to a very different audience: "Ignatius was writing for an elite of highly committed men; Calvin, for

---

13. Appropriately enough, the narrator of *Gilead,* John Ames, is a Congregationalist minister; his best friend, Robert Boughton, is a Presbyterian minister. Both are good men, but, as *Home* confirms, Ames is the better of the two.

anyone who could read him" (187). In the work of both men, "[t]he logical difficulties of their positions matter only if the question is understood in terms both explicitly reject" (188). This is, of course, true, and Robinson's insistence on understanding Calvin in his own terms is admirable. She does not, however, explain whether she holds this doctrine to be true or merely worthy of intellectual respect.[14] Nor does it explain whether what contemporary people might find valuable in Calvin is the doctrine itself or certain implications which, derivable from it, are nevertheless also to be found elsewhere. The doctrine of double predestination can indeed be, and historically has been, associated with the belief and practice of human equality, for human beings are all equally depraved, and the one distinction with real significance—whether one belongs to the elect or not—has to do with God's efforts, not ours. But it does not follow that those who affirm the political or moral value of equality must ground their arguments on its behalf in Calvin's work, even if it can be historically demonstrated that in the United States, Calvinism contributed much to creating a climate in which such values could thrive. Indeed, Robinson's account of Calvinism becomes suspiciously selective: everything that tends to affirm the liberal humanism that Robinson herself espouses is underscored, while everything that offends contemporary sensibilities must be explained away. Thus, Calvin's "extreme disparagements of the physical body" must be read not literally but as rhetoric "in the service of an extraordinarily exalted vision of the human soul" ("Marguerite" 182). Todd Shy's judgment that Robinson is in fact closer to Montaigne and Erasmus than to Calvin, to Renaissance humanism than to Reformed faith, seems borne out here (257–58).

---

14. Robinson's most explicit statement on the matter frankly indicates the difficulty: "I have never heard of even one persuasive case made for the compatibility of eternal damnation with the justice and mercy of God. But there it is, a conspicuous presence in Scripture and in tradition, and Calvin could hardly be expected to set it aside." Here, she speaks not of double predestination per se, but of the existence and eternity of hell—a Christian doctrine much more widely accepted than double predestination. She then goes on to argue, correctly, that predestination itself is not a doctrine first invented by Calvin, and that a consequence of the doctrine is "to make the categories 'redeemed' and 'unredeemed' profoundly mysterious to mortal eyes, to remove every basis for our making any such radical judgments about our fellows" ("Calvinism" 183). In short, instead of answering the question "is double predestination true?" Robinson responds with something like "Consider instead its implications for human equality." On whether *double* predestination is Calvin's opinion (which again leaves Robinson's own view of its possible truth unstated), Robinson astonishingly declares, "Whether predestination is 'double' or 'single' is a quibble with which Calvin was too honest to have patience" ("Polemic" 97). I would compare Robinson here with Newman, who similarly acknowledged that many Christian beliefs are also "beset with intellectual difficulties; and it is simple fact, that, for myself, I cannot answer these difficulties," but whose position on the consequences of this fact is far more straightforward: "[t]en thousand difficulties do not make one doubt, as I understand the subject; difficulty and doubt are incommensurate" (*Apologia* 155).

Perhaps another way to approach this problem would be to investigate how Robinson understands what Newman called "development of doctrine." To what extent do the doctrines of the Reformed faith prove capable of change, even change understood—to return to the terms that I invoked with respect to Vatican II—as continuity or deepening rather than as rupture? Robinson's humanism is, of course, about the possibility of human improvement: she is friendly, or wishes to be friendly, toward science and art, and she wants to regard the habitus of democratic culture as it developed in the United States as an ideal environment for its flourishing. She must therefore account for the fact that much in contemporary American culture appalls her, and she discerns the cause in large part in a deliberate decision to reject the Calvinist heritage, to misread it as illiberal and repressive. Much of the blame she lays at the feet of Weber, whose famous argument that Calvinism helped create "the spirit of capitalism" she detests:

> By comparison with Lutherans, Calvinists lack *gemütlichkeit*—they are not good fellows. Weber says you can see this in their faces. This is the new historical method. This is how *spirit* becomes a term suitable for use in economic analysis. I suppose I am unfair in saying that for Weber a prejudice is a proof. He offers none of the usual criticisms of capitalism itself—that it is exploitive, that it is crisis prone, that it creates extremes of wealth and poverty. His criticism is that, in its "modern" form, those who prosper from it do not enjoy their prosperity. He knows and says that Calvin did not encourage the accumulation of wealth, and that he insisted the "church"—in this sense, the elect—do not prosper in this world. . . . [Weber argues] that a social group defined by [him] as the people who adhere to or have been acculturated by a particular theology are, with generalizable and world-historical consistency, peculiarly inclined to behave in ways precisely contrary to the teaching of that theology. . . . Surely it is fair to wonder if any of this amounts to more than personal animus—which was the preferred historical method of much of the Western world at the beginning of this bitter century. . . . In fairness to Weber, he considered his conclusions in *The Protestant Ethic and the Spirit of Capitalism* to be merely tentative, likely to be superseded when "comparative racial neurology and psychology shall have progressed beyond their present and in many ways very promising beginnings." ("Introduction" 23–24)

Even if everything that Robinson argues here is correct, it does not necessarily invalidate Weber's thesis, and it raises the question of what alternative explanations for the evolution of capitalism might be more convincing.

If the hypercapitalist, morally priggish yet licentious, and aesthetically desensitized specter of contemporary American life *is* a dramatic departure from the nation's originally Calvinist ethos, rather than an unintended but retrospectively traceable consequence of this ethos, what enabled such dramatic changes? It is conceivable that it is precisely the democratic emphasis of Calvinist belief and practice that has facilitated the growth of capitalism and the lowering of aesthetic standards that Robinson deplores, contrary to her expectation that democracy should inculcate a high-minded humanism—some of Tocqueville's observations of nineteenth-century America and concerns about the nation's future, for instance, might be enlisted in support of such a claim.

Even if such an interpretation is not fully convincing, alternative accounts—Ann Douglas's thesis, for instance—might not necessarily be more congenial to Robinson. What if the pursuit of equality leads not to human flourishing but to a degraded mass culture, and what if Calvinism delayed the emergence of such a mass culture precisely to the extent that it impeded political equality (even as it undeniably affirmed the equality of human souls in relation to each other)?[15] In any event, the fact that capitalism has historically expanded the most rapidly and produced its most effective theorists in societies with long traditions of Calvinist belief and democratic polity (the United States, Scotland, the Netherlands) needs to be accounted for. Moreover, Robinson's attempt to discredit Weber by linking him to eugenics not only violates her own injunction to read thinkers in terms of their own historical moment rather than to apply contemporary standards to them but also seems continuous with her own hostility toward Darwinism, which might just as conceivably be described as a "prejudice" based on the fact that for strict Darwinists, talk of the human soul and even the mind is inadmissible. Surely a thinker whose own religious thinking is grounded in the primacy of certain individual experiences should be more careful about castigating the "individual" perceptions of others, even if these concern the presence or lack of *Gemütlichkeit* in certain faces.

---

15. Douglas shares Robinson's loathing for mass culture and her admiration for Calvinism, but not her sense that Calvinism and humanism are compatible: "Calvinism was a great faith, with great limitations: it was repressive, authoritarian, dogmatic, patriarchal to an extreme. Its demise was inevitable, and in some real sense, welcome. Yet it deserved, and elsewhere and at other times found, great opponents. One could argue that the logical antagonist of Calvinism was a fully humanistic, historically minded romanticism. Exponents of such romanticism appeared in mid-nineteenth-century America—one thinks particularly of Margaret Fuller and Herman Melville—but they were rare" (12–13). One might quarrel with the particulars of Douglas's description here—Robinson, I feel certain, would bristle at the characterization of Calvinism as "patriarchal to an extreme" (see "Marguerite" 184–87, in which Robinson defends Calvin against the charge of misogyny)—but her affirmation of a "fully humanistic, historically minded romanticism" sounds exactly like Robinson's own larger project.

In the most comprehensive situating of Robinson's fiction within the tradition of American Puritan writing thus far, Christopher Leise argues that Robinson "is consciously reading the Puritan tradition against itself," an approach that "looks at religion not as a stable entity at all but one that is fluid and—quite the opposite—actively destabilizing" (350). This overstates the case considerably. Leise's argument is grounded not on the particulars of Robinson's stated beliefs but rather on the theses of Derridean deconstruction as they are applied to religion via the work of Mark C. Taylor. Leise reduces the upshot of his argument to "[r]eligions are dynamic, not static" (351), but this, surely, is a fact and a platitude: one can endorse such a statement without writing off in principle, as Leise appears to do, the vexing questions of how one should understand which developments in a religious tradition are proper to it and which genuine departures. Robinson would, I am certain, describe her project as a faithful return to tradition rather than an ironic destabilization of it; she would also not be friendly to the implication that disagreements in how one understands a given tradition should simply be attributed to the inevitable self-undermining of any systems. Moreover, when she departs from the polemical strategy of her essays to the presentation of Calvinist Christianity in her two recent novels, Robinson is refreshingly free of the global irony that Taylor discovers in the phenomenon of religion—so free, in fact, that a common complaint from readers of *Gilead* it is that so good and sincere a man as John Ames is simply not credible.[16] This lack of global irony makes the novels, as instances of rhetoric, unusually effective: to those put off by the pugnacity and the thorny doctrinal questions associated with Calvinism, Robinson offers the serenity of a Calvinist milieu that is simply assumed. That she must set her novels in 1956 to make such a milieu convincing, however, suggests her readers of the novel may have to struggle with—or be open to—an implicit nostalgia in the two novels, a desire (rather like Updike's in *The Poorhouse Fair*) to return to a stronger, less riven America.

VI. The Primacy of Religious Experience in *Gilead* and *Home*

Gilead takes the form of a letter written by Reverend John Ames, the seventy-six-year-old Congregationalist minister of Gilead, Iowa, to his seven-year-old son, the child of a second marriage entered into after a long widowerhood. Diagnosed with heart trouble and not expected to live long,

---

16. Again, Siegel makes this argument in the strongest possible terms: "[T]hese people finally seem sprung from some moral vanity, some secret disdain for their flesh-and-blood particularity" (83).

Ames expects that as a grown man, his son will read the letter and learn "things I believe it becomes me as a father to teach you" (133–34). Throughout the novel, three lessons recur obsessively: the beauty of the world, charged as it is with the glory and love of God; the opacity of human beings, even when they have known and loved each other their entire lives; and, consequently, the dangers of moral judgment. These lessons are consistent with Ames's Jamesian conviction that "it is religious experience above all that authenticates religion, for the purposes of the individual believer" (145), and that it is therefore "presumptuous to judge the authenticity of anyone's religion, except one's own. And that is also presumptuous" (173). Many of the novel's loveliest passages, indeed, are affirmations of dailiness that authenticate Ames's own religious sense: a game of blowing bubbles with the pet cat, with its "effulgence of bubbles rising, and so much laughter" (9); a memory from childhood of a group of women singing in the rain and eating "the bread of affliction" (102) because their church has burned; the coming of dawn over the prairie (246). Knowing one's own luminous self-awareness, the novel implies, one has no right to deny others their own.[17] To think otherwise, Ames holds, would entail that "people are disabled from trusting their thoughts, their expressions of belief, and their understanding" (146).

In the course of writing his letter, Ames finds that these beliefs are tested when Jack Boughton, the son of John's best friend, returns to Gilead. As a child, Jack was constantly into "mischief only bordering on harm, generally speaking" (182); when he was older, he renounced his family's Christian faith. He is a frequent liar, as he admits, and he struggles with alcoholism. Most spectacularly of all, as a young man he got a very poor young woman pregnant and abandoned her, never publicly acknowledging the child, who died at the age of three of an infected cut. Jack, now forty-three, wishes to confide in Ames, but Ames is nervous: although he "see[s] the error of *assuming* a person is not speaking with you in good faith," he admits that "it is hard for me to see good faith in John Ames Boughton, and that is a terrible problem" (154). Indeed, one might suspect that the consistency of Jack's reprehensible behavior is intended to give credence to the Calvinist dogma of double predestination—for, as Ames also avows, "[g]enerally, a person's behavior is consistent with his nature" (151).

Both *Gilead* and *Home* reflect the degree to which Robinson regards total depravity—the doctrine that provides the precondition for predestination—

---

17. Robinson's notion of "self-awareness," as she describes it in *Absence of Mind*, is possibly relevant here: "I do not mean merely consciousness of one's identity, or of the complex flow of thought, perception, memory, and desire, important as these are. I mean primarily the self that stands apart from itself, that questions, reconsiders, appraises" (118).

as essentially democratic in its implications. Yet Robinson is aware that belief in it can also make for complacency, a certain impatience with distinctions that may nevertheless be meaningful, as Jack's sister Glory reflects in *Home:*

> Maybe she had never before known anyone who felt, or admitted he felt, that the state of his soul was in question. Whatever might transpire in her father's study, there had been only calm and confidence among his flock, to all appearances. Granting the many perils of spiritual complacency, and her father did grant them as often as Pharisees figured in the text, complacency was consistent with the customs and manners of Presbyterian Gilead and was therefore assumed to be justified in every case. Christian charity demanded no less, after all. Among the denominations of Gilead, charity on this point was not granted by all and to all in principle, but in practice good manners were usually adhered to, and in general the right to complacency was conceded on every side. Even her father's sermons treated salvation as a thing for which they could be grateful as a body, as if, for their purposes at least, that problem had been sorted out between the Druids and the centurions at about the time of Hadrian. He did mention sin, but it was rarefied in his understanding of it, a matter of acts and omissions so commonplace that no one could be wholly innocent of them or especially alarmed by them, either—the uncharitable thought, the neglected courtesy. While on the one hand this excused him from the mention of those aspects of life that seemed remotest from Sabbath and sunlight, on the other hand it made the point that the very nicest among them, even the most virtuous, were in no position to pass judgment on anyone else. . . . The doctrine of total depravity had served him well. Who, after all, could cast that first stone? He could not, he least of all. But it was hard to get a clear view of something so pervasive as to be total, especially if, as her father insisted, it was epitomized in his own estimable person. (111–12)

This description of the Protestant denominations of Gilead, divided theologically yet united in good manners, echoes Bottum's description of the days when mainline Protestantism set the tone for American life, creating a genuine sense of civic community even as it encouraged a possibly too complacent belief in American exceptionalism. All well and good, Glory seems to imply—such a regime indeed makes Gilead a fine place to live, at least for white Americans—but what about those whose sins place them so far beyond the pale that they may be incapable of repentance? Why emphasize only the salvation and not also the damnation that belief in predestination entails? Glory herself has been guilty of fornication with a man whom she intended to marry but who concealed his marriage from her, and she has never informed her family of the truth—they continue to believe that her marriage failed. Perhaps this experience makes her more skeptical of her father's complacency—and yet even she remains a believer who prays on her knees and reads her Bible every day. How to account for someone like Jack without seeing at least the likelihood of double predestination? Rowan Williams's claim that in Jack, "we see something absolutely vital to human integrity, the knowledge that I do not coincide with myself, that who and what I am is significantly out of my control," resonates with such a question and implies that Jack might find the doctrine of predestination "liberating" could come to accept it, because it declares that "our future is radically unknowable to us" ("Native Speakers").

Indeed, when Jack first approaches Ames, he wishes to discuss the claim that "some people are intentionally and irretrievably consigned to perdition" (*Gilead* 150). The subject, which Ames has discussed with many troubled souls, exasperates him, in part because "[n]ine-tenths of the time when some smart aleck starts in on theological questions he's only trying to put me in a false position" (152). More fundamentally, however, he is impatient with argument because of its inadequacy to match the reality of religious experience: "[M]y advice is this—don't look for proofs. Don't bother with them at all. They are never sufficient to the question, and they're always a little impertinent, I think, because they claim for God a place within our conceptual grasp" (179). Honest doubts, which come from one's own experience and observation, can be respected, as Ames shows through his appreciation for Ludwig Feuerbach, who recognizes "the joyful aspects of religion" and "loves the world" (24).[18] More often, though, doubts about religion are not really one's own but rather "the mustache and walking stick that happen to be the fashion of any particular moment" (179).

Ames's reflections here resonate with an entire tradition that holds Christianity to be not merely a set of beliefs, but a whole way of life, which cannot be "questioned" in the same way that one might question the logic of an argument. As Hungerford points out, Ames "does not say that arguments [against belief] are wrong, or mistaken, but that they do not participate in the religious practice of making experience open upon mean-

---

18. Indeed, in *Absence of Mind*, Robinson writes: "If I were not myself a religious person, but wished to make an account of religion, I believe I would tend toward the Feuerbachian view that religion is a projection of humanity's conceptions of beauty, goodness, power, and other valued things, a humanizing of experience by understanding it as structured around and mirroring back these values. Then it would resemble art, with which it is strongly associated" (127).

ing. . . . Belief here is imagined as a religiously understood reality that is simply other to arguments against it" (116). For Ames, this is so true that he even speaks of "[t]he oddness of the phrase 'believe in God'" (143)—presumably, because to use the word "belief" as a potential wedge between the reality of God and an individual experience of him (after all, a belief can be true or false) is already to falsify, or at least to cheapen, the experience. Jack suggests that the same imperviousness to argument is true of his own unbelief: "I don't even believe God doesn't exist, if you see what I mean" (220). Hungerford is to this extent justified in reading *Gilead*, despite its preoccupation with the content of Calvinist doctrine, as another illustration of the "postmodern belief" that she sees as central to American literature after 1960. The emphasis here, Hungerford proposes, is on belief as experience, as what Wittgenstein might call a "form of life," not on belief as meaning: "While scholars of lived religion have sidelined belief as a way of understanding religion, Robinson insists that belief is in fact something one experiences, just as thought is something that one experiences, and that the content of belief includes claims about the dignity of persons just as surely as it contains claims about God and God's relation to humanity" (116).

But what about the possibility of sincere inquiry about belief, coming from genuinely troubled, even desperate people who do not intend to be (even if in effect they often are) "smart alecks"? In *Home,* Jack's motive for the discussion is suggested when he tells Glory that of all the Christian doctrines, "perdition is the one thing that always made sense to me. I mean, it has always seemed plausible. On the basis of my experience" (119)—a statement that might call into question Williams's suggestion that belief in predestination is necessarily "liberating." Ames, to be sure, cannot discern Jack's motives in asking about predestination, and in the absence of further information—and in light of Jack's history—his suspicion that Jack is simply baiting him seems a plausible guess. But this does not relieve Ames of the responsibility of answering, and Jack's appeal to his personal experience here resonates with Robinson's own affirmation of the experiential—perhaps double predestination is precisely the means through which Jack might come to believe, if not necessarily (if readers take him at his word when he characterizes his own unbelief) to be *persuaded* of Christianity's truth. Intellectually, the upshot of Ames's response is that predestination is a great mystery, and that it is presumptuous to judge the authenticity of anyone's religion. Both statements may be true, but rhetorically, they have the effect of irritably brushing away the question—which is, as Jack himself points out, not "a mere word, a mere abstraction" (*Gilead* 150). As a minister's son, Jack is familiar with the theology that Ames professes; the pain of his apostasy is also the pain of discord within the family, and Hungerford is quite right to see that the "force of longing in *Gilead* is for Jack's return to the Boughton family, his reconciliation with those people, and that place, that formed his coherent moral context" (171). But how is such reconciliation to be achieved, if acquaintance with theology and the example of his own family—Jack does not seem particularly ironic when he declares to Ames, "We all love you, you know . . . You're all saints" (242)—have not sufficed? Jack's revelations about himself do serve to chasten Ames for his lapses in charity. However, they do not, it would seem, make any room for the efficacy of actual discourse that inquires into the truth of predestination—or, indeed, of any religious matters. If readers take Robinson and Ames at their word when they emphasize the irrefragability of religious experience, then this would include non-Christian religious experience as well and thereby frame her entire project within the discourse of the "spiritual."

A sort of reconciliation between Ames and Jack—though not between Jack and his father—is achieved in *Gilead* when Jack reveals that he has, in his long absence from home, married Della, an African American woman from Memphis, and become a father, despite fierce opposition from Della's family. In *Home*, Glory meets Della and her son when she comes searching for Jack, who has recently left, perhaps never to see his father and sister again, and the revelation of Jack's family and of their love for him moves Glory to an apparent conviction that Jack has found his redemption: the novel's final sentence is "The Lord is wonderful" (325). It is, perhaps, fitting that Robinson might choose interracial love and marriage as the index of whatever goodness Jack might possess, for in both novels, racial justice for African Americans is presented as the moral necessity that even the most upright of white Americans often fail to see. In *Gilead*, Ames reflects on his grandfather, an associate of John Brown, who was militantly against slavery and who thought his own son's pacifism to be a moral failing; this familial history is juxtaposed against a fire that destroys the only African American church in the town and the eventual departure of African Americans from Gilead—all despite Iowa's reputation as "the shining star of radicalism" (176). In *Home*, Jack makes his sympathy toward the civil rights protests in Montgomery clear, even though his father considers them provocations to violence (204); and when he tells his father that "colored people" in St. Louis have been "kind" to him, his father reminds him that "people judge you by your associations" and that he "could help [him]self by finding a better class of friends" (156, 157). While it would be inaccurate to state that Jack marries Della because he believes in racial justice, the marriage is symbolically appropriate because it suggests how far he is willing to offend conventional ideas in pursuit of a moral ideal. (Indeed, Della's family is, if anything, more opposed to the marriage than Jack's—not only because of the racial difference but also because Della's father believes that "all white men are atheists, the only difference is that some of them are aware of it" [*Gilead* 220]).

Jack's attitude toward race goes a long way to redeem him in the eyes of a twenty-first century audience, but it is noteworthy that the degree of risk he undergoes in marrying Della is, like the portrayal of Ames and Gilead itself, rendered credible primarily through the mere fact of its being set in 1956. Hungerford has suggested that "the work of both novels is to translate racial reconciliation into another mode of familial reconciliation" (119), so that "home" comes to serve as a metaphor for the nation's racial history. Yet this sense of the necessity for racial reconciliation seems difficult to reconcile with the atmosphere of nostalgia for home that permeates the two novels, with their almost defiant celebration of the provincial and their conviction that even so obscure a place as Gilead has, as Ames says, been the scene of unsung "heroes . . . saints and martyrs" (173). The year 1956 marks, on the one hand, a significant moment in a progressive historical narrative, when the evil of institutional racism is challenged and its end now glimpsed as a real possibility. On the other hand, it also marks the impending collapse of the world that has sustained such men as Ames— the world shaped by American mainline Protestantism, in which cultural homogeneity and shared values have produced much good, despite their tendency to produce complacency as well. In the essay "Puritans and Prigs," Robinson states that Puritanism "appears to me to have died early in this [that is, the twentieth] century" (150), and that she shares a "general sense that we are suffering a radical moral decline which is destroying the fabric of society, seriously threatening our sense of safety as well as of mutual respect and shared interest" (157). Like the Updike of *The Poorhouse Fair*, Robinson entertains the possibility that an older, more homogenous America may have been preferable to the contemporary United States, despite its evident failures. Affirming powerfully Calvin's call "to embrace the whole human race without exception in a single feeling of love" (qtd. in "Puritans" 172), and translating this call into the political commitments of liberalism, Robinson nonetheless fails to give a convincing answer to just how it is that a period that has seen the decisive triumph of many liberal ideals has also been a period of moral decline and social fragmentation. As a result, she runs the risk that some readers will discern in *Gilead* and *Home* little more than nostalgia, while others will view her religious commitments as subordinate to their usefulness in promoting equality—and to this extent, optional, private, and largely therapeutic in nature.

In *Absence of Mind,* Robinson mounts a powerful argument against Freud's conviction that "the mind is *not* to be trusted" (105) in terms that echo Ames's defense of the authenticity of religious experience in *Gilead.* She attributes Freud's errors to an understandable desire to reject not only the anti-Semitism that Jews suffered in early twentieth-century Vienna but all theories of civilization and culture that focused on racial and ethnic difference: "Rereading Freud, I have come to the conclusion that . . . very central features of his thought, most notably the murder of the primal father with all its consequences, were meant to confute theories of race and nation that were becoming increasingly predominant as he wrote. This is not to say that he was not persuaded of their truth, only that his deep concern that they be maintained as a bulwark against 'black mud,' that they should have seemed to Jung to have had something like a religious significance for him, is entirely understandable" (84). If my argument about Robinson is correct, then her own relationship to orthodox Christian doctrine and practice has a similar character. I do not doubt that Robinson is persuaded of the truth of Christian doctrine. I do, however, hold that the use she makes of this orthodoxy—the affirmation of human equality, of the power and reality of the human mind, and of the irreducibly individual nature of authentic religious experience—is far more important in her essays and her fiction than the question of whether Christian orthodoxy is true. For this reason, I see an essential continuity between *Housekeeping* and her overtly Christian novels—all are concerned with the authenticity of religious experience, whether that experience can be described as "Christian" or not. I also believe that this helps to account for her dismissive attitude toward Flannery O'Connor, whose orthodoxy is more evident than Robinson's but who shares little of Robinson's political liberalism.[19]

19. In "A World of Beautiful Souls," an interview with the Reformed journal *Perspectives,* Robinson casts doubt on whether O'Connor is a Christian writer in any meaningful sense: "For some reason it is not conventional for serious fiction to treat religious thought respectfully—the influence of Flannery O'Connor has been particularly destructive, I think, though she is considered a religious writer and she considered herself one." Robinson is not arguing here that people have misread O'Connor, seeing religious mockery where none is evident; she is instead insinuating that it is all too likely that O'Connor, whatever her intentions may have been, did not in fact treat religious thought with respect. I see in this statement evidence that Robinson is more complacent than O'Connor about religious matters, and that "respectful treatment" of religion for her means an unwillingness to call into question any religious experience by asking whether it is true. Because Robinson sees as her primary antagonist the thought that descends from Darwin, Marx, Nietzsche, and Freud, all of whom call the existence of the human mind into question, I am sympathetic to her position—but I do not believe that "experience" is the primary criterion of religious truth, and I believe that holding this belief leads Robinson into the error of disregarding a writer such as O'Connor, who is very much concerned with truth but just as opposed as Robinson to this kind of positivism.

In their respective uses of Christian orthodoxy, both Gordon and Robinson are characteristic novelists of their time. Shaped by religious cultures that from the current historical moment seem uniform and dogmatic—the pre–Vatican II, working-class milieu of American Catholicism and the civic-minded and small-town world of mainline American Protestantism—Gordon and Robinson seek to find ways to valorize what they consider to be the best of these cultures, whether aesthetic, ethical, or political, while holding at arm's length (or, in Gordon's case, actually dissenting from) many of the specific dogmas that these religious cultures affirm. Both seem haunted by the consciousness that the world has not turned out as they would have liked: as Gordon's feminist conception of sexual liberation and Robinson's deep commitment to political (and especially racial) equality recede as matters of felt historical conflict, the possibility that certain of their commitments, cut loose from a commitment to the primacy of Christian truth, may have actually led to social decline seems to be only grudgingly considered. Yet their work is valuable precisely because it attests to the deep attractions of Christian orthodoxy, its staying power even in a world uncomfortable with the proclamation of truth. It may be that until more people are willing to embrace truth as truth, the work of such writers will be useful as a rhetorical model akin to what Pascal described long ago—to make people see that Christianity is desirable, good, and not contrary to reason before they can come to be persuaded of its truth.

EPILOGUE

On Belief and Academic Humility

In 2005, Stanley Fish predicted that religion "would succeed high theory and the triumvirate of race, gender, and class as the center of intellectual energy in the academy" ("One University"). Eight years later, I can tentatively conclude that Fish was on to something. Religion has certainly not *replaced* these earlier foci, and its increased presence in the academy has not always entailed respect—certainly those who despise it, such as the New Atheists, have made the bigger splash in the mass media. Yet while a growing number of scholars, including Hungerford and John McClure, have focused welcome and generally respectful attention on the connections between literature and religion in the post–World War II period, it is still fairly rare for scholars to identify themselves as Christians—and even rarer for them to affirm Christian orthodoxy. The default assumption that intellectuals necessarily profess secular commitments has not been noticeably shaken.

Despite all the work that has been done on theories of secularization, I am not convinced that it is necessarily harder to believe today than it might have been in ages past, even if it is undeniable that political, social, and educational structures once did much more to promulgate and even to "enforce" Christian belief in the West than they do today. (Indeed, I am Kierkegaardian enough to suspect that Christian belief is healthier when it exists in tension with worldly powers than when it is cosseted and coopted by them.) Updike's Clarence Wilmot is probably close to the truth when he reflects, "Christ risen was no more easily embraced by Paul and his listeners than by modern skeptics. The stumbling blocks have never dissolved. The scandal has never lessened" (*Beauty* 18). While there is a long philosophical tradition that affirms the compatibility of a generalized theism with reason—acknowledged today both by the *Catechism of the Catholic Church* and by the formerly atheist but non-Christian philosopher Anthony Flew—the truly implausible claims of the Christian narrative (above all, Jesus' divinity and salvific death and resurrection) are apprehensible only through revelation. One accepts the testimony of the tradition that has handed news of these events down and believes in it, or one does not. Or—what seems to be the most common option today—one cobbles together a belief structure and lifestyle from what one likes in the tradition and rejects the rest.

I have focused on the post–World War II period not just because it remains, in many important senses, the time in which we live, but also because of its particular rhetorical challenges. Facing a dominant narrative of secularization that would claim that the "hard sayings" of Christianity are particularly incredible to modern (and postmodern) people, Christian writers concerned with orthodoxy have responded to this historical framing with varied strategies intended to lessen this sense of radical incompatibility with the consensus of human knowledge, to show that belief is and always remains possible. There is no denying, however, that such strategies can only go so far—especially if I am correct that the difficulty of accepting Christianity has less to do with empirical questions (considerable though these may be) than with its challenge to self-esteem. As Ralph Wood puts it:

> [We] must confront the hard truth that the Story here retold is not obvious but scandalous. It is not the story that we would tell ourselves. Such a story would make excuses for our massive crimes and tiny misdemeanors. It would justify our many misdeeds, both great and small. It would exonerate us from all final blame. It would offer solutions, whether simple or complex, that we could ourselves accomplish. Above all, it would not offend by telling us that we are unable to save ourselves. The Christian Story refuses to pursue all of these easier paths. It is indeed an offensive and scandalous Story. It does not report what we *want* to hear, but something far better—what we *ought* to hear and thus, at the deepest level, what we truly long to learn. (viii)

Such obstacles, I would argue, formidable enough for human beings to overcome at any time, are particularly so for most inhabitants of the academy today—often, precisely the people who have the greatest belief in the value of their own intelligence and the greatest resentment against a larger society that refuses to confirm their worth through appropriate remuneration or status.

There is a considerable irony in the fact that in the last few decades, scholars of literature, in part as a reaction to the prestige of the sciences in the contemporary university, have frequently professed a version of epistemic humility. Influenced by the endless deferral of meaning that Jacques Derrida took as his keynote, or by the absolute responsibility toward the Other that Emmanuel Levinas enjoined, much recent thought has suggested that the pursuit of knowledge often amounts to a morally dubious attempt to master others, and that the desire for certainty is totalitarian. Such thinking continually emphasizes how little it knows, rarely asserts a proposition without profuse reminders of its provisional nature, and adeptly casts a disapproving eye at those who have the temerity to assert their claims as truth. Though the contradictory nature of such discourse has been exposed time and time again—dare one claim that it is "true" that "truth" is so harmful?—it has lost none of its appeal.

Writers with orthodox Christian concerns confront this climate, for a narrative that claims to be the truth necessarily offends such a position. Perhaps the apparent contrast between O'Connor and Robinson is most instructive here: O'Connor, who assumes the hostility of her audience and assaults her readers with the shocking implications of the Christian narrative, assumes that her audience will be no less convinced of its own "truth" (whether it grounds this truth in science or in uncertainty) and will require humiliation, while Robinson, professing Christian belief, emphasizes the exalted conception of human nature that it affirms ("Marguerite" 183–84) against what she sees as a general belittlement of human capacities caused by a materialist worldview and abetted by capitalism. O'Connor, it might be said, doesn't think much of human beings' claims for themselves; Robinson wishes that human beings would engage in "the rigorous imagination of a higher self" ("Marguerite"183) and thus confirm her own high estimation of them.

I would attempt to resolve this contrast by arguing not for epistemic humility but for Christian humility. I see little evidence that "epistemic humility" even exists—one believes what one believes, no matter how much one attempts to hold these beliefs at a distance, and the fact that one can imagine believing otherwise (the condition that defines Charles Taylor's "secular age") in no way implies that one believes less firmly. Newman's work on assent and certainty corresponds to the structure of human belief as one encounters it; it confirms that *all* people are believers, if not in Christianity, then in some set of ultimate principles, however much they may disavow such belief. Genuine humility has nothing to do with a reluctance to profess one's belief; it has instead to do with how one conducts oneself in the practice of this belief and with whether one admits one's unworthiness. The ironic community that Booth envisages, created through an invitation for human beings to leave their former selves behind is, I would like to believe, sustained through its gratitude for gifts undeserved and incomparable. In Evelyn Waugh's historical novel *Helena* (1950), St. Helena expresses such a sense of gratitude in a prayer to the three magi who brought gifts to the Christ child: "You are my especial patrons . . . and patrons of all late-comers, of all who have a tedious journey to make to the truth, of all who are confused with knowledge and speculation, of all who through politeness make themselves partners in guilt, of all who stand in danger by reason of their talents" (224). The writers I have discussed in this book understand the attractions of such a Christian community, and as writers of literary fiction, they write to an audience composed largely of just the sort of people with whom Helena identifies herself. Though O'Connor, Spark, Updike, Percy, Gordon, and Robinson differ in the rhetorical efficacy of their arguments and in the degree to which they represent Christian belief faithfully, their efforts have much to teach about the rhetoric of fiction, the use of narrative as argument on behalf of Christianity. I venture no prediction as to whether the academy will, as Fish suggests, become friendlier toward such efforts—though I hope, ardently, that it will prove up to the challenge.

WORKS CITED

Agamben, Giorgio. *Homo Sacer: Sovereign Power and Bare Life.* Translated by Daniel Heller-Roazen. Stanford, CA: Stanford University Press, 1998.

Anderson, Benedict. *Imagined Communities: Reflections on the Origin and Spread of Nationalism.* Rev. ed. London: Verso, 1991.

Appiah, Kwame Anthony. *Cosmopolitanism: Ethics in a World of Strangers.* New York: Norton, 2006.

Apostolou, Fotini E. *Seduction and Death in Muriel Spark's Fiction.* Westport, CT: Greenwood Press , 2001.

Aristotle. *Poetics.* Translated by Leon Golden. In *The Critical Tradition: Classic Texts and Contemporary Trends,* edited by David H. Richter, 42–64. Boston: Bedford, 1998.

Asals, Frederick. *Flannery O'Connor: The Imagination of Extremity.* Athens: University of Georgia Press, 1982.

Atlas, James. "An Interview with Walker Percy." In *Conversations with Walker Percy,* edited by Lewis A. Lawson and Victor A. Kramer, 182–86. Jackson: University Press of Mississippi, 1985.

Augustine. *Confessions.* Translated by Garry Wills. London: Penguin, 2009.

———. *On Christian Doctrine.* Translated by D. W. Robertson. New York: Prentice Hall, 1958.

Bacon, Jon Lance. *Flannery O'Connor and Cold War Culture.* Cambridge: Cambridge University Press, 1993.

Badiou, Alain. *The Century.* Translated by Alberto Toscano. Cambridge: Polity, 2007.

———. *Saint Paul: The Foundations of Universalism.* Translated by Ray Brassier. Chicago: University of Chicago Press, 2003.

Bakhtin, Mikhail. *Problems of Dostoevsky's Poetics.* Translated by Caryl Emerson. Minneapolis: University of Minnesota Press, 1984.

Baldanza, Frank. "Muriel Spark and the Occult." *Wisconsin Studies in Contemporary Literature* 6 (Summer 1965): 190–203.

Berger, Peter L. "Secularization Falsified." *First Things* 180 (February 2008): 23–27.

Bloom, Harold. "Introduction." In *Modern Critical Views: John Updike,* edited by Harold Bloom, 1–8. New York: Chelsea House, 1987.

Booth, Wayne. *The Company We Keep: An Ethics of Fiction.* Berkeley: University of California Press, 1988.

———. *The Rhetoric of Fiction.* 2nd ed. Chicago: University of Chicago Press, 1983.

———. *A Rhetoric of Irony.* Chicago: University of Chicago Press, 1974.

Boswell, Marshall. "The World and the Void: *Creatio* [sic] *ex Nihilo* and Homoeroticism in Updike's *Rabbit Is Rich.*" In *John Updike and Religion: The Sense of the Sacred and the Motions of Grace,* edited by James Yerkes, 162–79. Grand Rapids, MI: Eerdmans, 1999.

Bottum, Joseph. "The Death of Protestant America: A Political Theory of the Protestant Mainline." *First Things* 180 (August/September 2008): 23–33.

Boyle, Nicholas. *Sacred and Secular Scriptures: A Catholic Approach to Literature.* Notre Dame: University of Notre Dame Press, 2005.

Brooks, Peter. *Reading for the Plot: Design and Intention in Narrative.* New York: Knopf, 1984.

Browning, Robert. "The Bishop Orders His Tomb at St. Praxed's Church." In *Selected Poems,* edited by Daniel Karlin, 45–49. Harmondsworth: Penguin, 2001.

Catechism of the Catholic Church. Chicago: Loyola University Press, 1995.

Cheyette, Bryan. *Muriel Spark.* Tavistock: Northcote House, 2000.

Christensen, Jerome C. "*Lancelot:* Sign for the Times." In *Walker Percy: Art and Ethics,* edited by Jac Tharpe, 107–20. Jackson: University Press of Mississippi, 1980.

Ciuba, Gary M. *Walker Percy: Books of Revelations.* Athens: University of Georgia Press, 1991.

Cohn, Dorrit. *The Distinction of Fiction.* Baltimore: Johns Hopkins University Press, 1999.

Cox, Harvey. *The Secular City: Secularization and Urbanization in Theological Perspective.* New York: Macmillan, 1965.

Crews, Frederick. *The Critics Bear It Away: American Fiction and the Academy.* New York: Random House, 1992.

Crowe, Marian E. *Aiming at Heaven, Getting the Earth: The English Catholic Novel Today.* Lanham, MD: Lexington, 2007.

Douglas, Ann. *The Feminization of American Culture.* New York: Knopf, 1977.

Dunn, Allen, and Thomas F. Haddox. "The Enigma of Critical Distance; or, Why Historicists Need Convictions." In *The Limits of Literary Historicism,* edited by Allen Dunn and Thomas F. Haddox, xi–xxv. Knoxville: University of Tennessee Press, 2011.

Dupuy, Edward J. *Autobiography in Walker Percy: Repetition, Recovery, and Redemption.* Baton Rouge: Louisiana State University Press, 1996.

Eagleton, Terry. *The Ideology of the Aesthetic.* Oxford: Blackwell, 1990.

———. *Literary Theory: An Introduction.* 2nd ed. Minneapolis: University of Minnesota Press, 1996.

Edgecombe, Rodney Stenning. *Vocation and Identity in the Fiction of Muriel Spark.* Columbia: University of Missouri Press, 1990.

Edmondson, Henry T., III. *Return to Good and Evil: Flannery O'Connor's Response to Nihilism.* Lanham, MD: Lexington, 2002.

Eliot, T. S. *For Lancelot Andrewes: Essays on Style and Order.* London: Faber and Gwyer, 1928.

Ellul, Jacques. *The Humiliation of the Word.* Translated by Joyce Main Hanks. Grand Rapids, MI: Eerdmans, 1985.

Fetterley, Judith. *The Resisting Reader: A Feminist Approach to American Fiction.* Bloomington: Indiana University Press, 1978.

Fish, Stanley. "One University under God?" *The Chronicle of Higher Education* 51, no. 18 (7 January 2005): C1.

Flew, Anthony. *There Is a God: How the World's Most Notorious Atheist Changed His Mind.* New York: HarperOne, 2007.

Freud, Sigmund. "On Narcissism: An Introduction." In *The Freud Reader,* edited by Peter Gay, 545–62. New York: Norton, 1989.

Gandolfo, Anita. *Testing the Faith: The New Catholic Fiction in America.* Westport, CT: Greenwood, 1992.

Gardner, John. *On Moral Fiction.* 1978. New York: Basic Books, 2000.

Garsten, Bryan. *Saving Persuasion: A Defense of Rhetoric and Judgment.* Cambridge, MA: Harvard University Press, 2006.

Gentry, Marshall Bruce. *Flannery O'Connor's Religion of the Grotesque.* Jackson: University Press of Mississippi, 1986.

Giannone, Richard. *Flannery O'Connor: Hermit Novelist.* Urbana: University of Illinois Press, 2000.

———. *Flannery O'Connor and the Mystery of Love.* Urbana: University of Illinois Press, 1989.

Giles, Paul. *American Catholic Arts and Fictions: Culture, Ideology, Aesthetics.* Cambridge: Cambridge University Press, 1992.

Girard, René. *Deceit, Desire, and the Novel.* Translated by Yvonne Freccero. Baltimore: Johns Hopkins University Press, 1965.

Gordon, Mary. *Circling My Mother.* New York: Pantheon, 2007.

———. *The Company of Women.* New York: Random House, 1980.

———. *Conversations with Mary Gordon.* Edited by Alma Bennett. Jackson: University Press of Mississippi, 2002.

———. "The Deacon." In *The Stories of Mary Gordon,* 65–83. New York: Pantheon, 2006.

———. *Final Payments.* New York: Random House, 1978.

———. "Getting Here from There: A Writer's Reflections on a Religious Past." In *Good Boys and Dead Girls and Other Essays,* 160–75. New York: Viking, 1991.

———. *Pearl.* New York: Pantheon, 2005.

———. *Seeing Through Places: Reflections on Geography and Identity.* New York: Scribner, 2000.

———. *The Shadow Man.* New York: Random House, 1996.

———. *Spending: A Utopian Divertimento.* New York: Scribner, 1998.

Guardini, Romano. *The End of the Modern World: A Search for Orientation.* New York: Sheed and Ward, 1956.

Haddox, Thomas F. "The City Reconsidered: Problems and Possibilities of Urban Community in 'A Stroke of Good Fortune' and 'The Artificial Nigger.'" *The Flannery O'Connor Review* 4 (2005): 4–18.

———. *Fears and Fascinations: Representing Catholicism in the American South.* New York: Fordham University Press, 2005.

Harpham, Geoffrey Galt. *Language Alone: The Critical Fetish of Modernity.* New York: Routledge, 2002.

Harrison, Bernard. "Muriel Spark and Jane Austen." In *Critical Essays on Muriel Spark,* edited by Joseph Hynes, 131–50. New York: G. K. Hall, 1992.

Hawkes, John. "Flannery O'Connor's Devil." *Sewanee Review* 70 (Summer 1962): 395–407.

Hawthorne, Nathaniel. *The Scarlet Letter.* 1850. In *Collected Novels,* edited by Millicent Bell, 115–345. New York: Library of America, 1983.

Hemingway, Ernest. *The Sun Also Rises.* New York: Scribner, 1926.

Hendin, Josephine. *The World of Flannery O'Connor.* Bloomington: Indiana University Press, 1970.

Hungerford, Amy. *Postmodern Belief: American Literature and Religion since 1960.* Princeton, NJ: Princeton University Press, 2010.

Iannone, Carol. "The Secret of Mary Gordon's Success." *Commentary* 79 (June 1985): 62–66.

Jameson, Fredric. *The Political Unconscious: Narrative as a Socially Symbolic Act.* Ithaca, NY: Cornell University Press, 1981.

Jarraway, David. "Future Interior: Subjective (A)voidance in John Updike's "Rabbit" Novels." *Canadian Review of American Studies* 40 (2010): 45–63.

Kermode, Frank. "Muriel Spark's House of Fiction." In *Critical Essays on Muriel Spark,* edited by Joseph Hynes, 29–32. New York: G. K. Hall, 1992.

Kimball, Roger. "Muriel Spark, RIP." *The New Criterion* 24 (May 2006): 1–2.

Kundera, Milan. *The Unbearable Lightness of Being.* Translated Michael Henry Heim. New York: Harper and Row, 1984.

Lake, Christina Bieber. *The Incarnational Art of Flannery O'Connor.* Macon, GA: Mercer University Press, 2005.

Lasch, Christopher. *The Revolt of the Elites and the Betrayal of Democracy.* New York: Norton, 1995.

Lawler, Peter Augustine. *Postmodernism Rightly Understood: The Return to Realism in American Thought.* Lanham, MD: Rowan and Littlefield, 1999.

Leise, Christopher. "'That Little Incandescence': Reading the Fragmentary and John Calvin in Marilynne Robinson's *Gilead.*" *Studies in the Novel* 41 (Fall 2009): 348–67.

Lodge, David. "Post-Pill Paradise Lost: John Updike's *Couples.*" In *Modern Critical Views: John Updike,* edited by Harold Bloom, 29–36. New York: Chelsea House, 1987.

———. "Time-Shift." *The Art of Fiction.* Harmondsworth: Penguin, 1992.

Lyotard, Jean-François. *The Postmodern Condition: A Report on Knowledge.* Translated by Geoff Bennington and Brian Massumi. Minneapolis: University of Minnesota Press, 1984.

MacIntyre, Alasdair. *Whose Justice? Which Rationality?* London: Duckworth, 1988.

MacKay, Marina. "Catholicism, Character, and the Invention of the Liberal Novel Tradition." *Twentieth-Century Literature* 48 (Summer 2002): 215–38.

Maley, Willy. "Not to Deconstruct? Righting and Deference in *Not to Disturb.*" In *Theorizing Muriel Spark: Gender, Race, Deconstruction,* edited by Martin McQuillan, 170–88. Houndsmills: Palgrave, 2002.

Mano, D. Keith. "Doughy Middleness." In *Critical Essays on John Updike,* edited by William R. Macnaughton, 74–77. Boston: G. K. Hall, 1982.

Maritain, Jacques. *The Peasant of the Garonne: An Old Layman Questions Himself about the Present Time.* New York: Holt, Rinehart, and Winston, 1968.

Mattessich, Stefan. "Drifting Decision and the Decision to Drift: The Question of Spirit in Marilynne Robinson's *Housekeeping.*" *Differences: A Journal of Feminist Cultural Studies* 19.3 (2008): 59–89.

Mayne, Richard. "Fiery Particle—On Muriel Spark." In *Critical Essays on Muriel Spark,* edited by Joseph Hynes, 47–54. New York: G. K. Hall, 1992.

McClure, John. *Partial Faiths: Postsecular Fiction in the Age of Pynchon and Morrison.* Athens: University of Georgia Press, 2007.

McQuillan, Martin. "'I Don't Know Anything about Freud': Muriel Spark Meets Contemporary Criticism." In *Theorizing Muriel Spark: Gender, Race, Deconstruction,* edited by Martin McQuillan, 1–31. Houndsmills: Palgrave, 2002.

Merton, Thomas. "Flannery O'Connor: A Prose Elegy." In *Raids on the Unspeakable*, 37–42. New York: New Directions, 1965.

Michaels, Walter Benn. *The Shape of the Signifier: 1967 to the End of History*. Princeton, NJ: Princeton University Press, 2004.

Milbank, John, Catherine Pickstock, and Graham Ward. "Suspending the Material: The Turn of Radical Orthodoxy." In *Radical Orthodoxy: A New Theology*, edited by John Milbank, Catherine Pickstock, and Graham Ward, 1–20. London: Routledge, 1999.

Miller, D. Quentin. *John Updike and the Cold War: Drawing the Iron Curtain*. Columbia: University of Missouri Press, 2001.

Montgomery, Benilde. "Spark and Newman: Jean Brodie Reconsidered." *Twentieth-Century Literature* 43 (Spring 1997): 94–106.

Morris, Charles R. *American Catholic: The Saints and Sinners Who Built America's Most Powerful Church*. New York: Times Books, 1997.

Morris, Wright. *The Territory Ahead*. New York: Harcourt Brace, 1958.

Nadel, Alan. *Containment Culture: American Narratives, Postmodernism, and the Atomic Age*. Durham, NC: Duke University Press, 1995.

Neuhaus, Richard John. "While We're At It." *First Things* 88 (December 1998): 65–80.

Newman, John Henry. *Apologia Pro Vita Sua*. 1908. Mineola, NY: Dover, 2005.

———. *An Essay in Aid of a Grammar of Assent*. 1870. New York: Longmans, Green, 1947.

———. *An Essay on the Development of Chrisitan Doctrine*. 1845. New York: Longmans, Green, 1949.

Novak, Frank G., Jr. "The Satanic Personality in Updike's *Roger's Version*." *Christianity and Literature* 55 (Fall 2005): 3–26.

Nussbaum, Martha. "The Professor of Parody." *The New Republic* 220 (22 February 1999): 37–45.

O'Connor, Flannery. "The Artificial Nigger." In *The Complete Stories*, 249–70. New York: Farrar, Straus, and Giroux, 1971.

———. "The Catholic Novelist in the Protestant South." In *Mystery and Manners: Occasional Prose*, edited by Sally and Robert Fitzgerald, 191–209. New York: Farrar, Straus, and Giroux, 1969.

———. "Everything That Rises Must Converge." In *The Complete Stories*, 405–18. New York: Farrar, Straus, and Giroux, 1971.

———. "The Fiction Writer and His Country." In *Mystery and Manners: Occasional Prose*, edited by Sally and Robert Fitzgerald, 25–35. New York: Farrar, Straus, and Giroux, 1969.

———. "The Geranium." In *The Complete Stories*, 3–14. New York: Farrar, Straus, and Giroux, 1971.

———. "A Good Man Is Hard to Find." In *A Good Man Is Hard to Find and Other Stories*. 9–29. New York: Harcourt, 1955.

———. *The Habit of Being: Letters of Flannery O'Connor*. Edited by Sally Fitzgerald. New York: Farrar, Straus, and Giroux, 1979.

———. Introduction to *A Memoir of Mary Ann*. In *Mystery and Manners: Occasional Prose*, edited by Sally and Robert Fitzgerald, 213–30. New York: Farrar, Straus and Giroux, 1969.

———. "Judgement Day." In *The Complete Stories*, 531–50. New York: Farrar, Straus, and Giroux, 1971.

———. "The Lame Shall Enter First." In *The Complete Stories*, 445–82. New York: Farrar, Straus, and Giroux, 1971.

———. Manuscript drafts of "The Artificial Nigger." Flannery O'Connor Collection, Files 157b, 157c, and 158. Georgia College Library and Instructional Technology Center, Georgia College, Milledgeville, Georgia.

———. "Novelist and Believer." In *Mystery and Manners: Occasional Prose,* edited by Sally and Robert Fitzgerald, 154–68. New York: Farrar, Straus, and Giroux, 1969.

———. "On Her Own Work." In *Mystery and Manners: Occasional Prose,* edited by Sally and Robert Fitzgerald, 107–18. New York: Farrar, Straus, and Giroux, 1969.

———. "Parker's Back." In *The Complete Stories,* 510–30. New York: Farrar, Straus, and Giroux, 1971.

———. "Revelation." In *The Complete Stories,* 488–509. New York: Farrar, Straus, and Giroux, 1971.

———. "Some Aspects of the Grotesque in Southern Fiction." In *Mystery and Manners: Occasional Prose,* edited by Sally and Robert Fitzgerald, 36–50. New York: Farrar, Straus, and Giroux, 1969.

———. *Wise Blood.* 2nd ed. New York: Farrar, Straus, and Giroux, 1962.

O'Gorman, Farrell. *Flannery O'Connor, Walker Percy, and Catholic Vision in Postwar Southern Fiction.* Baton Rouge: Louisiana State University Press, 2004.

Olesky, Elzbieta. "A Talk with Walker Percy." In *More Conversations with Walker Percy,* edited by Lewis A. Lawson and Victor A. Kramer, 72–83. Jackson: University Press of Mississippi, 1993.

Pascal, Blaise. *Pensées.* Edited and translated by Roger Ariew. Indianapolis: Hackett, 2005.

Percy, Walker. *Conversations with Walker Percy.* Edited by Lewis A. Lawson and Victor A. Kramer. Jackson: University Press of Mississippi, 1985.

———. *Lancelot.* New York: Farrar, Straus, and Giroux, 1977.

———. *The Last Gentleman.* New York: Farrar, Straus, and Giroux, 1966.

———. *Lost in the Cosmos: The Last Self-Help Book.* New York: Farrar, Straus, and Giroux, 1983.

———. "The Message in the Bottle." In *The Message in the Bottle: How Queer Man Is, How Queer, Language Is, and What One Has to Do with the Other,* 119–49. New York: Farrar, Straus, and Giroux, 1975.

———. *More Conversations with Walker Percy.* Edited by Lewis A. Lawson and Victor A. Kramer. Jackson: University Press of Mississippi, 1993.

———. *The Moviegoer.* New York: Knopf, 1961.

———. "Questions They Never Asked Me." 1977. In *Signposts in a Strange Land,* edited by Patrick Samway, 397–423. New York: Farrar, Straus, and Giroux, 1991.

———. *The Second Coming.* New York: Farrar, Straus, and Giroux, 1980.

———. *Signposts in a Strange Land,* edited by Patrick Samway. New York: Farrar, Straus and Giroux, 1991.

———. *The Thanatos Syndrome.* New York: Farrar, Straus, and Giroux, 1987.

Phelan, James. *Living to Tell about It: A Rhetoric and Ethics of Character Narration.* Ithaca, NY: Cornell University Press, 2005.

Piper, Wendy. *Misfits and Marble Fauns: Religion and Romance in Hawthorne and O'Connor.* Macon, GA: Mercer University Press, 2011.

Plato. *The Republic.* In *The Dialogues of Plato,* translated by B. Jowett. Vol. 2. New York: Bigelow, Brown, 1892.

Prickett, Stephen. *Narrative, Religion, and Science: Fundamentalism versus Irony, 1700–1999.* Cambridge: Cambridge University Press, 2002.

Proust, Marcel. *Remembrance of Things Past.* Translated by C. K. Scott Moncrieff, Terence Kilmartin, and Andreas Mayor. 3 vols. New York: Random House, 1981.

Quinlan, Kieran. *Walker Percy: The Last Catholic Novelist.* Baton Rouge: Louisiana State University Press, 1996.

Rawls, John. *Political Liberalism.* New York: Columbia University Press, 1996.

Ricoeur, Paul. *Time and Narrative.* Translated by Kathleen McLaughlin and David Pel-
lauer. Vol. 1. Chicago: University of Chicago Press, 1984.

Rieff, Philip. *My Life among the Deathworks: Illustrations of the Aesthetics of Authority.*
Volume 1 of *Sacred Order/Social Order.* Edited by Kenneth S. Piver. Charlottesville:
University Press of Virginia, 2006.

———. *The Triumph of the Therapeutic: Uses of Faith after Freud.* New York: Harper and
Row, 1966.

Robinson, Marilynne. "Calvinism as Metaphysics." *Toronto Journal of Theology* 25 (Fall
2009): 175–86.

———. *Gilead.* New York: Farrar, Straus, and Giroux, 2004.

———. *Home.* New York: Farrar, Straus, and Giroux, 2008.

———. Interview with Sarah Fay. *The Paris Review* 186 (Fall 2008). Available online
at http://www.theparisreview.org/interviews/5863/the-art-of-fiction-no-198-
marilynne-robinson.

———. "Marguerite de Navarre." In *The Death of Adam: Essays on Modern Thought,*
174–206. Boston: Houghton Mifflin, 1998.

———. "Onward, Christian Liberals." *The American Scholar* 75 (Spring 2006): 42–51.

———. "The Polemic against Calvin: The Origins and Consequences of Historical
Reputation." In *Calvin and the Church: Papers Presented at the 13th Colloquium of the
Calvin Studies Society.* Grand Rapids: CRC Services for the Calvin Studies Society,
2002.

———. "Psalm Eight." In *The Death of Adam: Essays on Modern Thought,* 227–44. Boston:
Houghton Mifflin, 1998.

———. "Puritans and Prigs." In *The Death of Adam: Essays on Modern Thought,* 150–73.
Boston: Houghton Mifflin, 1998.

———. "The Tyranny of Petty Coercion." *Harper's* 309 (August 2004): 13–17.

———. "A World of Beautiful Souls." *Perspectives: A Journal of Reformed Thought.* May
2005. Available online at http://www.rca.org/page.aspx?pid=3584. Accessed 18
July 2011.

Rorty, Richard. *Consequences of Pragmatism: Essays, 1972–1980.* Minneapolis: University
of Minnesota Press, 1982.

———. *Contingency, Irony, and Solidarity.* Cambridge: Cambridge University Press,
1989.

Sandner, David. "Between Eucatastrophe and Grace: J. R. R. Tolkien and Flannery
O'Connor." *Soundings: An Interdisciplinary Journal* 89 (Spring/Summer 2006): 171–
98.

Searles, George J. "*The Poorhouse Fair:* Updike's Thesis Statement." In *Critical Essays on
John Updike,* edited by William R. Macnaughton, 231–36. Boston: G. K. Hall, 1982.

Shy, Todd. "Religion and Marilynne Robinson." *Salmagundi* 155/156 (Summer 2007):
251–66.

Siegel, Lee. "The Believer." *New York Magazine* 37 (December 6, 2004): 82–83.

Smith, Christian, and Melinda Lundquist Denton. *Soul Searching: The Religious and
Spiritual Lives of American Teenagers.* New York: Oxford University Press, 2005.

Spark, Muriel. *The Abbess of Crewe.* New York: Viking, 1974.

———. *The Comforters.* 1957. London: Macmillan, 1966.

———. *Curriculum Vitae.* Boston: Houghton Mifflin, 1993.

———. "The Desegregation of Art." In *Critical Essays on Muriel Spark,* edited by Joseph
Hynes, 33–37. New York: G. K. Hall, 1992.

———. *The Driver's Seat.* New York: Knopf, 1970.

———. *The Girls of Slender Means.* London: Macmillan, 1963.

————. Interview with Sara Frankel. *Partisan Review* 54 (1987): 441–57.

————. *Loitering with Intent.* New York: Cowan, McCann, and Geoghegan, 1981.

————. "My Conversion." In *Critical Essays on Muriel Spark,* edited by Joseph Hynes, 24–28. New York: G. K. Hall, 1992.

————. *The Prime of Miss Jean Brodie.* London: Macmillan, 1961.

————. *Reality and Dreams.* London: Constable, 1996.

————. "'The Same Informed Air': An Interview with Muriel Spark." By Martin Mc-Quillan. In *Theorizing Muriel Spark: Gender, Race, Deconstruction,* edited by Martin McQuillan, 210–29. Houndsmills: Palgrave, 2002.

Stannard, Martin. *Muriel Spark: The Biography.* New York: Norton, 2010.

Steiner, George. "Supreme Fiction." *The New Yorker.* 11 March 1996. 105–6.

Stephens, Martha. *The Question of Flannery O'Connor.* Baton Rouge: Louisiana State University Press, 1973.

Stevens, Wallace. "The Idea of Order at Key West." In *Collected Poetry and Prose,* edited by Frank Kermode and Joan Richardson, 105–6. New York: Library of America, 1997.

Taylor, Charles. *A Secular Age.* Cambridge: Belknap, 2007.

Taylor, Mark C. *After God.* Chicago: University of Chicago Press, 2007.

Tocqueville, Alexis de. *Democracy in America.* Translated by Arthur Goldhammer. New York: Library of America, 2004.

Tolson, Jay. *Pilgrim in the Ruins: A Life of Walker Percy.* Chapel Hill: University of North Carolina Press, 1992.

Updike, John. *Couples.* New York: Knopf, 1968.

————. "Fellatio." *Midpoint and Other Poems.* New York: Knopf, 1969. 73.

————. Foreword. *The Poorhouse Fair.* New York: Knopf, 1977. i-xx.

————. "Hawthorne's Creed." In *Hugging the Shore: Essays and Criticism,* 73–80. New York: Knopf, 1983.

————. *In the Beauty of the Lilies.* New York: Knopf, 1996.

————. *Marry Me: A Romance.* New York: 1976.

————. *Memories of the Ford Administration.* New York: Knopf, 1992.

————. *A Month of Sundays.* New York: Knopf, 1975.

————. "One Big Interview." *Picked-Up Pieces.* New York: Knopf, 1975. 491–519.

————. "Pigeon Feathers." 1962. In *Pigeon Feathers and Other Stories,* 116–50. New York: Knopf, 1980.

————. *The Poorhouse Fair.* 1959. New York: Knopf, 1977.

————. *Rabbit Is Rich.* New York: Knopf, 1981.

————. *Rabbit, Run.* New York: Knopf, 1960.

————. *Rabbit Redux.* New York: Knopf, 1971.

————. "Remarks upon receiving the Campion Medal, bestowed by the Catholic Book Club, in New York City, on September 11, 1997." In *More Matter: Essays and Criticism,* 850–52. New York: Knopf, 1999.

————. *Roger's Version.* New York: Knopf, 1986.

————. *Self-Consciousness: Memoirs.* New York: Knopf, 1989.

————. *Terrorist.* New York: Knopf, 2006.

————. "Top-Notch Witcheries." In *Hugging the Shore: Essays and Criticism,* 341–50. New York: Knopf, 1983.

Walczuk, Anna. "Text into Text: An Intertextual Reading of Muriel Spark's *Reality and Dreams.*" *Anglistik* 15 (September 2004): 89–97.

Waldmeir, John C. *Cathedrals of Bone: The Role of the Body in Contemporary Catholic Literature.* New York: Fordham University Press, 2009.

Waldron, Ann. *Close Connections: Caroline Gordon and the Southern Renaissance.* New York: Putnam, 1987.

Walker, Alice. "Beyond the Peacock: The Reconstruction of Flannery O'Connor." In *In Search of Our Mothers' Gardens: Womanist Prose,* 42–59. San Diego: Harcourt Brace Jovanovich, 1984.

Wallace, David Foster. "Certainly the End of *Something* or Other, One Would Sort of Have to Think: Re John Updike's *Toward the End of Time.*" In *Consider the Lobster: And Other Essays,* 51–59. New York: Little, Brown, and Company, 2005.

Walsh, Richard. *The Rhetoric of Fictionality: Narrative Theory and the Idea of Fiction.* Columbus: The Ohio State University Press, 2007.

Waugh, Evelyn. *Helena: A Novel.* Boston: Little, Brown, 1950.

Weaver, Richard M. *The Ethics of Rhetoric.* Chicago: Henry Regnery, 1953.

Weil, Simone. "Reflections on Quantum Theory." Translated by Richard Rees. In *On Science, Necessity, and the Love of God,* 49–64. London: Oxford University Press, 1968.

Whittaker, Ruth. *The Faith and Fiction of Muriel Spark.* London: Macmillan, 1982.

Williams, Rowan. "Native Speakers: Identity, Grace, and Homecoming." Delivered at the University of Notre Dame's Centre in London on 15 July 2011. Available online at http://www.archbishopofcanterbury.org/articles.php/2136/archbishops-speech-at-conference-on-christianity-and-literature. Accessed 1 February 2012.

Wills, Garry. *Bare Ruined Choirs: Doubt, Prophecy, and Radical Religion.* Garden City, NJ: Doubleday, 1972.

Wood, James. "John Updike's Complacent God." In *The Broken Estate: Essays on Literature and Belief,* 227–35. London: Jonathan Cape, 1999.

Wood, Ralph C. *The Comedy of Redemption: Christian Faith and Comic Vision in Four American Novelists.* Notre Dame: University of Notre Dame Press, 1988.

———. *Flannery O'Connor and the Christ-Haunted South.* Grand Rapids, MI: Eerdmans, 2004.

———. "Into the Void: Updike's Sloth and America's Religion." *Christian Century* 113 (April 24, 1996): 452–57.

———. *Literature and Theology.* Nashville, TN: Abingdon, 2009.

———. "*The Thanatos Syndrome:* Exciting, Disappointing, Horrifying." *Christian Century* 104 (October 7, 1987): 857–58.

Yaeger, Patricia. "Flannery O'Connor and the Aesthetics of Torture." In *Flannery O'Connor: New Perspectives,* edited by Sura Rath, 183–206. Athens: University of Georgia Press, 1996.

Žižek, Slavoj. *On Belief.* London: Routledge, 2001.

———. *The Puppet and the Dwarf: The Perverse Core of Christianity.* Cambridge: The MIT Press, 2003.

INDEX

Tocqueville, Alexis de, 46, 92–93, 119, 172, 194
Tolson, Jay, 126n2, 139n10, 143n12, 144
tragedy, 31, 36n4
transcendence, 129, 137
Transcendentalism, 109
transubstantiation, 5, 168, 169
truth, 6, 7–10, 11n13, 27, 29–30, 58–59, 72, 82, 88, 134, 153, 188, 203, 206

Unamuno, Miguel de, 87
universalism, 30, 89, 108
Updike, John, 6, 10, 14, 15, 17, 75, 85–124, 158, 172–73, 201, 205, 207; and American exceptionalism, 19, 90–92, 95, 101–3, 106; and Christian orthodoxy, 1, 2, 18, 19, 96, 165, 173, 191; and ethics, 89–90, 93, 96, 105, 110–11, 113–14, 117; rhetoric of narcissism of, 19, 20, 85–89, 92–95, 97, 117, 122–23, 126, 165–66. *See also* Protestantism
urbanism, 26, 43–44

Vatican II, 19, 20, 73, 74, 75, 125, 141, 161–63, 166–69, 170n7, 173, 176, 180, 182, 185, 193, 203
violence, 18, 24, 30, 34–35, 45–48, 64, 126, 134–36

Violent Bear It Away, The (O'Connor), 33n3, 96

Walczuk, Anna, 79
Waldmeir, John, 169–70, 178–79
Walker, Alice, 25, 48
Wallace, David Foster, 85, 86n2
Walsh, Richard, 8–9, 86, 86n3
Watt, Ian, 32
Waugh, Evelyn, 15, 207
Weaver, Richard, 6
Weber, Max, 2, 3, 129, 188, 193–94
Weil, Simone, 6, 129n5
Whitman, Walt, 93, 106
Whittaker, Ruth, 57, 75n14
Williams, Rowan, 198
Wills, Garry, 161n1, 162
Wise Blood (O'Connor), 26, 32, 33n3
Wittgenstein, Ludwig, 199
Wolfe, Thomas, 105
Wood, James, 106, 110, 112
Wood, Ralph, 4, 16, 20, 46–48, 48n10, 90, 113, 117, 122, 158, 160, 205
Wordsworth, William, 106

Yaeger, Patricia, 24

Žižek, Slavoj, 11n14, 21, 27–28

LITERATURE, RELIGION, AND POSTSECULAR STUDIES
Lori Branch, Series Editor

Literature, Religion, and Postsecular Studies publishes scholarship on the influence of religion on literature and of literature on religion from the sixteenth century onward. Books in the series include studies of religious rhetoric or allegory; of the secularization of religion, ritual, and religious life; and of the emerging identity of postsecular studies and literary criticism.

Hard Sayings: The Rhetoric of Christian Orthodoxy in Late Modern Fiction
    Thomas F. Haddox

Preaching and the Rise of the American Novel
    Dawn Coleman

Victorian Women Writers, Radical Grandmothers, and the Gendering of God
    Gail Turley Houston

Apocalypse South: Judgment, Cataclysm, and Resistance in the Regional Imaginary
    Anthony Dyer Hoefer